C000281786

THE HISTORY OF
WEXFORD FESTIVAL OPERA,
1951–2021

Nora Sourouzian, Gerard Powers
and Wexford Festival Chorus
in *Pénélope*, 2005

IN A PLACE LIKE NO OTHER

THE HISTORY OF WEXFORD FESTIVAL OPERA, 1951–2021

Karina Daly

Karina Daly
2021

FOUR COURTS PRESS

Set in 11 on 14 pt Garamond for
Four Courts Press, 7 Malpas Street, Dublin 8, Ireland
www.fourcourtspress.ie
and in North America for
Four Courts Press
c/o IPG, 814 N Franklin St, Chicago, IL 60610

A catalogue record for this title
is available from the British Library.

ISBN 978-1-84682-997-0

Book design and typesetting by Anú Design, Tara
Printed in Spain by Grafo S.A.

'In this age of global economics, travellers may have more difficulty than ever seeking out a place that is like no other. For me, one of those places is Wexford … home to Wexford Festival Opera, one of Europe's most distinctive musical institutions.'

Brian Kellow, *Opera* magazine, 2016.

CONTENTS

PREFACE

Wexford Festival Opera is a truly unique cultural event. Celebrating its 70th anniversary in 2021, the fact that it has managed to survive so many significant challenges over 70 years and continues to flourish is a testament to the incredible efforts of those at the helm and the spirit of resilience that is synonymous with the Wexford community. It is a tribute to the phenomenal efforts of so many people who have gone to remarkable lengths to ensure that Wexford remains a bright, if unlikely, light on the world opera stage. This book is written for those who have enjoyed Wexford Festival Opera over many years, travelling from all over the world because of their love of little-known operas, the standard of Wexford's Festival repertoire and the unique welcome and atmosphere for which Wexford is renowned. I would like to thank all of those who have shared their experiences, material and memories of what went on behind the scenes, far away from the bright lights of festival time. I would also like to thank the Board of Wexford Festival Opera for their support of me in my journey to complete this history.

There are many people whose help has been invaluable to me in putting together the story of this remarkable Festival – Gráinne Doran, Wexford County Archivist, was so helpful in facilitating access to the Wexford Festival archival material, particularly in the challenging environment of Covid-19 restrictions; Denise O'Connor-Murphy gave me permission to use photographs from her father Denis O'Connor's archive and Padraig Grant kindly allowed me to use his images of the 2020 Festival. I am grateful to John Ironside and Derek Spiers who gave me access to their production photos; Clive Barda was selfless with his time in helping me to choose images and kindly provided many photos, including the beautiful image on the cover; Kevin Lewis and Miles Linklater gave me invaluable help with editing opera titles and naming singers from the archival records.

I would also like to thank Tom Mooney who reviewed a draft of my book and was always on hand to provide content and context on events. Professor Richard Aldous also reviewed drafts of my book and, having inspired me to write the first version of the history of Wexford Festival Opera in 2004, has been unceasingly supportive and always a source of very sound advice.

Many people shared their experiences with me and helped me to understand the context to key moments in the Festival's history. Joe Csibi, Joe Vaněk, Billy

Sweetman, Eithne Healy and Nora Cosgrove provided insightful stories, while Rosetta Cucchi and David McLoughlin were also generous in sharing their experiences of Wexford Festival Opera over the last number of years – a time of great change at Wexford. Victoria Walsh-Hamer provided me with her father's archival material and also provided important context, particularly of earlier years, along with reviewing drafts of my book. The contributions of former chairpersons Peter Scallan and Ger Lawlor and current chairperson Mary Kelly gave me a great understanding of the leadership role at Wexford, while Ger also gave me invaluable help by restoring and reproducing old photographs and allowing me to use his photographs in the book.

David Agler was instrumental in encouraging me to take on this project, was extremely generous with his time and provided me with valuable material along the way. Terry Neill was another source of encouragement in writing this book and has been incredibly supportive throughout. Paul Hennessy, too, has been endlessly supportive and generous with his time, reading drafts of my book and helping me to chart the history, particularly the intricacies and negotiations relating to the building of the new Opera House.

Others kindly agreed to contribute by providing their own memories of Wexford Festival Opera which are included in the epilogue – President Michael D. Higgins, Geoffrey Wheatcroft, Terry Neill, Angela Meade and John O'Donoghue. Their reflections have added hugely to the book.

I am particularly grateful to Colm Toibín for his generosity in writing his reflections of Wexford Festival Opera for inclusion in the book. Colm has been a true friend of Wexford Festival Opera for many years and remains so today. I really appreciate his generous support.

I would like to thank Anthony Tierney and Martin Fanning of Four Courts Press for taking on this project. It has been a pleasure to work with them and their support and advice has been invaluable.

I would like to particularly thank my family – my father Michael, my sister Irene Michelle and my brother, Derek, who were always on hand with practical suggestions and advice. My mother, Irene, spent countless hours assisting me, pulling together research material and reviewing many drafts.

Finally, I would like to make special mention to John who has supported my every endeavour since we studied together at University College Dublin. His support was vital in enabling me to find the time to carry out the research and write this history. He commented on many drafts and was always on hand with sound advice and words of encouragement. He has never turned down a challenge and has encouraged me to adopt the same approach in life.

This book is dedicated to John and my gorgeous children
Abigail, Eli, Tara Faye, and Cassie. x

Tom Walsh (1930s) in
Wexford production of
The Gondaliers.

PROLOGUE

by Bernard Levin

writing in the 1989 Festival programme book

If you are reading this, you are holding in your hands the Wexford Festival programme book, as the orchestra tunes. If Tom Walsh had not lived, you would not be, because there would be no Wexford Festival programme book, because there would be no Wexford Festival. It is as simple as that.

Mind you, it wasn't at first. Tom thought there should be an opera festival in Wexford, and when he mentioned the subject, other music-lovers agreed. But when he made clear that he was going to create one, in a town of 11,000 people, and a town very far from prosperous, too, heads were shaken, temples tapped, smiles hidden behind hands. Tom was written off as a visionary.

So he was; he had seen a vision. But his enthusiasm, his energy, his silver tongue, his unwavering determination, his implacable unwillingness to accept defeat — these combined to keep his vision clear and bright. All he had to do then was to raise the money, prepare the theatre, find the artists, engage the orchestra and tell the world. A madman, certainly: but what are you holding in your hands? ...

The Festival opened, on time. It continued, it waxed, it became known, it became *well* known, it became famous. Tom's enchanting smile grew wider — not from the knowledge of his operatic paternity, but for the joy he had brought to so many visitors. All music festivals have their 'regulars', who return every year; it is probable that the proportion of regulars at Wexford is greater than any other in the world.

Why? Because Tom built to last. His greatest magic was to inspire the town to spread happiness before its visitors like a red carpet before royalty. In Wexford at Festival time you cannot go round a corner without meeting an old friend, nor round another without making a new one, and Irish hospitality is at its warmest in this town of tiny streets and great hearts ...

A man like Tom Walsh cannot be lost by death; his spirit will live on in the town he loved, the town he taught the world to love, too, and his achievement, the Wexford Festival, is now deep-rooted and will endure.

The tuning is finished. The lights will soon go down. Close the book. *Si monumentum requires, circumspice.*

CHAPTER 1

THE MOST AMBITIOUS VENTURE IN YEARS

1951

'My own favourite festival is Wexford', wrote William Mann in the *Times*.

> The town is small, as is the opera house. That, straight away, means that it is very select and catering for a small public. But the operatic repertory is wide, French, German, Italian. The productions are tasteful and immaculate. It's small scale but totally delectable. The place is small enough to surround you with new friends all the time, if you were sociable. Food, drink and gossip are everywhere on tap at all times. Salzburg in the early 1920s must have been like this. It is how an opera festival should be.[1]

It has been the source of utter amazement to those who visit the Festival on an annual basis that it has survived and prospered in a town like Wexford. Even

Murray Dickie, Dermot O'Hara and Maureen Springer, 1951

more amazing is the fact that it was set up in the first place – for Dr Thomas J. Walsh created an opera festival in a land without classical music.

In mid-twentieth-century Ireland, grand opera was associated with the old values of the Ascendancy and the Anglo-Irish. Much of the Irish population did not care for an operatic tradition and were even against the idea of introducing any art form that had filtered through to Ireland from Britain. Opera formed no part of the Irish character. There had been few important Irish composers. Even those whose music still survived, like Vincent Wallace of Waterford and Michael Balfe of Dublin, had aimed primarily at an audience outside of Ireland. Opera houses themselves were hard to come by, as many had been turned into cinema houses or theatres to entertain a greater demand.[2]

This was partly explained by the Irish political situation. After Independence in 1922, Ireland entered a period of cultural decline. There was a sense of anti-intellectualism, even. The arts in particular suffered as they were seen, at best as an elite pastime, and at worst, as 'anti-Irish'. As John F. Larchet, Professor of Music at University College Dublin, wrote of Dublin:

It possesses no concert hall, good or bad, and no permanent orchestra which could be called a symphony orchestra ... Most of the people have no knowledge of Strauss, Brahms, and the great volume of modern orchestral music. Few are acquainted with any important works of later date than Wagner's *Ring of the Nibelungen.*

Little interest is taken in chamber music or choral music; a large percentage of music lovers in Dublin have never heard a string quartet ... In such circumstances, it is inevitable that Dublin should contribute nothing to the support or progress of music.[3]

Imagine, then, what it was like in Wexford. It was against this backdrop of cultural stagnation that Dr Tom Walsh introduced opera to provincial Wexford.

Walsh was born in 6 Upper George Street, Wexford, in 1911. Educated at the town's Christian Brothers School, he began his medical studies at University College Dublin in 1930. He did not qualify until 1944, his time at college being disrupted, firstly due to the death of his father, a local publican, and then because Walsh himself developed tuberculosis. He married Eva Cousins, a lady considerably older than himself and a leading member of the local light opera society. She was well off and a member of a family who owned a mineral water business in Wexford town. Eva was a skilled pianist, and her love of music naturally complemented her husband's interest in music and opera. During his time at University College Dublin, Walsh studied singing with the prestigious A.G. Viani at the Royal Irish Academy of Music. This served him very well indeed, particularly with regard to his acute ability later on to recognize the potential of singers for productions at Wexford. Viani, an Italian-born music teacher, was one of the leading figures in the establishment of the Dublin Operatic Society in 1928 and was responsible for the performance of opera at the Gaiety Theatre until 1936.

According to Nellie Walsh, her brother's love of music and opera began at an early age, when both of them used to listen to opera on gramophone records and, later, on the radio. Walsh was a member of the Wexford Musical Society and had taken part in many local productions.[4] His childhood memories of Wexford were that it was a 'dull country town' and he said that he was lured to the local theatre because 'there was light there'. The first opera he remembered attending was *Rigoletto*. It had been produced in Wexford in 1921 by a touring company, and it had left an indelible mark on his taste for opera, because, as he admitted, he had nothing to compare it to at that stage.[5]

When Walsh came home to work as a medical doctor following his studies in Dublin, he kept up his favourite pastime of listening to opera. Friends began to call around to his house when they realized what an impressive collection of gramophone recordings he had built up. Although this was only a hobby, being a man of serious ambition, Walsh was not satisfied with this arrangement. He wanted to extend the gathering to offer other opera lovers the opportunity to listen to such music.

In 1950, he set up the Wexford Opera Study Circle to bring opera lovers together. The Circle was merely an extension of the gatherings at his home.[6]

Walsh's love of opera was so intense that he was not content with simply listening to recordings. He was deeply knowledgeable about singers and opera and he wanted to stage his own production in his own town. Although a crazy idea, Walsh had seen what his music teacher in Dublin, Viani, had achieved with the founding of the Dublin Operatic Society.

Walsh was not alone in his enthusiasm once he discussed his proposal with some close friends – Eugene McCarthy, the owner of White's Hotel, Wexford; Seamus O'Dwyer, a local postman; Dr Jim Liddy and Dr Des Ffrench, who were both medical doctors. Walsh's wife, Eva, was also extraordinarily optimistic that her husband's dream could be achieved. The group met often to discuss their project, each time becoming more and more convinced that it was feasible. While all this was going on, Walsh was holding down a full-time job as a general practice doctor, and was at the same time acting as anaesthetist to the Wexford County Hospital.

In a Wexford Arts Newsletter of 1977, Walsh wrote an article on his memories of how the festival began. The inspiration, he said, came from an old programme book of Benjamin Britten's Aldeburgh Festival which he found in Foyle's Bookshop in London. It was not the Aldeburgh Festival itself that inspired Walsh, but merely the image of the boats at Aldeburgh that reminded him of similar scenes on the quay front at Wexford.

The fact that Aldeburgh had begun a festival from very humble beginnings gave Walsh the confidence to discuss his proposal with Sir Compton Mackenzie, editor of the famous *Gramophone* magazine. In 1950 he wrote to Mackenzie, describing himself as 'an amateur of opera endeavouring to revive an interest in the art, traditional to our town up to the year 1938, since when the old touring companies have ceased to visit us'.[7]

He invited Mackenzie to give the opening lecture to the Wexford Opera

Frank Stafford and James White at the art exhibition during the 1951 Festival

Study Circle. Mackenzie consented and went on to become the President of the Wexford Festival of Music and the Arts in its inaugural year and an invaluable source of publicity for the Festival in England.[8] It was interesting that the first president of the Festival was not an Irishman, but was British. Mackenzie had suggested to Walsh that the Festival should perhaps have a local, or at least an Irish president. Walsh disagreed, later commenting that 'we owe a deep debt to Sir Compton. He was a political friend of this country when it was neither popular nor profitable to be so, and as long as we have a festival Sir Compton will be its president'.[9]

Although Mackenzie was enthusiastic, interest was not forthcoming locally. Walsh and his aides began by finding out how many local businesses and local people would become subscribers to the proposed Festival. The target was 500 guineas but only 200 guineas were collected. Walsh later recalled that

> to a man everybody voted against it, on the perfectly sensible grounds that there was obviously insufficient interest in the project to make it a success. Whereupon, I decided we would hold the Festival anyhow.[10]

Throughout the summer of 1951, leading up to the first Festival, Walsh admitted that he was at times unsure as to how the venture would be received publicly. 'In fact, thinking back on it the reaction of most of the townspeople was to look upon the whole business as a joke, and outside Wexford, nobody [had] even heard of us,'[11] he said, smiling.

Walsh was certainly ambitious. He set out to enlist the help of the English conductor Sir Thomas Beecham. Beecham was at first baffled that a medical doctor should be so enthusiastic about opera. This was strangely ironic because Beecham himself was essentially an amateur musician, although he was a world-famous one by 1951. 'But you are a doctor, why are you so interested in

Audience attending the first Wexford Festival, 1951

opera?' Walsh recalled Beecham asking him. 'Sir Thomas, do you ever go to football matches?' Walsh retorted. Instantly he realized what Walsh meant and, as Walsh relayed, 'his eyes twinkled and, poking me in the chest with his finger, he said, "With your team winning? I know, I know!"'

Walsh had taken the important decision of choosing the opera for his so-called Festival – Balfe's *The Rose of Castile*.[12] The opera told the story of conspiracy and intrigue with a classic twist of romantic fate. Walsh explained that he had chosen this opera for its melodious music so as to attract an Irish operatic audience. Besides, he knew that Balfe had connections with Wexford, having spent part of his early life there, and the fact that performance of the said opera was a rarity heightened its interest factor for Walsh, who wanted to present a little-known work.[13] *The Rose of Castile* had been first produced at Drury Lane in October 1857.

Walsh then set about putting together the production, beginning with the chorus. The chorus started out as an entirely amateur and local group (apparently many of them could not even read music)[14] – a fact which led people to think that Walsh might be taking on too much. For the orchestra, he managed to convince Radio Éireann, the national broadcaster, to provide its Light Orchestra. The decision to seek help from a public, professional organization such as Radio Éireann marked the start of a trend in the history of the Festival.

Walsh's relationship with the broadcasting administrators was a difficult one. They came to describe him as 'a martinet and ruthless perfectionist, who because of fiery temperament enjoys a love-hate relationship with journalists'.[15] They appeared to respect the work he was doing in the organization of the Festival, but they were wary of the amateur nature of the project. Still, the Wexford Festival soon came to rely on successful collaboration with this national and professional institution.

Contact with Radio Éireann was first made as early as February 1951. Walsh suggested in a letter to Fachtna Ó hAnnracháin, Director of Music, that the principal artists would come from London and Dublin, and the chorus would be local; and he asked if the orchestra might be the Radio Éireann Light Orchestra. He also indicated that the producer would perhaps come from London and the scenery and costumes would be specially designed for the production. He pointed out to Ó hAnnracháin that 'neither expense nor trouble will be spared to make this an artistic venture of national importance'.[16]

Clearly very confident about what he expected to achieve, Walsh tried to impress his professional attitude upon Ó hAnnracháin. He even calculated for Ó hAnnracháin the expected loss of the venture, stating that it would be in the region of £250 to £500, which he predicted would be covered by local subscriptions. He hoped that the Director of Music would agree to one or two broadcasts as a means of promoting the Festival. Failing this, he requested the recording of a performance from the fringe events. This recording was to be broadcast at a later date, so as not to run the risk of people simply staying at home and waiting for the broadcast version.[17] Ó hAnnracháin was quick to point out that if Radio Éireann did get involved, the station must have full rights of broadcasting or recording for broadcasting at a later date.[18]

Because the Festival had been guaranteed against loss of up to £350, Ó hAnnracháin considered it relatively safe for Radio Éireann to collaborate. Further, he agreed to make enquiries to help the organizers find suitable singers, and to obtain the orchestral music that was available from the agents Goodwin and Tabb in London. He seemed content with the arrangement between himself and Walsh, in view of the fact that, as he recalled, the organizers were willing to pay for a good team of soloists as well as a first-class producer.[19] But their commitment was equivocal.

Seamus O'Dwyer, a postman who was working closely with Walsh on the Festival project, suggested that Radio Éireann give Walsh himself the chance of a short broadcast, in the form of an interview, to help promote the Festival.[20] Yet Radio Éireann declined, saying that they could possibly include a 5–7 minute script by Walsh in a fortnightly series due to begin in October, entitled *Music Magazine*.[21] It was obvious at this early stage that Radio Éireann was not entirely comfortable with its association with this proposed Festival.

By May 1951 Walsh had secured Ria Mooney as producer for the opera and Michael O'Herlihy as designer of the sets. Mooney was a distinguished Abbey Theatre actress, who, in the period 1943 to 1948, had produced new plays at the Gaiety Theatre, Dublin. She subsequently worked at the Abbey again as a producer from 1948 to 1963. The problems of obtaining soloists had not yet been solved, but Walsh had placed advertisements in the daily papers in the hope of uncovering some more possibilities.[22]

Still, by June, the principal roles for *The Rose of Castile* had not been filled. It was not until July that Walsh managed to get an agreement from Maureen Springer to sing one of the principal roles. She, in turn, put Walsh in touch

James Nolan, Murray Dickie and Michael Nolan, *The Rose of Castile*, 1951

with her agents, Harold Holt Ltd, London, in the hope of finding suitable singers for the other roles. Ironically, given her later involvement, Veronica Dunne was turned down for the main part of Elvira, because Walsh believed her to be 'a lyrico-spinto rather than a coloratura', while also stressing that his Council was 'anxious to have at least one "Star" name on the bill'.[23]

Getting these 'star' names led to the first disagreements between Walsh and Ó hAnnracháin. Ó hAnnracháin told him disdainfully that he seemed:

> to imply that we are trying to keep the 'Star' names out of the bill; whereas, I have been insisting from the beginning that all solo parts should be given to really good singers only. Unless, therefore, we have your written agreement that in the event of our failure to secure satisfactory singers locally, suitable singers will be found elsewhere, we cannot see our way to proceed in the projected collaboration.[24]

Erskine Childers, Dr Tom Walsh and Sir Compton Mackenzie with cast, 1951

Walsh was exasperated by Radio Éireann's attitude. The broadcasting station was trying to take over, and he was far from willing to relinquish any control. Ó hAnnracháin also insisted that Walsh consult Mairéad Pigott, Radio Éireann's assistant for Vocal Programmes, before making any offers of solo parts. The auditions were to begin at the Radio Éireann premises in Dublin without further delay. At this point, Radio Éireann was not sure if the Wexford project would ever be launched and its directors were not keen about the idea of being part of an enterprise that was doomed to fail.

Walsh insisted that he had not, in fact, implied that Radio Éireann had wanted to exclude 'star' names from the cast, but went on to declare, during a meeting at which Dermot O'Hara, conductor of the orchestra, Ria Mooney and Walsh himself were present, that it had been decided that 'it was better policy to engage, let us say – second rate Irish artists than third raters and "has beens" from England'.[25]

Walsh was concerned lest English singers might arrive at the Festival with a very 'imperfect knowledge' of their parts or, worse still, that they might break their contracts altogether. Most of the singers would be unfamiliar with Balfe's opera and may not have thought it worth their while learning the parts. Walsh, however, stressed to Ó hAnnracháin that the Council had managed to secure prestigious artists such as pianist Joseph Weingarten and violinist Jaroslav Vaněcěk to give recitals. Moreover, the National Gallery had, for the first time, agreed to loan pictures for an Irish exhibition, and this exhibition would be part of the Wexford Festival. An exhibition of rare gramophone records and prints of famous singers would also be on display, prepared by the National Museum. Walsh was trying to impress upon Ó hAnnracháin that the Wexford enterprise would in fact succeed and that Radio Éireann's efforts on their behalf would not be wasted. This was evident in his explanation of the work done thus far:

> For our opera we have engaged one of the best producers in Ireland, with settings and costumes designed by an artist who has been described as Ireland's leading theatre designer. To my knowledge no operatic production in this country has had scenery and costumes specially designed for it by an artist of Mr O'Herlihy's calibre for well over a hundred years.[26]

The engagement of singers continued to cause immediate problems for Walsh and his Festival Council. Walsh even suggested to Ó hAnnracháin that he would contact the Dublin Operatic Society, whose season occurred before the Wexford one, to enquire whether Wexford could retain some of its artists.[27] At this stage, Walsh and his team were unsure as to how to go about finding suitable singers. It was even put forward that music teachers be contacted to identify appropriate singers. Still, he wanted to maintain control over selection of singers, and was keen to keep Radio Éireann's involvement in the selection process to a minimum. Walsh did not need someone from Dublin to tell him how to run his Festival: 'We fully understand the enterprise we have undertaken,' he told Ó hAnnracháin angrily, 'and we have no intention of mounting any production that will not alone bring credit to Radio Éireann and to Wexford but honour to Ireland'.[28]

By the late summer of 1951, preparations of the first Wexford Festival were in place. The principal artists had at last been decided upon – Maureen Springer, coloratura soprano at the Edinburgh Festival, along with Murray Dickie, a tenor who had excelled at Covent Garden, Glyndebourne and Rome.[29] An agreement had been drawn up regarding the performance of the Radio Éireann Light Orchestra for the first opera season that was to take place between 1 and 4 November. The agreement was very specific. The Director of Broadcasting, C.E. Kelly, agreed to provide not less than thirty members of the Radio Éireann Light Orchestra and a conductor. Tucked away in the contract was the condition that the opera, *The Rose of Castile,* must be put on by a professional producer and that the chosen primary artists be acceptable to the Director of Broadcasting himself. Even as late as September, this was still causing stress. Ó hAnnracháin was adamant that Walsh's choice of producer – an amateur – was unacceptable. Further, Radio Éireann had full permission to record any or all of the performances of the opera and the concert free of charge as it so wished. Although the Broadcasting Service was providing the orchestra free of charge, the Festival was responsible for covering any travelling or hotel expenses of the orchestra and conductor. The number of rehearsals, their duration and the actual personnel of the orchestra were to be decided upon jointly by Radio Éireann and the Festival Council.[30]

Eventually, Walsh visited Ó hAnnracháin in Dublin to discuss the production of *The Rose of Castile.* Radio Éireann settled upon John Stephenson as producer.[31] Walsh was dissatisfied with this decision being taken by Radio Éireann after he had personally approved Ria Mooney for the position. But Radio Éireann had made its point about a professional producer clear. However, when Stephenson was approached, he turned Wexford down flat; '£40' he said, was a fee that 'no professional producer would accept'. He added sarcastically that he was sorry not to come in order 'to learn all Doctor Walsh has to show me about the "style of Operatic Production at the Opera Comique Paris", and to incorporate these ideas as far as possible into the production of *The Rose of Castile*'.[32]

Stephenson's rejection of the offer raised tensions between Radio Éireann and Walsh, not least because Walsh was now threatening to take charge of the production himself. Ó hAnnracháin wrote to the Council in September, stridently setting out Radio Éireann's position:

> I feel that I must point out that I made it quite clear to Dr Walsh when he first discussed the project of the Wexford Festival with me that Radio Éireann could collaborate only on the assurance that a professional producer of standing would be engaged. I was rather amazed yesterday therefore, to learn that Dr Walsh had proposed

Dr Tom Walsh, Eva Walsh, Sir Compton Mackenzie and Erskine Childers, 1951

to undertake the responsibility of production himself without even mentioning the matter to me ... I should be grateful if in all future notices you would use the words Radio Éireann Light Orchestra and not Radio Éireann Orchestra ... Naturally [Dermot O'Hara, conductor] will not go to Wexford again until the question of production is solved to the mutual satisfaction of the Wexford Festival Organising Committee and Radio Éireann.[33]

Walsh relented, and at the end of the month engaged Powell Lloyd to produce *The Rose of Castile*. Lloyd had been resident producer at Sadler's Wells from 1941 to 1945 and producer–designer with the Dublin Grand Opera Society in 1948, 1949 and 1950.[34] Radio Éireann accepted this compromise.

The rows continued in the weeks leading up to the first night. Just days before the opening night, the Director of Broadcasting, C.E. Kelly, told the Wexford Festival Council that the pit in the theatre was too small for the agreed 30 players and that a lesser number would be used.[35] Walsh was furious,

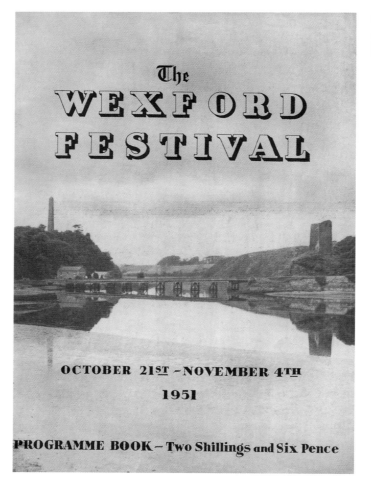

believing it would compromise the power of the performance. But while Radio Éireann continued its lukewarm support, public interest at home and abroad was growing. Was it really possible that a small harbour town in the south-east of Ireland was about to put on its own opera festival?

The English press was clearly intrigued by this opera festival, which, until after the first season, it knew very little about. As early as 9 October 1951, the London *Times* music critic, Frank Howes, announced that he was coming over to Wexford to witness the atmosphere of the Festival for himself. Ironically, it was the English press that first printed news of the Wexford Festival of Music and the Arts. On 11 October, the *Times* had reported news of the Festival and immediately the Irish correspondent of the *Times* contacted Walsh for the story. The *Evening Herald* in Dublin tried to justify their delay in reporting the events at Wexford, by declaring that

> the remarkable feature of the event is the silence, almost secrecy, with which the plans were conceived and brought along to fruition. Too often have we trumpeted about our inherent love of music and culture, but the only suitable notes to comfort our efforts in most cases would be 'The Last Post'.[36]

One of the aspects that the press picked up on was the importance of the Festival at Wexford as an educational aid to children. Schoolchildren were to attend a concert held by Radio Éireann Light Orchestra, as part of the Festival activities. The Department of Education deduced that since the concert was being given on a Saturday morning – outside of primary school hours – there was no problem with children attending. With regard to secondary schools that did hold classes on Saturdays, the decision was left to the discretion of the Principals who could decide permission of attendance. It was even agreed by the Department of Education that the Inspector of Music in the Secondary branch of the Department, Peadar Ó Collín, would attend the concert and give a short lecture to the students.

Yet despite all the hard work, it was clear that experience of organization was minimal. The 1951 Festival programme book, for example, boasted of acquiring Joan Denise Moriarty – the 'prima ballerina'.[37] Moriarty felt she was treated as anything but an important member of the cast. She aired her discontent in a letter to the Council:

> The dance which I had composed had to be entirely scrapped for lack of space on the stage, and it seemed clear from the beginning that no dancing was wanted by the producer in the opera. As a result only improvisation was possible; for the few minutes of my appearance I had to forgo an entire week's work in Cork so that the fee originally agreed upon could be no source of profit, apart from the worry and disappointment of the whole engagement.[38]

Walsh did his best to appease the cast in the days leading up to the opening

Des Ffrench and Sir Compton Mackenzie

night, but there was so much going on and it was difficult to stay on top of all matters. The press was beginning to ask Walsh what his association with the tourist industry was, seeing as the Festival had the potential to attract tourists to this small seaside town. He was quick to dispel the notion that the Festival was somehow an attempt to promote tourism in Wexford: 'I don't know how people come to think I'm in the tourist business,' he declared:

> but I'm not interested in tourism at all. I have enough on my plate trying to bring the opera. Let somebody else bring the tourists. I'm sure the Festival [will help] the tourist industry – how much or how little, is not my pigeon. I just want to put on opera.[39]

Finally, after all the preparations and a turbulent few months, the Wexford Festival of Music and the Arts opened on 1 November. It was a marvellous occasion: opera goers arrived to the narrow street that housed the Theatre Royal donned in black tie; artists scurried up the street and into the theatre already in costume, as the dressing room space in the theatre was entirely inadequate.

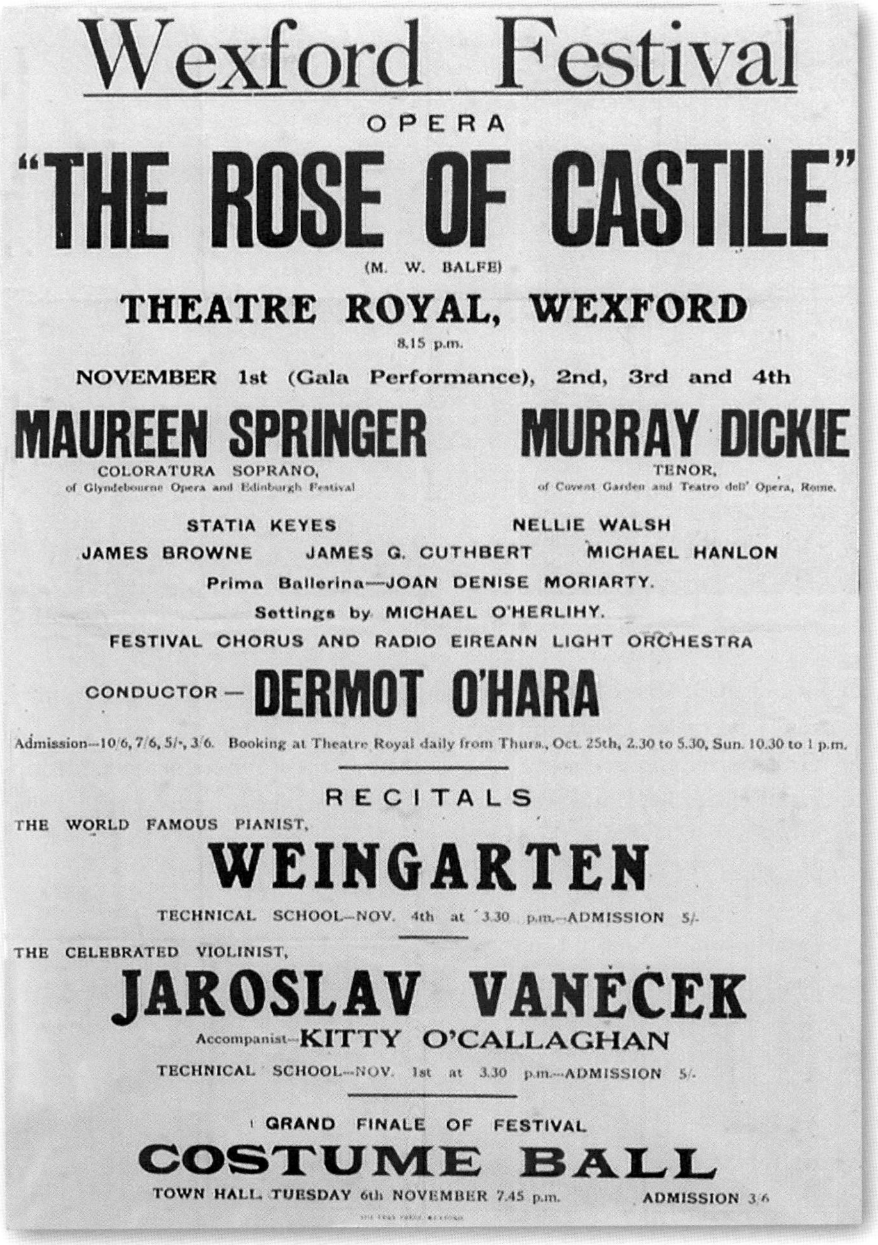

Poster for *The Rose of Castile*, 1951

Children were draped from every window in this tiny street to catch a glimpse of the unusual and entirely novel creatures that were congregating in the theatre across the street from where they lived. The sound of English accents was audible and caused further excitement. Doubtless those who came to investigate the situation did not recognize the Musical Director of Radio Éireann, Fachtna Ó hAnnracháin, or the Director of Broadcasting, C.E. Kelly. Lt.-Col. Bill O'Kelly, chairman of the Dublin Grand Opera Society, was also present. Erskine Childers, the then Minister for Posts and Telegraphs and later President of Ireland, had also made his way to Wexford for the great occasion.

The Rose of Castile was a successful choice, with performances every night from 1 to 4 November. As Walsh appeared on the stage following the performance on each of the four nights, the audience sprang to their feet spontaneously to show its appreciation for what he had achieved. He was naturally delighted. The press was bemused by the entire affair, recognizing that it had been an outstanding amateur success, yet not quite knowing how it had come about. Perhaps one of the most gratifying compliments came from that great arbiter of taste in England, and the Festival's president, Sir Compton Mackenzie, when he declared that 'the Festival [has] ended in glory as indeed it deserved to ... At the rate you are going you'll be competing with Salzburg before long'.[40] He congratulated Walsh personally on the positive financial result of the Festival, which Mackenzie described as 'remarkable'.[41]

What was really remarkable was that the first Wexford Festival of Music and the Arts received acclaim from all over the world. At home, the *Evening Herald* commented that:

> the town of Wexford has shot into the limelight, having planned a Festival on an ambitious scale ... Their courage and determination should not go unapplauded by the rest of the country.[42]

The *Irish Independent* followed in November 1951, by declaring that:

> Wexford has just given a lead which could with great cultural benefit be followed by other towns throughout this country ... Those towns which are prepared to show as much enterprise ... may confidently expect support from the directors of the National Gallery, from the controllers of the Radio Éireann Orchestra, and from singers, speakers,

and lecturers of the distinguished calibre of those who graced the Wexford Festival.[43]

The London *Times* described it as:

> the most ambitious venture of its kind in years. Mr Compton Mackenzie, the Festival President, is to be there this week. He should be not a little tickled at the thought that a talk on opera that he gave in Wexford last winter planted the seed that has brought forth so flourishing a cultural plant.[44]

News of the Festival even reached the United States. The *Boston Globe* reported that

> Wexford's Festival of Music and Art … was so great a success and its promise for the future is so encouraging that Irish art circles hold it to have been the most constructive cultural step taken by the nation since the founding of the Abbey Theatre 50 years ago.[45]

Help from other sources was highlighted in the acknowledgments of the first Wexford Festival Programme. The Festival Council expressed its appreciation to the Minister for Posts and Telegraphs, for allowing the Radio Éireann Light Orchestra to perform for the operas. Other members of the broadcasting team who were singled out for thanks were C.E. Kelly, Margaret Pigott and Fachtna Ó hAnnracháin.[46]

This had been a triumph for Walsh. He had the personality and courage needed to make a cultural venture succeed in Ireland in the 1950s. As the journalist Fanny Feehan pointed out:

> It takes a remarkable and strong personality to achieve anything in Ireland if it is of a cultural nature; and then he needs the gods on his side. If it is to happen in the provinces a monstrous determination is needed to combat the lethargy and inertia.[47]

He may well have been a 'martinet and ruthless perfectionist',[48] as described by Feehan, but it was that authoritarian personality that would turn his amateur and private venture in the south-east corner of Ireland into a world-acclaimed festival.

CHAPTER 2

AN AMATEURISH AFFAIR

1952–5

It was almost taken for granted that the Festival would continue into its second year. The 1952 programme incorporated four operatic nights of Donizetti's *L'elisir d'amore,* with the Radio Éireann Light Orchestra conducted again by Dermot O'Hara. Peter Ebert, son of the prestigious Carl Ebert of Glyndebourne fame, was the producer; Joseph Carl was the designer.[1] It was to be Dermot O'Hara's last year to work at Wexford, apparently following an episode where he requested the curtain to be lifted after the performance where he proceeded to blame the local chorus for not knowing their music in front of an audience that was just beginning to leave the theatre.[2]

Despite being deemed a success, as Walsh himself admitted, *The Rose of Castile* had been presented the previous year amid much criticism. Some people questioned his choice of opera, suggesting that *Maritana* might have been a more popular choice. But Walsh was not interested in popular opera. This was soon understood with the production of *L'elisir d'amore.* Walsh himself admitted that his choice of opera 'nearly broke the Festival'. Only on the last night was the theatre full, and this was because of the talent of the tenor chosen by Walsh, Nicola Monti.[3] With the engagement of four Italian singers, three of whom boasted La Scala reputations,[4] Walsh ensured that Wexford would be included on the international circuit of opera festivals.[5]

Following the success of another season, the Minister for Posts and Telegraphs, Erskine Childers, commented that Radio Éireann's involvement with the Wexford Festival was its most important function outside of Dublin. He praised the initiative of Walsh and his Council and said that the Festival was comparable to other significant cultural events that were taking place on the Continent. Childers further intimated that he would like to see other counties in Ireland taking the lead from Wexford. He promised that Radio Éireann would give any such enterprise as much help and support as possible. The Wexford Festival, he noted, had already acquired a positive reputation for standards achieved, and he hoped that it would continue on into the future.[6]

And continue it did. Donizetti's *Don Pasquale* was the opera chosen and the conductor for the 1953 season was Bryan Balkwill, a man who described his experience at Wexford as 'a pioneering job'. Balkwill commented later on that he had taken the job because, in his opinion, Wexford already had a good name. The sense of being in on something from the beginning added to the whole experience for Balkwill. He had worked on the Continent, at Glyndebourne and at the Cambridge Theatre, as had Peter Ebert the producer, and he noted that Walsh had been extremely impressed with the results at Glyndebourne.[7] This third season again witnessed certain strains between the Festival Council and Radio Éireann. Ó hAnnracháin told Walsh that although the Light Orchestra was available for the 1953 season, Radio Éireann would not guarantee its services for further festivals;[8] Radio Éireann was evidently still unsure about the future of the Festival and had no intention of being associated indefinitely with a faltering venture. For this season also, Radio Éireann agreed to provide its Symphony Orchestra for a concert,[9] with a children's concert on the Saturday morning, provided it did not upset travel arrangements and did not exceed the allocated one hour and thirty minutes.[10]

By the end of April, relations between Radio Éireann and the Festival Council had worsened. Disagreements arose over the matter of allowing the Wexford public into the theatre to view the dress rehearsals of the operas. Ó hAnnracháin registered his opposition to this practice and added that arrangements needed to be made for the acoustic treatment of the pit as had been done for the 1952 season.[11] He obviously did not realize the significance of allowing local people to attend

Nicola Monti in
L'elisir d'amore,
1952

the dress rehearsals. Wexford needed to use the operatic dress rehearsals to gain support, financial and otherwise, for the enterprise locally, but Ó hAnnracháin appeared to be taking charge of the Radio Éireann involvement in the Festival, thus making life very difficult for the amateur Festival Council.

Walsh was naturally extremely anxious about this objection put forward by Radio Éireann:

> I am considerably worried at your suggestion that members of the public cannot attend at any rehearsal of our Opera. As you are undoubtedly aware, we charge a small fee to the public for our dress rehearsal, which enables us to make a little extra money, which I am sure you can understand, we particularly need in running our Festival. I cannot understand your objection to this and must point out that

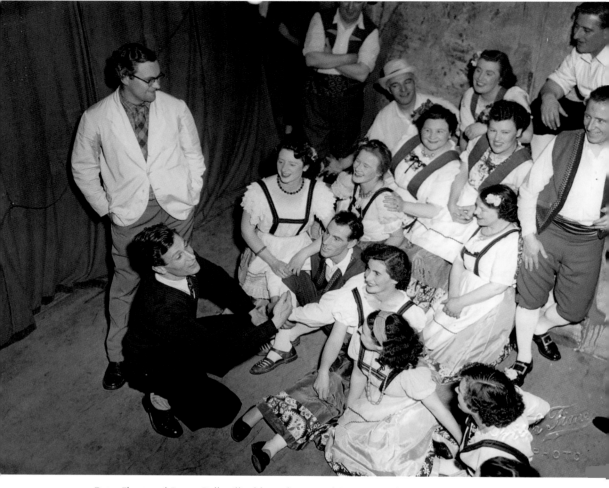

Peter Ebert and Bryan Balkwill address the cast of *Don Pasquale*, 1953

both myself, and, I am satisfied, the Festival Council, will protest strongly against this new arrangement. What is your objection to it?[12]

Of course Ó hAnnracháin's objection was obvious. He made the point that it would nearly always be necessary to stop during a dress rehearsal in order to tweak the performance. The conductor or producer would often feel it necessary to make a comment to a performer – which would not be appropriate in front of an audience. Singers, too, might well prefer not to 'sing out' during a rehearsal, that is, give of their best, and this privilege would be lost if an audience was present. Of the previous season's example, Ó hAnnracháin said:

> Last year's dress rehearsal in Wexford showed clearly how impossible it is to rehearse satisfactorily with the Theatre full of people. Your point about enabling 'the poorer people' of the town to hear first class opera can hardly have been put forward seriously and if it is a question of money we think some other way must be found.[13]

This was a huge difference of opinion that needed to be overcome before the Festival could presume to continue. After all, the principal artists had already been engaged and it was not feasible to cancel the production if there were insurmountable differences between the amateurs at Wexford and the professionals in Dublin.[14] Walsh did not agree that the dress rehearsal would be ineffective if an audience was present; the public was fully aware of the possible necessity to stall the performance at any stage. And, although the Italians were noted for merely 'marking' their parts at a rehearsal, under the agreement at Wexford each singer had given a guarantee that he or she would sing out fully at the rehearsal performance.[15] Walsh stressed the importance to the town of allowing the local public to sample opera at a reduction of the normal price:

> The question of money for the dress rehearsal is naturally of importance to us but is one which can be surmounted. My point about the poorer people of the town hearing first class opera is however insurmountable; in fact, so important is it that if the dress rehearsal is not open to them at these nominal prices so great would be the ill-feeling in the town that it would mean the end of the Wexford Festival. As one who saved pennies to hear opera in Wexford I would think it a most despicable business that people in the town who could never have the opportunity of hearing a great tenor such as Monti should be precluded from doing so *for no reason whatsoever.* I would further point out that when entering into your agreement with us this year as in the two previous years you made no mention of this very

important new factor. If you had, we could then have decided if it were feasible to hold our Festival.[16]

Walsh went on to say that the dress rehearsal would go ahead on 26 October, whether the Radio Éireann Light Orchestra would participate or not. A compromise was consequently reached, with both parties agreeing to add an extra dress rehearsal, for the benefit of the public.[17] An overt clash had been averted, but even so, Ó hAnnracháin managed to undermine Walsh's authority. The Music Director insisted that he had spoken to soloists about the arrangement of allowing the public to attend the dress rehearsal, and that they agreed that they had never come across such an arrangement before.[18] He furthermore commented that

> surely a rehearsal which is likely to be full of imperfections and lacking in continuity should not be described as first class opera and furthermore the 'poorer people of the town' (as you choose to describe them) are surely as worthy of the best as any other section of the community.[19]

One of the 1953 principal artists, Nicola Monti, was requested by Radio Éireann to perform with the Radio Éireann Symphony Orchestra for a concert to be held in Dundalk and also in its Promenade Concert on 8 November.[20] Walsh had written to Monti on behalf of Radio Éireann, but noted in a letter to Ó hAnnracháin that the Wexford Festival Council had booked the services of Monti as early as the Festival the previous year and that he may not be available at such short notice, due to his growing popularity on the Continent.[21] In the event, Monti agreed to assist Radio Éireann, for a fee of £100 for each performance.[22]

The 1953 Wexford Festival of Music and the Arts was another success. Patrick J. Little, who had been Minister for Posts and Telegraphs from 1943 to 1948, opened the Festival proceedings. It was significant that a political figure had agreed to do so: it showed a growing confidence in the enterprise, even at this early stage. Little was also chairman of the Arts Council at the time. 'I think the people of Wexford have come to recognize the festival as not only good for the town and county, but for the country as a whole,' Walsh told the press in the same year.[23] The *Irish Independent* made the important point

Cristiano Dalamangas, Nicola Monti, Afro Poli and Elvina Ramella in *Don Pasquale*, 1953

that the Festival had already become an outstanding event in Irish cultural life. Compton Mackenzie told the audience at a Festival Forum, in reply to a query about the future of the Festival, that:

> it is something so alive and so big, like living poetry, that nothing can interfere with it now. It is an idle question to ask if it will go on. Of course it will go on, and I am as proud of the honour of being President as I am of anything in my whole career.[24]

Mackenzie paid tribute again to the Festival from the theatre stage following the final performance of *Don Pasquale*:

> I want to pay tribute to this magnificent company. Watching the opera tonight, I could not help feeling that we were linked with Europe and the opera houses of Italy. I can't think of a single town in Scotland,

Cristiano Dalamangas and Nicola Monti in *Don Pasquale*, 1953

Wales or England, which could carry off such an achievement as we have seen tonight.[25]

By 1954 things seemed to be on a sure footing. There were no particular problems that threatened the Festival's immediate existence. The opera chosen was *La sonnambula* by Vincenzo Bellini. There was no change in either conductor, producer or designer in that year.[26] The *Irish Press* summed up the curious success of opera in a town like Wexford:

> In Wexford things are different. Here a real war for decent values has begun, and with real prospects of success because the people behind it know what the fight is all about. People elsewhere have been content to follow the pattern of what has been done before, so there are pleasant drama festivals in many small towns around the country, with the usual plays, many of which in their time were box office stuff and are still capable of drawing the crowd, but most of which have

little artistic value and very little relation at all to life in Ireland ...
[But] Wexford puts the standard first.

The Radio Éireann Light Orchestra again took part, despite its scepticism the year before, and Wexford enjoyed four operatic nights and a public dress rehearsal for a local paying audience.

By this stage, the full enormity of Walsh's success was being recognized at home and abroad. An extract from the periodical *Creation* paid tribute to what Walsh had achieved:

> [Walsh] combines genuine devotion to music – and [Wexford] – with an encyclopaedic knowledge of opera, tremendous drive, and a single-minded tenacity of purpose. It may be several generations before the people of Ireland fully recognize and appreciate all he has done to bring international prestige to the little town of Wexford.
>
> Dr Walsh has in fact achieved the impossible. And he has wrought this miracle in the face of true Irish scepticism.

As Walsh himself declared in 1954, 'The first year it was a joke. The second year it was no longer a joke – it was impossible.'[27]

At this stage it was still the valuable cultural aspect of the Festival that occupied the thoughts of those at the fore. Financial considerations were dealt with more as a necessity rather than as an issue central to the success of the Festival. An expenditure account of the 1955 season indicated that the bulk of the money spent on production by the Festival Council went to the producer, conductor and designer, and the artists themselves. This amounted to £4,150, nearly half of the overall expenditure for the season. In total, taking into consideration the opera performances, the Radio Éireann Symphony Concert, recitals, exhibitions and lectures, along with advertising and administration, the expenditure account totalled at £8,350.[28] The receipts for the income account signified that members' subscriptions accounted for over one third of the total income to the Festival. The deficit for 1955 was £2900,[29] obviously not a crippling amount, as the Council prepared for its coming year.

For the first time ever at Wexford, the 1955 Festival managed to combine two operas into an extended season of two weeks. It was certainly an achievement, and the Council deserved more than a little recognition, not only for maintaining the high standard of the festival, but also for expanding its seasons' repertoire. The operas were alternated every second night, beginning on 30 October with *Manon Lescaut* by Puccini and followed by Lortzing's *Der Wildschütz.* Anthony Besch produced both operas, while the designer, Peter Rice, had the responsibility for both works.[30]

The Wexford Festival Chorus had remained a loyal and valuable part of the productions, and Walsh, though not always on amicable terms with the Music Director of Radio Éireann, managed to secure the services of the Radio Éireann Light Orchestra for each consecutive year.[31] From a peripheral perspective, the continued success was both astounding and baffling:

> Like its founder, the festival is indeed somewhat eccentric, a mixture of fashion and familiarity, high professional quality and endearingly homespun. It began against all the odds, but has survived and prospered. And the town has prospered around it. Wexford has never become an imitation of other glossier European festivals,[32]

the *New York Times* said later although the notion was particularly apt in 1955.

Walsh was honest about the amount of help he had received from Glyndebourne and what an inspiration Glyndebourne had been as Wexford planned its own Festival. To those who were not aware of any connections, Walsh declared that:

> since I had first visited Glyndebourne Festival Opera before the war I had recognized from what I had seen there that opera was not just a platform for singers, but an art form in which singers, chorus, orchestra, production, scenery, costumes and lighting all had their place in creating what in Germany they call 'gesamtkunstwerk' – a total work of art.[33]

Walsh and his Council had managed to keep very quiet about the fact that the Wexford Festival was helped enormously by the Glyndebourne Festival, especially by what Walsh himself had learned from the East Sussex experience. Ireland in the 1950s was still showing signs of retaining suspicions about high culture, but Glyndebourne became the name immediately associated with the Wexford Festival. Carl Ebert said of Wexford that it was:

Bryan Balkwill, Peter Ebert and the cast of *La sonnambula*, 1954

just like Glyndebourne at the beginning. Nobody then believed that
we could successfully run an opera festival just two hour's journey from
London. The success of Wexford is, of course, due to the passion and
artistic knowledge of its director Dr Tom Walsh, plus the wonderful
support which it gets from the local people.[34]

With Carl Ebert's son, Peter Ebert, producing three of the operas so far between
1951 and 1955, it was obvious that a Glyndebourne influence was infiltrating
into the make-up of the Wexford productions. In musical and operatic circles,
it was not a problem but an honour to be associated with such a prestigious
organization, even if it was English. But some voiced strong objection to the
very hint of a connection:

In Tom Walsh's day many of us felt, and sometimes said, that he was
slightly prejudiced against things Irish and tended to rely too much

Halinka de Tarczynska,
Gwyn Griffiths, Marilyn Cotlow,
Nicola Monti and Thetis Blacker, 1954

upon people from England. To what extent that impression was a matter of his personality, and to what extent a basic logistic necessity of Walsh-standard opera, is un-discoverable. But this dependence upon England seems to be increasing,

Charles Acton remarked in a newspaper article entitled 'Wexford needs to stress Irishness'.[35]

Although most of the correspondence between Glyndebourne and Wexford was not preserved at Wexford,[36] information from the Glyndebourne archives highlighted the fact that Wexford and Glyndebourne were joined closely in cultural circles and benefited greatly from each other's assistance. In 1955, Moran Caplat, who had become general manager at Glyndebourne in 1945, commented that he was immensely impressed with what he saw at Wexford.

I enjoyed myself very much and I congratulate you all not only on the success but on the vitality of the Wexford Festival … I shall look forward to seeing you at Glyndebourne …

he wrote in the wake of the 1955 season.[37] Caplat was a contributor to the Festival Forum – a discussion forum that was part of the Festival events – and was particularly useful in promoting the Wexford Festival in England. For the 1956 Festival Forum, the host, Fintan O'Connor, requested that Caplat put forward some possible questions for discussion. John Raymond of the *New Statesman* was to accompany Caplat and Mackenzie onto the Forum platform for 1956.[38]

Wexford had also sought Glyndebourne's help with the formation of Loc Garmain [sic] Enterprises in 1955, which became, the following year, Wexford Festival Limited. The Festival Council had agreed that it would be in its best interest to form a limited liability company, to be called 'The Wexford Festival Limited'; it was aware that Glyndebourne had formed two organizations, a limited company and also a trust. O'Connor wrote to Caplat to request permission to view the memorandum and articles of association of the company and the trust document.[39] Glyndebourne readily shared its experience with Walsh and Eugene McCarthy, who were named as the original shareholders and directors of Wexford Festival Limited, with one share each.[40]

Marilyn Cotlow,
1954

The press soon picked up on the negative aspects of Wexford's relationship with Glyndebourne. Charles Acton noted that Wexford had been described as 'the Irish Glyndebourne', and he went on to say:

> There is this danger that the image and feel of Wexford Opera should come to have some of the cosiness and smugness that some people associate with Glyndebourne, so that in Ireland, and even more in England, Wexford should be thought of, rightly or wrongly, as Glyndebourne's provincial branch.[41]

This was not a criticism of the operatic performances or indeed any aspect of the Festival. It was the association with a type of aristocratic Englishness that was viewed with suspicion.

Esther Réthy in *Manon Lescaut,* 1955

A criticism that was made of Wexford's association with Glyndebourne was the fact that using artists from abroad inevitably reduced Wexford's own involvement in the production of the operas. 'Wexford's super-dependence on the Glyndebourne connection [is] both convenient and administratively useful', wrote reporter John Mulcahy, 'but it inevitably replaces the search for local talent and the fostering of native resources'.[42] Still, the chorus was mainly local, the voluntary workers were local, and the Radio Éireann Light Orchestra was based in Dublin.

Minutes of the Council meetings indicated that the number of local members of the chorus had dropped and was continuing to do so, forcing a greater reliance on members of the Glyndebourne chorus to fill the places.

This fall-off in local help was inevitable, however: the Wexford voluntary chorus could not indefinitely commit to the Festival as a firm commitment would mean surrendering much time to rehearsals each year. On the other hand, the Glyndebourne chorus members were paid for their efforts.[43] Walsh was fortunate to have such a strong relationship with Glyndebourne which essentially allowed the Wexford Festival to progress year after year. The *RTÉ Guide* alluded to this fact:

> Glyndebourne early on took an interest in Wexford, and their help, in many little ways, was undoubtedly a prerequisite for Wexford's continuing success. And after all, Glyndebourne did for opera in England before the war what Wexford has done for opera in Ireland – shown just what good opera can really be ... That Wexford could be mentioned in the same breath as Glyndebourne and that Glyndebourne would go talent-spotting in Wexford had a lot to do with Ireland becoming known on the operatic map of the world.[44]

Elizabeth Lindermeier, Monica Sinclair and Thomas Hemsley in *Der Wildschütz*, 1955

CHAPTER 3

THE BURDEN OF CARRYING IT ON

1956–9

Preparations for this annual Festival continued into 1956, culminating in the production of *Martha* by Friedrich von Flotow and *La Cenerentola* by Gioachino Rossini. Bryan Balkwill conducted both operas, and the designer was Joseph Carl. Peter Potter, a new addition to the Wexford Festival staff, produced *Martha* and Peter Ebert returned after a year's interlude to produce *La Cenerentola*.[1] Mackenzie had promised to write an article about the Festival for the Tourist Board in England and wrote to Walsh in April to request specific details about the coming festivities.[2]

Although the operas continued to be successful and their popularity was reflected in the admirable attendance at each performance, a loss was incurred in 1956. The accountant and auditor, Joseph Busher, produced a balance sheet which showed that the deficit remained at £2,900[3] which was not a huge amount, and the words of Mackenzie on this subject served as some consolation

Dr Tom Walsh and Eugene McCarthy at a London press conference

for those working so hard, yet struggling to keep the financial side afloat:

> I am sorry to hear you had such a loss – though in fact it is very little
> for what was achieved. Edinburgh lost £30,000 last year. Anyway I am
> sure you will override all difficulties.[4]

At a Council meeting in June of 1956, Walsh made the claim that the Wexford Opera Festival had managed to become the third-largest festival in England, Ireland, Scotland and Wales, preceded only by Edinburgh and Glyndebourne. The Festival must be run 'on business lines', he argued; otherwise its future would be in jeopardy. He also pointed out that the entire liability of the Festival was being carried solely by Walsh himself, Eugene McCarthy and Des Ffrench.

The question of how to finance the growing amateur venture was a real concern. Further, how was the Festival going to progress from here? The proposed solution to the financial situation was to find at least twenty people who were willing to guarantee £50 towards liability. It was decided that since the Festival had achieved so much for the county, if the local people wished for the prosperity to continue they should agree to guarantee the money. As an incentive to those who would contribute, they would automatically become members of the Council. At this point, Walsh, McCarthy, Jim Liddy and Des Ffrench put their names forward as guarantors. It was also decided that each member of the Council would try to enlist another person as guarantor of the Festival.[5] Walsh enlisted his wife, Eva, who then automatically became a Council member.[6]

Another pressing issue was the poor condition of the Theatre Royal. The issues of rain leaking through the roof and the condition of seating needed to be addressed. As Walsh warned, '[the] dressing rooms are in such poor condition that it is difficult to get artists to come and sing in the place'.[7]

Given the seasonal nature of the Festival, the repairs to the Theatre tended to be temporary measures, each year the roof being repaired and the seating attended to for use during Festival week. But a limited liability company, Theatrical Entertainments Ltd, owned the theatre and could not afford major

Marco Rothmüller and Men's Chorus in *Martha*, 1956

Constance Shacklock and Marco Rothmüller in *Martha*, 1956

renovations. Luckily, a local timber company agreed to take care of the repairs for the 1956 season free of charge. These offers of help were vital. A suggestion was made that the Wexford Festival should seek assistance from Bord Fáilte, Ireland's tourist board, for the permanent renovation of the theatre and as a result, a loan of £5,000 was sought.[8]

In October 1956 a letter was received from the Director General of Bord Fáilte stating that it would be willing to make a grant of just £1,000 for the renovation of the Theatre Royal.[9] Although less than hoped for, this news was welcomed. However, the success and even continuance of the Festival still depended to a large extent on its 'wealthy admirers', as admitted by Walsh in 1956. These supporters of Walsh's efforts offered to buy the plot of land at the back of the theatre for the benefit of the Festival. Walsh was also offered £250 on the assumption that the Council could provide a further £800 for the renovation of the theatre.[10] But the Council was naturally not prepared to spend large sums of money on a theatre that might not be available for its use in the future. As they could obviously not afford to purchase the building, it was suggested that Wexford Festival Limited obtain a long lease of the theatre from Theatrical Entertainments Ltd, thereby ensuring that any money spent on its renovation would benefit the Festival directly.

The Council's time was increasingly taken up with the important issue of financing the coming season. The cost of producing opera was increasing steadily. In 1956, the notion of insuring the artists was discussed. It was agreed that insurance was an absolute necessity to guard against the failure of artists to perform.[11] This served as an added expense for the Council – an expense that had not been considered in the earlier years. Eva, Walsh's wife, had even suggested that funding could be raised by the setting up of a 'Silver Circle' that involved collecting money locally in Wexford but also from the rest of the country.[12] Schemes to extract money from the community were generally high on the agenda at the Council meetings, but realistically the bulk of the income was donated by the Council members and private sponsors at this stage. Little reference was made to the Arts Council subsidy; nevertheless it continued to contribute annually.

The Council was promised a subsidy from the German government in December 1956.[13] This was because Wexford was employing German musicians and the subsidy represented part-payment of the artists' fees. Walsh, moreover, received a letter from the editor of the German magazine, *Festival*, stating that a number of staff members were interested in visiting the Wexford Festival, with a view to doing a piece on cultural life in Ireland generally. No doubt it served the Festival well to be deemed a representative of progressive cultural life in Ireland. On receiving the letter, Walsh immediately contacted Bord Fáilte who was the sponsor of visiting journalists to Ireland.[14]

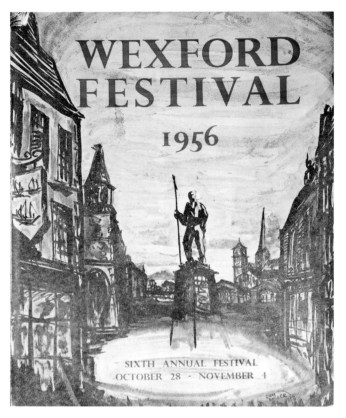

Wexford Festival programme book, 1956.

In 1956, too, officers of Bord Fáilte in Britain began to take a real interest in the Festival. Terry Sheehy, who was general manager of Bord Fáilte in Britain at the time, recalled a meeting held at the Café Royal in London to publicize and promote the Festival; the meeting, which took the form of a type of conference or luncheon, was attended by Walsh, Eugene McCarthy, with Mackenzie in the chair. This panel was joined by the top music critics in Britain. London editors of papers such as the *Irish Times*, the *Irish Press* and the *Cork Examiner* were also present. Considering the power and prestige of Britain's music critics, this was a huge affair, essentially creating for Walsh and Wexford an air of importance that they so richly deserved.

The BBC, too, had a keen interest in the affairs at Wexford, and ran programmes about the Wexford Festival. Sir Huw Wheldon, who later became Managing Director of BBC Television, had personally visited Wexford to experience the Festival, thus lending weight and credence to the enterprise. The Irish Tourist Board paid for other invited guests to attend.

The Irish Tourist Board in London set up a 'Wexford Festival window' for the purpose of promoting the venture. Sheehy later pointed out that the Dublin Grand Opera Society was *not* aided by the Tourist Board for the simple reason that it held no international attraction on account of it being introverted. It was just a typical opera society, unlike Wexford, where the unusual location, budget, management and local chorus gave weight to the claims that it was a unique event.[15] As Moran Caplat of Glyndebourne pointed out, 'the venerable Dublin Grand Opera Society was in the habit of hiring established productions from abroad and slapping them on, miserably unrehearsed, with singers ranging from the excellent to the execrable'.[16]

Later on, the *Wexford People* claimed that:

> the Tourist Board had made it clear to them that they were not particularly interested in the work of the Festival as a promoter of the arts, but, they were more concerned with encouraging a bigger flow of people to this country from abroad.[17]

But Sheehy himself refuted this, and declared that Wexford had brought out the cultural side of Ireland. Intellectuals were going there to see opera, and it had waves of meaning for the country.[18]

The Wexford Festival Council had managed to uphold its policy of producing rare operas, or certainly ones that had not been produced elsewhere in Ireland or Britain. Of course, this constituted much of the charm at Wexford for the visitors, and undoubtedly there were many who were assured that they would not be able to witness the same production at Glyndebourne or Covent Garden. For 1957 the Council had chosen another Rossini opera, this time *L'italiana in Algeri* and also Gaetano Donizetti's *La figlia del reggimento*.[19] The Council was particularly proud of the fact that the earl and countess of Harewood attended this year's festival.[20]

With the deficits incurred increasing each year, it was a distinct possibility that the Festival would be forced to fold. This was alluded to in the Council minutes where it was requested that discussions regarding the possibility of not holding a Festival in 1957 should not be mentioned to the public.[21] It was at this point that the first indication of Walsh's intention to resign became evident. Just as the musical repertoire had reached a solid point, financial troubles were beginning to take hold. Work was being carried out on the theatre for a new season but Walsh was reluctant to utilize the funding by donors for a project that might not reach fruition. It was reported that:

> owing to the question of future Festivals being in doubt [Walsh] did not want to involve the Donors into a liability if the Festival were to cease this year. As the offer had been made by the donors to him, Dr Walsh considered that the responsibility was on him to see that the deal would only be carried out if the Festival were to continue.[22]

It is significant that at this juncture, the first signs of division in the Council became apparent. Walsh requested that a professional organizer be appointed for the 1958 Festival, and also threatened his resignation. He was persuaded, however, to reconsider, given that the Council did intend to employ someone to assist him with the direction of the Festival. Reverend M.J. O'Neill had taken on the role of chairman of the Council by this stage. Meanwhile, every option was considered with regard to extra funding and there was an ongoing application for funding from the Shaw Trust.[23] Sir Alfred Beit, a former Conservative MP now living at Russborough, Co. Wicklow,[24] was investigating the possibility of obtaining a grant for the Festival from the Gulbenkian Foundation.[25]

Beit's interest in the Festival marked an important turning point in its affairs. He was an extremely wealthy man and had come to live in Ireland in 1952, where he housed a remarkable collection of paintings at his home. His knowledge and interest in opera was immense, beginning, like Walsh, when he was ten years old. Beit had a high regard for Verdi and Puccini and also for French and German composers.[26] He had moved to Co. Wicklow to retire from active political life.[27] Moran Caplat of Glyndebourne has claimed that it was he who had encouraged Beit to become involved in the Festival. They met at Wexford and Caplat outlined to Beit the significance of the Wexford Festival.[28]

Despite the growing financial concern, 1958 was another successful year in ticket sales, with the production of *I due Foscari,* composed by Verdi, and *Anna Bolena*, by Donizetti.[29] Manchester's Hallé Orchestra had been invited over to perform in concert and the orchestra's performance was very well received.[30] It was no surprise to anyone that Walsh was beginning to feel the strain. He was tired of the financial burden of the Festival. Money issues were arising year in, year out, but were never resolved. Described by the *Evening Herald* as a 'star

Paolo Pedani in
La Cenerentola, 1956

Gisela Vivarelli and
Constance Shacklock
in *Martha*, 1956

matador', he attended a press conference in July 1958, only to be described as embodying 'the bland expression of one who knows that the Press must have their little fling; his the face that launched a thousand Press conferences'.[31]

The confidence of achievement and sense of purpose of the man who had launched such an important cultural event no longer carried the same air of optimism. Each new idea and new season was fraught with financial strain. Of course, the financial accounts of the Wexford Council were not publicly known and therefore the press continued in its praise of the festival.

But there was a more personal reason for Walsh's nonchalance at this time. Walsh lost his beloved wife, Eva. It was no surprise that Festival activity was not his priority at this time following his loss. Eva had complemented Walsh's role in the Festival, playing a very active part. She too, had a musical background, and she had played hostess to many who had visited the Festival since 1951. The Reverend M.J. O'Neill paid tribute to her enormous influence on her husband's Festival:

> Eight years ago in those first uncertain years of Festival planning – or perhaps one should say – improvisation, when friends were few, Eva rallied to her husband's side and by her encouragement and

Patricia Kern, Graziella Sciutti, Geraint Evans and cast in *La figlia del reggimento*, 1957

Mario Spina, Bryan Balkwill, Patricia Kern, Graziella Sciutti and Peter Ebert in *La figlia del reggimento*, 1957

prudent, practical judgement helped to make the venture possible. To fit an International Festival of Music and the Arts into Wexford was, indeed, a difficult undertaking. With Tom she realized that artistic standards must be raised to the highest level, but she also realized – with that feminine intuition, which husbands rarely appreciate, but always use – that high standard alone would not assure success. She foresaw that what Wexford lacked by way of a Vienna Staatsoper or a Salzburg Felsenreitschule must be masked by establishing a genuine Irish spirit of friendliness and hospitality, so that celebrities, patrons and all visitors would be made to feel at home when they came here.[32]

Compton Mackenzie, who had known Eva well through his association with the Festival, echoed these sentiments:

Tom Walsh has been the dynamo of the Festival, but he could never have achieved what he has so remarkably achieved without the help of his wife, and to lose her like this is a heartbreak for him and for all those who loved her.[33]

Grief dimmed Walsh's enthusiasm as the next season loomed. At the Council meetings, however, serious reorganization of the entire Festival was being discussed. It was suggested that the administration should be divided into five sections – artistic, business, theatre and box office, finance, and illuminations.[34] Walsh would naturally be head of the artistic section, with Eugene McCarthy dealing with the business aspect.[35] This reorganization came in the wake of Walsh's threatened resignation and may have been a direct result of it. Now he was responsible solely for the artistic aspects of the Festival. This was a telling indication that the Wexford Festival was becoming more professional in outlook. The golden amateur period was destined to end, as the days of amateur production became more difficult to sustain; the involvement of the Radio Éireann Light Orchestra was already in place, and now Walsh had made it clear that he could not personally oversee the smooth running of all aspects of the Festival.

Bord Fáilte guaranteed the 1958 Festival up to a maximum of £2,000[36] and the Arts Council provided a guarantee against loss of up to £430,[37] but the Festival Council had failed to negotiate with the Gulbenkian Trust for the 1958 season.[38] Nevertheless Alfred Beit advised Walsh to continue negotiations for future years.[39] Beit was becoming increasingly involved in Council affairs and he offered to donate money towards the cost of re-upholstering seats in the theatre.[40] Meanwhile Walsh had just returned from Milan where he had travelled for the sole purpose of auditioning singers.[41]

Walsh's genuine love of opera and his dedication to the Festival could never be disputed, but the task of presenting opera was becoming more difficult, as he himself intimated at a Council meeting in January 1959. He pointed to the added competition of the newly established Dublin Festival that would inevitably affect his own enterprise.[42] In the absence of any solid proposals, it was suggested that the 1959 Festival be postponed. Yet the Council was aware that they would lose out drastically if they allowed the Dublin Festival to become established in the absence of a Wexford Festival season; indeed Wexford might not be able to recover its past support at all in the future. As reported in the minutes of the Council meeting:

> [it was] understood that Dr Walsh would not be willing to act as Director for another Festival without the dressing rooms. To which Dr Walsh said that it was not his willingness in this matter but the fact that it would be impossible to get artists to come and work under

the conditions as in the past[43] ... At this stage Dr Walsh suggested that if the members could not see their way to be responsible for the provision of the money, it would be well to consider winding up the Festival now on a high note.[44]

This feeling was also evident in a letter to Ninette Hant, a week later, when he disclosed that the financial situation was becoming too difficult to rectify. Walsh had met Ninette on a cruise, and they were subsequently married in February 1960. Ninette's daughter, Victoria, was to play a central role in her new stepfather's life. Aside from Festival considerations, it was a time of transition personally for Walsh. It was at this time too that Walsh retired from general practice and took up the full-time appointment of Anaesthetist at the Wexford County Hospital. Not surprisingly, he became dejected with the amount of work and fundraising that was expected of him. He wrote:

> This year a further £3,000 was needed for dressing room and back stage accommodation. I saw our bank manager who said, 'If you can get guarantees for £2,000 I will advance you the extra £1,000'. David Price and I agreed to guarantee to raise £500 each which we can by doing a certain amount of work ... There the matter stuck with the remainder sitting on the fence and waiting for me as on many occasions heretofore, saying alright I'll find the remaining £800. The meeting on tomorrow night is to discuss the motion 'That the Wexford Festival should be discontinued' – it will be if I don't agree to take over the responsibility. But after eight years I have become sick and tired of finding money.
>
> I will have to decide tomorrow night either to let the Festival end, or to accept the burden of carrying it on. On the other hand, I may be wrong about what will transpire tonight, and maybe they will find the money – I don't know.[45]

As Walsh had inferred, the dire financial situation had, yet again, the potential to put an end to the Wexford Festival.

A letter from Mackenzie to Walsh in February 1959 indicated that, in the interest of the financial well-being of the festival, Mackenzie suggested his own retirement, citing old age. This would leave the position open for Alfred

Paolo Pedani in
I due Foscari,
1958

Beit. Beit was, at this stage, vice-president of the Festival. The very fact that Mackenzie was considering retirement from his position as president of the Festival Council suggested that the financial situation had deteriorated rapidly:

> I say again what I have already said: if you think that in view of the finance you ought to make Sir Alfred Beit President, you are to let me know and I'll make it quite easy by resigning on score of old age.[46]

Giorgio Tadeo, Janet Baker, Nicola Monti, Mariella Adani, Elizabeth Bainbridge and the cast of *La gazza ladra*, 1959

Beit was obviously in a strong financial situation and his potential for assisting the Festival could not be ignored. When considering Mackenzie's immense value to the Festival from the very beginning, the situation that the Festival Council found itself in was all the more poignant. Walsh had described Mackenzie as 'the first person who made me realize – and I was then just 39 – that all I ever dreamed about, was possible, and for that I will always love him'.[47]

Walsh was becoming increasingly infuriated with the financial situation that faced the Festival. Although the Council was in contact with Bord Fáilte regarding the possibility of receiving an interest-free loan, Walsh had set the Council a deadline, before which time he expected them to have a number of solutions to the financial problem.[48] His deadline was January 1959 and he refused to budge on this. It was an unfortunate situation, considering that the Festival was in danger of folding simply because it was an amateur, middle-class venture. This had been its very charm from the beginning. Walsh had decided, not for the first time, that his position as artistic director was being compromised, as he was expected to deal with the business side of the Festival as well as the artistic side.

It was surprising then, that in February Walsh presented himself at a Council meeting only to declare that he was willing to run the Festival in 1959 despite all he had said before and despite the lack of dressing rooms. He did suggest, however, that he would not be free to give as much time to the organization of the Festival as he had in previous years. The Council members also agreed that the burden of financing the Festival should not rest with him. He was busy enough in any case with the artistic direction as the artists were proving difficult to obtain. Walsh subsequently took a trip to London to interview various agents.[49]

The situation seemed to be in a somewhat healthier state with the confirmation from Bord Fáilte that the Minister for Finance had agreed a loan of £3,500 to the Festival. This money was to be utilized to build dressing rooms and in the general renovation of the Theatre Royal.[50] The Gulbenkian Foundation also guaranteed that the sum of £5,000 would be available for the renovation of the building.[51] The funding was invaluable, and for the first time the Council considered the possibility of making the public aware that there might not be a Festival the following year, in order to gauge the local interest in keeping the Festival going. After all, the feeling was that if the local people were disinterested, there was little hope of expecting 'outsiders' to contribute.[52]

The fact that money was needed was obvious, even in media circles, but most believed it was for the improvement and extension of the Festival, not for its survival. The cultural significance of the Festival was always stressed in the reports. The *Wexford People*, in October 1959, printed part of a sermon by Fr M.J. O'Neill, at the Church of the Immaculate Conception, Rowe Street, Wexford. O'Neill spoke of the Wexford Festival, not only as a means of entertainment, but also as a means of educating the public in the appreciation of higher and more finely developed forms of music and the arts.[53]

> While we are justly proud of our own national culture, [the Festival] was humble enough to learn from the great masters of other nations.

Mariella Adani and
Paolo Pedani in
La gazza ladra, 1959

They had as their honoured guests some of the most eminent artistes of Europe. The very high standard of their artistic performances should be an incentive to them all to raise their own cultural standards and make them more worthy of the Irish Catholic Nation. A nation might very rightly be judged by its culture. They could, therefore, realize how important it was that they should, on the one hand, foster and support all that was genuinely artistic and beautiful, and, on the other hand, should reject and despise all that was vulgar and degrading ...[54]

Why Fr O'Neill used the Wexford Festival as a symbol of Catholic nationality was unclear, yet his desire to stress the Festival's Irishness and more directly its community spirit was prominent.

'Here you have something which was created by local effort and was continued by local effort', stated M.J. O'Driscoll, Director General of Bord Fáilte, guest speaker at the inaugural night of the 1959 Wexford Festival, 'a festival which from being a matter of pride for the town of Wexford, has become something of which the country is proud, and something which is establishing abroad the good name of our people and our country'.[55] In front of an audience that included prestigious figures such as An Tánaiste, Seán MacEntee, the Italian ambassador and Prince and Princess Caracciolo, Verdi's *Aroldo* was performed on four nights of the season. The second work performed this year at the Theatre Royal was *La gazza ladra* by Rossini.[56]

The prestige of the Festival was augmented this year by the presence of the BBC Symphony Orchestra at the Abbey Cinema. Help from Glyndebourne for the 1959 season was recorded in the *Irish Times* in October of the same year. While praising the local chorus and its participation in the success of the Festival, the paper reported that:

> inevitably there have to be a few professional leaders engaged from Glyndebourne, who give added confidence to the chorus. Though some of these will always be necessary, it is the Wexford people themselves who really are the chorus, who earn the praise, whom every conductor extols.

A combination of private initiative, public aid and British help had thus produced a spectacular effect at Wexford, ensuring, as the *Irish Times* put it, that the town was at last 'on the musical map of the world'.[57]

CHAPTER 4

ON THE MUSICAL MAP
OF THE WORLD

1960–3

The first indication that the Festival would perhaps be taking a different route in the future was Walsh's admission in October 1959 that the Festival had 'grown up' and it:

> should be in a position to look forward three years ahead. It was now considered that certain changes in the Festival would have to be made, but these would not alter the original character of the Wexford Festival.[1]

It was obviously a huge disappointment to Walsh and the Festival Council then, that there was no Opera Festival in 1960. It was decided in January of that year that it would be necessary to have entire renovations carried out on the theatre before the next Festival and this could not be done by October.[2] The Council

Moran Caplat and Dr Tom Walsh, 1960s

had managed to produce nine consecutive years of opera, but at this stage it was forced again to consider the permanency of its venture. Its meetings continued regularly, and matters were discussed with the same enthusiasm in the hope that the lapse of one year would not result in permanent disbandment.

The transition from an amateur event to a professional one was subtly introduced by Beit, as his part in the work of the Festival Council became increasingly authoritative. A confidential memo sent from Beit to Walsh set about trying to improve the situation in order to ensure the Festival's continued success. The Council had no choice but to heed him. Beginning with an overview of the financial situation, Beit indicated that the Council now had £8,500 for the purpose of building dressing rooms (artists had often changed into costume in their hotel rooms because of lack of changing facilities at the theatre) and enlarging and redecorating the Theatre Royal. Beit suggested that a further £6,000 would be needed to complete the task. He suggested that this be sought, not by appealing to the public, but by targeting large business enterprises in Ireland and then a select number of individuals who would be also willing to help. At the same time Beit questioned the very suitability of the

Theatre Royal as the primary venue for the opera performances. He displayed his distaste for the theatre itself, commenting that 'the more I see of the Theatre Royal, the less I like it'. He complained that the noise of singers in full flow in the tiny space was something little short of 'deafening'. Beit noted also that some of the singers had made complaints of this nature to the *Sunday Times* and to the *Financial Times*,[3] which was bad publicity for the Festival. It was important for Wexford to satisfy its cast, and the Festival was obviously reliant on its international singers.

Beit turned his attention then specifically to the Abbey Cinema, which he felt should be used for productions during the Festival. He offered to enquire about the availability of the building, not knowing whom it belonged to. He suggested that the Festival Council should either enter into a contract to rent the Abbey for perhaps a period of a fortnight each year for five years, including some time for rehearsals. Other rehearsals, he added, could be held at the Theatre Royal. He mentioned that if any work needed to be done to the Abbey Cinema, dressing room extensions or orchestra pit, the Gulbenkian Foundation and the Irish Tourist Board would surely agree to use their grant and loan respectively on the Abbey Cinema instead. He added that the economic situation should improve due to the increased number of seats available at the Abbey.

Beit recognized that, with the recent conclusion of the 1959 season, the bank overdraft would probably be in the region of £5,000. However, he first dealt with the problem of meeting all future running costs. According to him, the Tourist Board had agreed to provide £2,000 for each Festival for the next three years and it was assumed that the Arts Council would not renege on its grant of approximately £400. A press report suggested that the Tourist Board grant would be provided on a £1 to £1 basis and Beit was keen to investigate whether this was true or whether an unconditional grant of £2,000 was being offered.

Most importantly, Beit himself agreed to anonymously guarantee up to £1,000 a year for the next three years, but the guarantee was conditional. First, Wexford town (the Chamber of Commerce, the town council and private guarantors) had to guarantee a similar amount. Second, Beit requested that the Council no longer engage the Radio Éireann Light Orchestra. He also demanded that an executive committee of the Festival Council should be formed, which would be responsible to the Council itself and would plan all details of the Festival in the future. The demands made by this prestigious outsider to the group were indeed stringent, but Walsh was in no position to bargain.

Beit expanded on his requests, particularly with regard to the retention of the Radio Éireann Light Orchestra in future years by saying:

> The second condition regarding the orchestra may be controversial but in my opinion is essential if the Festival is to maintain its reputation, let alone increase it. I have heard enough to be able to state that conductors of the calibre we engaged this year will be reluctant or may even refuse to appear again with an orchestra of such exceptionally low quality. If, therefore, a new one is to be found I see only two alternatives. The first and the most obvious is that a new approach be made, possibly by a deputation, to obtain approximately 30 of the best players from the Radio Éireann [Symphony] orchestra itself. They are not heavily engaged at the particular season we want them and a new approach based on the money to be spent, and the improvements which will result, should be worth trying. Failing this an English Chamber Orchestra, such as the Boyd Neel or the Goldsborough, might be engaged.

Relations between the public enterprise of Radio Éireann and the private, amateur organization were on the verge of breaking down again, this time due to the demands of Beit, who had ironically appeared on the scene to ensure the Festival's permanency.

The final condition, which Beit had touched on in his memo, had the potential to cause great distress within the ranks of the Festival Council. The suggested creation of an executive committee implied that the Festival Council itself could not cope with rising financial problems. According to Beit, the committee should consist of some six or seven persons, among whom Walsh and Beit himself would take priority seating. Two or three more from the original Council, those 'who take a real interest in the Festival', would be asked to join this committee. In addition, other individuals, not at that time members of the Festival Council, would be asked to join. One addition to the committee, suggested by Beit, but not obviously publicized, was Moran Caplat, as representative of the Glyndebourne Festival for the purpose of maintaining 'the useful liaison that has been established between the two centres' (the link was important and no one acknowledged this more than Walsh himself). The executive committee would essentially plan each Festival, the engagement of its

Eugene McCarthy and Éamon de Valera, 1961 Wexford Festival

singers, conductors, producers, designers and its orchestra. As Beit pointed out in his memo, probably to the distaste of those already serving on the Festival Council and certainly to Walsh, the committee would:

> largely confirm the work which Dr Walsh himself undertakes, but in view of the growing size, cost and importance of the Festival and the additional financial burden borne by a wider circle of people or institutions it should have a final say in all matters of artistic policy.

Beit concluded his memo by dealing with the immediate overdraft incurred by the Festival just ended. Believing that it was not feasible to expect the public 'to make gifts of money to pay off the debts of the past', Beit suggested that a reduction in the overdraft could gradually be brought about over a period of years by organized events such as bazaars, lotteries and dances. Of course, the exact intentions of the committee in this area would not be publicized; merely the public would be made aware that such organized enterprises and events would be for the benefit of the Wexford Festival. In this way, they could see their money being utilized in present and future festivals.[4]

Beit's memo was confidential for obvious reasons, but Walsh distanced himself from it.[5] The public at large was oblivious to the disarray in the ranks; to them the Festival was apparently under complete control. Following Beit's stern indication that money urgently needed to be guaranteed to ensure a successful Festival in the future, Raymond Corish, auctioneer and insurance broker, named, in a letter to Walsh, those Council members who were willing to guarantee the sum of £750 for the next three years.[6] But opera was an expensive business and this gesture was not in itself sufficient. As Walsh commented:

> Opera *must be* grandiose. The simple small-scale production may work occasionally as a novelty, but in the end it loses out on concept.[7]

Walsh informed his Council members what had transpired between himself and Beit. He disclosed that Beit and his allies, including Lord Donoughmore, were willing to form a trust in order to ensure the continuation of the Festival. They would underwrite the present debt of approximately £2,500 and would provide £1,000 each year for the next three years towards the cost of running the Festival. Walsh also noted that a second trust would be formed to deal with artistic and business affairs, and although the Festival Council in its present form would remain in operation, the newly formed trust would reserve the right to make final decisions on any given matter. He mentioned that he and McCarthy would join the trust with a guarantee of £200 each against the Festival's overdraft, while assuring the Council members that all would have the opportunity to join, provided that they were willing to also guarantee £200 against the overdraft in addition to paying £100 each year for the next three years. Walsh also stipulated that the artistic standards of the Festival must be improved.[8]

Beit's involvement with Festival affairs increased again when, in early 1960, he offered to lend the necessary money in excess of the Gulbenkian grant, in order that work on the theatre could begin as soon as possible.[9]

By 1961, it was certain that a Festival would be held that year, but as James O'Connor, press officer to the Festival, pointed out, the Irish were 'creatures of habit' and after a year of operatic lapse, ticket sales were very poor in 1961.[10] This was to be the first Festival undertaken without the co-operation

Alain Vanzo,
Andrea Guiot and
Jean Borthayre in
Mireille, 1961

of the professional Radio Éireann Light Orchestra. There was no discussion in the Council minutes as to why Walsh had decided to engage the Liverpool Philharmonic Orchestra in place of the Radio Éireann Light Orchestra.

Beit's growing influence must be duly noted in this instance. His criticism of the Radio Éireann Light Orchestra at Wexford obviously did not go unheeded, and the very fact that he stipulated that all the criteria in his memo be met before he would agree to act as guarantor for the Festival, served to heighten suspicions that he was now at the head of the organization at Wexford.

The operas performed this year were Verdi's *Ernani* and Charles Gounod's *Mireille*. Along with the Liverpool Philharmonic Orchestra, the Wexford Festival Chorus participated in all performances.[11] Peter Ebert returned to produce *Ernani*. It was conducted by Bryan Balkwill, another Glyndebourne man, and the designer was Reginald Woolley. Gounod's work was produced by Anthony Besch and was designed by Osbert Lancaster.[12] It was conducted by Michael Moores who was a new addition to Wexford. The 10th Wexford Festival lasted from 24 September to 1 October 1961.[13]

In a magazine article of November 1961, Marese Murphy tried to outline the reasons for the fall-off in ticket sales in the first year following the renovation of the theatre:

> Possibly due to the change of date – a month earlier than usual – or, perhaps, to the lapsed year, or the almost simultaneous incidence of similar events in Dublin and Cork, this was not the gayest of Wexford Festivals until the latter half of the week. Throughout, however, it was the most artistically successful to date and, with the impeccable co-operation of the Royal Liverpool Philharmonic Orchestra, the operas

Alain Vanzo, Andrea Guiot and
Franco Ventriglia in *Mireille*, 1961

achieved a higher all-round standard than in any other year of my experience.[14]

Schemes were discussed immediately to combat the problem of falling ticket sales. This problem was perhaps unforeseen by the Council members whose main priority had been to ensure that sufficient funding would be available to allow the Festival to go ahead.

Walsh had taken ill during the immediate Festival preparations and Moran Caplat was contacted to suggest a replacement for him. In the end, Walsh was able to continue as artistic director for 1961 but the experience served as a reminder to the Council that Walsh played a huge part in the annual Festival preparations and that replacing him would be no easy task.[15]

The total cost of the 1961 Festival was estimated at £16,600. A deficit of £3,770 was recorded after the consideration of grants and guarantees and it was concluded that this deficit could only be regulated by increased membership and admission charges.[16] It was an ongoing concern that financial support was not forthcoming from the town itself. Walsh was of the opinion that members of the Council even, should do more to help the Festival, considering the value of the Festival to the locality, and declared at a Council meeting:

> I think some other members of the Council who are business men may realize the value of the Festival to the town, especially since Wexford as a tourist centre has begun to be stressed. The value of a £16,000 to £17,000 promotion lasting eight days plus the attendant publicity must be of considerable value from a business point of view.[17]

Beit continued to play his part, this time by paying for advertisements in three of the Dublin morning papers, the *Cork Examiner* and the *Belfast Telegraph* at the end of August 1961, and in the *Kerryman* and the *Limerick Leader*. The cost of these advertisements amounted to £136. Beit did not think it proper for him to be compelled to pay his £125 guarantee in addition to this sum, so he did not do so. He made it known that all the trustees of the Festival had already agreed to guarantee the amount of £125, thus bringing in the sum of £875.[18] Beit further suggested that the method of arranging a Guarantee Fund, of the sort devised by both the Dublin Grand Opera Society and the Dublin Theatre Festival, would have worked very nicely at Wexford, had Walsh and his Council employed the method. 'On reflection, a mistake we probably made was in not arranging for a Guarantee Fund some time ago to cover possible losses', he admitted.

> Having myself been a guarantor of both these for some years I have found that they have never yet asked for the full amount. Since our accounts were based on the assumption, which you now think is faulty, that the theatre would be booked out, we must in future have some guarantee fund of this nature.[19]

As well as becoming chairman of the Executive Council for the Festival, Beit had become the financial mentor at Wexford, a post at which he excelled, and it was not surprising that Walsh handed over this particular burden without much regret. Money remained devastatingly important to the successful continuation of the Festival. Wexford, unlike Glyndebourne, lacked, in the first decade of its existence, a rich patron to privately fund the amateur venture. Now, with Beit, they had one.

Beit's continued dominance of Council affairs left little room for discussion as the original Festival Council realized in the wake of the 1961 Festival. The gross deficit was estimated at £8,500 and it was generally agreed that local guarantors had reached their limit. At this stage, even, two guarantors of £50 each had aired their discontent at having no say in the choice of programme for the Festival each year. They pointed out that if they were to continue paying this sum annually, they should have a small say in the running of the Festival.[20] Again the professionalization of the Festival was becoming evident, with criticism arising from the fact that an Executive Council had been formed and the original team were left with very little power to affect policy changes. The complaint was noted at a Council meeting and the views of certain Council members were duly aired:

> There was no function for the Council any more except to provide voluntary workers and they felt that this was evident during the past year. While they were not objecting that the Trust should run the Festival and make major decisions, since they were financially responsible, and in any event they were made aware of this when the Trust was formed, they were at the same time left to understand that

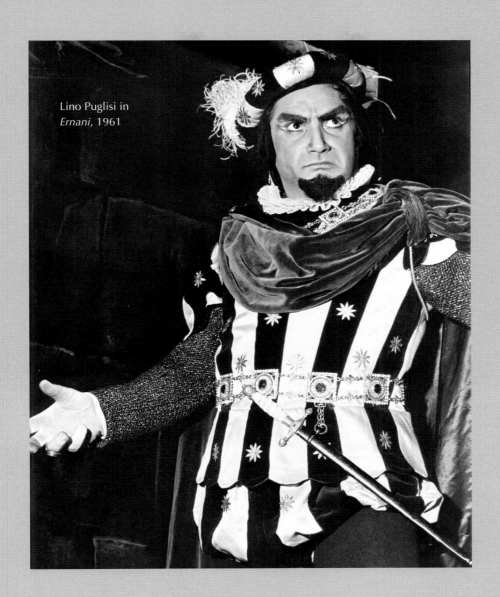

Lino Puglisi in
Ernani, 1961

Mirella Freni in *I puritani*, 1962

they would have some say in certain matters but instead they were just told that the decisions had been made and that was all. Also more often than not they were not aware of what was happening ...[21]

This feeling continued into the new season and saw the steady dissolution of the old Festival Council in the place of the new Executive Council.[22] The preparations for the 1962 Festival witnessed a marked change in artistic policy. Walsh had stipulated in earlier years that it was his desire to produce little-known operas at Wexford, hence increasing the sense of uniqueness at what was being achieved. But for the first time, Walsh set out before the Festival Council, at Beit's request, the proposed plan for the 1962 Festival, which included the presentation of two operas, one unusual and one popular. It was unanimously agreed by the Council that it was a good idea to combine the popular with the unique, probably because the ticket sales had proved so slow the previous year. Inevitably, it would contradict Walsh's designated plan to keep the Festival exclusive in its productions, but at this point, in order to ensure its survival, all options had to be explored. Walsh was evidently in agreement with the production of a popular opera at this stage.

Films and lectures as usual were produced as fringe events, and the Festival took on a new title in 1962, the 'Wexford Festival Opera'. Perhaps the subtle title change was an attempt to focus on the importance of opera rather than the actual Festival and its fringe events. It was also agreed by the Council members that the Festival would have to be produced for £9,000 – that all possible grants and funds had been extended to their limits.

The hiring of the Liverpool Philharmonic Orchestra in the place of the Radio Éireann Light Orchestra had served its purpose well, and the Council realized in 1962 that Radio Éireann was willing to make available its Symphony Orchestra for the Festival, for a fee considerably less than that of the Liverpool Philharmonic.[23] The Wexford Festival Council, particularly Walsh who dealt directly with Radio Éireann, had taken a substantial risk by choosing to employ the Liverpool Orchestra over Ireland's national orchestra, but Wexford benefited from its no-tolerance tactic at this point. Beit had initiated this shift, but the standard of the Radio Éireann Light Orchestra had consistently fallen short of the expectations of Walsh who aimed to produce opera to the highest standard possible. In the end it transpired that even the first desk players from the Radio Éireann Symphony Orchestra were available for the Festival in 1962 at an inclusive fee of £1,700.[24]

The artistic direction of the operas, which was, in effect, Walsh's responsibility, was discussed more frequently than ever at the Council meetings. Walsh felt his position compromised as Beit strayed from his financial direction, to propose specific operatic productions. In a letter to the Council that was read out in Beit's absence, Beit had stated that:

> while I agreed to your suggestion that we should put on one popular opera I personally could not agree in any circumstances that we should put on a hackneyed opera such as *Traviata, Rigoletto, Trovatore, Aida, Lucia di Lammermoor, La Bohème, Madame Butterfly, Tosca, Cav.* [*sic*] and *Pag.* [*sic*] and the like.

He went so far as to suggest that *Simon Boccanegra* would be an excellent choice.[25] It must be taken into account, however, that Beit had donated £500 to the Festival and had guaranteed a further £500.[26] His private funding was absolutely essential to the Festival's success into the future.

It was again a telling sign that Walsh was far from satisfied with the direction and financial instability of the Festival, when in January of 1962, he reasserted that he would not remain on the Council as artistic director unless Bord Fáilte's grant was assured and the financial liability of the theatre reconstruction was resolved.[27] It was not the first time that the Council members had been faced with the possibility of replacing Walsh with a professional artistic director. Walsh's main grievance had been that he felt they left the financial burden for him to resolve, presuming that he would find a solution each year – and he did. His threatened resignation was really the only strong card that he could play, for the notion of finding and then paying a professional artistic director had potential to put a permanent end to opera in Wexford.

By this stage, the old Council had practically disbanded, with the Executive Council functioning in its place. Many of the same members remained but those on the new Council were now more financially committed to the Festival's progression. Walsh had to point out in January 1962, however, that matters discussed by the Council should remain confidential. He had met a 'traveller from Dublin' in Wexford who was able to relay to him, in full detail, the points discussed at an earlier meeting. This was obviously not a satisfactory manner of conducting business, and it was agreed that in future the subject matter of Council meetings would not be disclosed.[28]

It was becoming increasingly difficult to encourage voluntary workers to dedicate time to the Festival. The local chorus was voluntary but was augmented considerably by paid singers from Glyndebourne.[29] Backstage workers, an integral part in Festival proceedings, were all volunteers. The importance of voluntary work to the survival of the Festival was stressed by Walsh, who stated that only the officially appointed staff could be paid.[30]

As chairman of the Executive Council, Beit outlined the position regarding a Festival for 1962. He explained to the Council that there was a moral obligation to run a Festival in view of the commitments to the Gulbenkian Foundation and to Bord Fáilte in respect of their grant and loan to the theatre. He explained that if the Festival was to fold, the Executive Council would have to return any monies that had been subscribed to the theatre by the same parties. If this were done, the outstanding liabilities on the theatre would create a serious problem.

Despite all the considerations facing the Executive Council, it was decided that the Festival should go ahead in 1962.[31] Council members who were paying subscriptions continuously requested the privilege of having some small say in the choice of operas. Beit, too, remained considerably interested in artistic choice at Wexford. He had extensive opera knowledge, partly due to the fact that he was a travelled man, and this would inevitably have given him the opportunity to experience opera elsewhere.[32] By 1962 then, Walsh found himself again in the position of being compelled to discuss his artistic direction at the

Council meetings. An example of this was recorded in the minutes of one such meeting on 10 April 1962:

> Dr Walsh referred to *The Lily of Killarney* and said that 1962 was the centenary of the opera. However there would be difficulties – the orchestral parts would be out of print although possibly the BBC might have them, the libretto was very bad and would have to be re-written ... An Irish character tenor and possibly Veronica Dunne would have to be kept strictly to the budget. With regard to the Italian opera, Dr Walsh asked for possible alternatives so that he could fit in artists etc. It was decided that the first choice would be *I Masnadieri* by Verdi, second choice would be *Duca d'Alba* by Donizetti, third would be *Favorita,* fourth *Linda de Chamounix* and fifth *Puritani.* Dr Walsh was to set about getting singers as soon as possible, and then *report back* to the Executive Council.[33]

Walsh must surely have noted this decisive shift away from his total control of artistic decision-making, to communal artistic proposals being put forward by an Executive Council. It was no wonder that the notion of resigning was never far from his mind.

Promotion of the 1962 Festival was seen as a key element for the success of the event. Beit had communicated with members of the Dublin Festival and both he, as representative of the Wexford Festival Opera, and the Dublin Festival put forward suggestions to Bord Fáilte to improve the advertising of their respective festivals in the British press. They also inquired about the possibility of obtaining a public relations officer to promote those festivals in Great Britain.[34] The crux of the matter seemed to be that, coupled with a lack of money, there seemed to be a level of apathy – at home and abroad. With the reduction in membership fees, it was hoped that there would be a significant increase in membership, but this had not materialized.[35]

The Festival began on 21 October with Mascagni's *L'amico Fritz*,[36] accompanied by the Radio Éireann Symphony Orchestra and the Wexford Festival Chorus[37] whose local members had lessened dramatically since 1951. This opera had not even been considered at the time of the April Council meeting, when options were discussed. The season finished on 28 October with Bellini's *I puritani*,[38] with Mirella Freni singing the part of Elvira in the

Nicola Monti, Bernadette Greevy, Paolo Pedani and Veronica Dunne in *L'amico Fritz*, 1962

production. Both she and her agent were satisfied that the experience she would gain at Wexford would benefit her career abroad.

Walsh delivered an ultimatum in November 1962. He stated that if certain conditions were not met, he would not be prepared to remain as artistic director with the Festival. He insisted that the financial budget be in place by 1 January 1963 (this was a condition that he had constantly sought, but which

Bernadette Greevy in
L'amico Fritz, 1962

the Council had never achieved). He also stressed that the opera policy should be decided by the Council by the same date. He was prepared to put on two operas and two films for the week only, the choice of operas being decided by the Council as long as they were in Italian, French or German.[39]

At this point, Walsh's authority was threatened by Beit as chairman, who decided that policy statements should not be issued in this way. This was the first recorded disagreement between Beit and Walsh, and Beit went on to give his policy proposals for the 1963 Festival. He favoured two operas, *four* films and one or two symphony concerts.[40] Walsh was opposed to Beit's suggestions for a number of reasons. He pointed out that opera selection was an extremely difficult process. The restriction of language affected, in some cases, the availability of singers. Covent Garden had failed to release any singers to perform at Wexford and continued to turn down all requests to do so. Russian and Bulgarian operas presented distinct language barriers for the chorus. Walsh also noted that two symphony concerts would pose enormous rehearsal difficulties.[41] But Beit's financial aid was absolutely essential and no one was more aware of this fact than Walsh.

In an attempt to make the town of Wexford more aware and involved in the progression of the Festival, the Senior Chamber of Commerce had held a special meeting on 12 August, to meet with Council members of the Festival. It pledged full support for the Festival and its members, while airing some criticisms. Beit, for the most part, agreed with the Chamber's points. It was reported that:

> One member of Senior Chamber of Commerce stated that he felt that the atmosphere had been destroyed by the fact that the singers did not perform in the hotels after the opera. This was fully discussed by the Festival Council members. The chairman, Sir Alfred Beit, stated that he was very much in sympathy with this view. He felt that our Festival was not a Salzburg or a Munich, and that we had drifted from the fun in the old days. Several members expressed the opinion that it would be good for the Festival to try and bring back the old atmosphere ... A member of the Senior Chamber stated that he felt that the public should know more about the Festival.

It was ironic that Beit should be in agreement with the Festival returning to the 'fun in the old days', as he had not been part of the Festival Council at that stage. He was, however, named among the first of subscribers in 1956. It was true that Walsh had put a stop to singers entertaining guests at their hotels, as he felt it would strain their voices and their performances might suffer as a consequence. It was even written into each singer's contract that it was forbidden for them to sing outside the Theatre Royal without the permission of Walsh himself. Walsh indicated to the Senior Chamber and to Beit, however, that he would be willing to grant permission to singers in certain instances, to sing at their will, but those who did so without his permission would be fined.[42]

The 1963 Festival witnessed for the first time the production of three operas in one season – Donizetti's *Don Pasquale*, Ponchielli's *La Gioconda* and Balfe's *The Siege of Rochelle*.[43] Walsh's original idea was to engage Irish singers to sing for this Irish composer's opera, but he found it impossible to do so. He wrote to Gerard Victory, the Director of Music at Radio Éireann, to air his discontent:

> It was impossible to get a cast of Irish singers, the reason for this being that some of our best Irish singers were tied up with Sadler's Wells, and some were simply not interested. In the circumstances, I decided where good Irish artists were not available, to engage English artists, who were more than pleased to sing this opera.[44]

So, along with the engagement of Glyndebourne singers for the chorus, it was easier to entice English singers to sing at Wexford than it was to get Irish artists. Of course, many artists could not justify singing at Wexford for the fees that Wexford was prepared to pay.

In the aftermath of the Festival, Beit congratulated all involved, stating that the Festival had been 'a considerable artistic and social success'. Bookings had increased once again and it was noted that there was a general revival of interest in the 1963 Festival. Financially, however, it was an unfortunate consequence that all guaranteed sums of money had to be utilized in full.[45]

> I started the Festival when I was younger and much more enthusiastic. I continue it now because we have a good theatre and an excellent organization but more especially perhaps because I love opera more than ever,

Alfonz Bartha and Margherita Rinaldi in *Don Pasquale*, 1963

Walsh told the *Irish Independent* in July 1963.[46] Walsh was indeed the last of the great amateurs, and this was becoming clear as the Festivals were produced year after year, with a progressively professional outlook. It was inevitable of course that Walsh would lose his grip on the affairs at Wexford, because the more renowned and public the Festival became, the more it required this professional approach. This would never have happened at Glyndebourne in John Christie's time, incidentally, because Christie was funding the venture himself – a luxury that Walsh could not have afforded. Christie had handed over the running of his opera festival to a professional team and he allowed them to carry out their work without interference. But Walsh was the artistic director, a position that was pivotal to the production of an opera festival.

The difference between the aristocratic and the middle-class venture became strikingly clear at this point. Beit was perhaps the rich patron of Wexford but, realistically, the extent to which the Festival relied on its grants from Bord Fáilte and the Arts Council ensured that Beit would never assume complete authority over the Festival.

Walsh made a statement again in November 1963 to the effect that he was quite unsure if he would remain as artistic director for the following season. At this point, however, the mention of his resignation was greeted with little surprise:

> Dr Walsh explained that, as already mentioned, there was a 50/50 chance of his not being available next year to act as artistic director. He said that he would be quite prepared to give as much help as he could as a Council member, but pointed out that he did not consider it practical for anybody to act as director for a certain period, and then leave, as the artistic director had a responsibility both *for* the artists and to the artists. He also mentioned that he did not consider that a change in the Festival policy at this stage would be a bad thing. The chairman said that he thought it would be extremely difficult to replace Dr Walsh either from Wexford or elsewhere in Ireland and he said he thought it would be a good plan to write to George Christie of Glyndebourne [son of John Christie] to ask about the possibility of engaging a professional artistic director with their assistance. It was finally agreed, after discussion, that the chairman should do this and that the matter should then be considered further.

Peter Ebert was the suggested replacement for Walsh, but it was thought that he would be too expensive.[47] Walsh had implied that a 'change of policy' might be necessary in future but he did not suggest what this new policy should be. Perhaps he wanted the Festival to change utterly following his resignation as artistic director, so that his private and amateur policies could be easily distinguished from the air of professionalism that was beginning to surround the Festival.

No decision was reached by Walsh regarding his future with the Festival, and by December 1963, he concluded that it would be impossible to produce operas of 'the established standard' within their budget of £8,000. He added that he personally did not wish to be involved in directing 'second-rate productions'. He again alluded to the fact that another group of people might wish to take over the Festival and run it in a different way. It is uncertain whether he had a specific group of people in mind when he put this suggestion to the Council. In any case, Beit agreed that the Festival Council in its present form did not wish to lower the standard of operatic productions to satisfy budgetary figures; he suggested therefore that the Council should resign as a body, if no other solution were found.[48]

By 27 December, it was decided that the Festival should return to its original title of 'Wexford Festival of Music and the Arts',[49] but this was a premature decision, as on 5 February 1964, a unanimous vote by the Executive Council concluded that, because of inadequate funding, there should be no Festival in 1964.[50]

CHAPTER 5

WALSH AND WEXFORD, ANTONY AND CLEOPATRA, BACON AND EGGS

1964–9

The coming to an end of Tom Walsh's era at Wexford marked a significant turning point in the whole make-up of the Festival. The *Irish Times* reported in 1964 that 'if there is one man who is irreplaceable in the Irish musical world, that man is Tom Walsh'. This was certainly a true reflection of Walsh's worth to Wexford Festival Opera, and the Executive Council was more than aware of this. No one would deny that he had ruled with an autocratic hand – or that that had not been absolutely essential. As Tony Grey pointed out in his article written eight years after the inaugural Festival:

> perhaps Dr Walsh has been a bit autocratic in his handling of the operatic material of the Festival, but if he has, again it has paid off.

Too many festivals fall by the wayside because the organizers cannot agree among themselves.

You know the old definition of a camel – a horse designed by a committee. There is none of that sort of indecision and compromise at Wexford. The pattern of the Festival has been firmly set, and Dr Walsh and the committee are not going to depart from it to chase after shadows.[1]

But the entire organization had changed dramatically, and had been forced to do so by the crippling debts, not least those debts as a result of the renovation of the Theatre. Although a decision had been taken that there would be no Festival in 1964, the Executive Council continued to explore avenues to make a season possible after all.

The press soon became aware of the fact that Walsh was unhappy with the Festival Council's policies and was considering withdrawing his support for this year's proposed Festival. Walsh told the *Irish Independent* in February of 1964:

I wrote to the members concerned, saying that I realized that certain members wished to have a change of policy and that I thought that they should have it. I said that if the next Festival was better than the twelve which went before, then they were right; if it was not, then I was right. It was what might be termed a friendly disagreement.

'My job', he added, 'was that of artistic director. I felt that when the policy was changed I was not directing'. Walsh implied that these policy changes of the Wexford Council had nothing to do with the financial difficulties that the Festival continued to face. 'If we ran it for a hundred years we would still be without money', he vehemently declared.

The ambiguity surrounding Walsh's proposed departure was heightened by conflicting reports to the national newspapers, including reports by Walsh himself. The notion that the Council wished to change policy against Walsh's will was not apparent in the minutes of the Executive Council meetings, and it was indeed out of character for Walsh to discuss Council policies at such an early stage with the press. While Walsh was saying one thing, James O'Connor, public relations officer for the Festival, was saying the opposite: in the same *Independent* article O'Connor reaffirmed that there was no dispute between

Karola Ágai in *Lucia di Lammermoor*, 1964

Walsh and the Festival Council: 'the Council have at all times supported Dr Walsh in maintaining the tremendously high standard for which the Wexford Festival is now famous'.[2]

Walsh, on the other hand, was reported in the *Evening Standard* the following day as having declared that:

> If I am to be an artistic director of the Festival, I must have full powers. Should there be a lowering of standards because of a change of policy, then I would be held responsible for that falling-off in standards ... I can see the right of the Council to take a decision to alter policy. If I cannot agree with that policy, then I have the right to withdraw as artistic director.

The press reported ad nauseum on the proposed ending of an era of opera at Wexford, when the 1964 season still hung in the balance. A letter to the

The cast in *Il Conte Ory*, 1964

Irish Times in February of 1964 portrayed the dismay by some at the proposed ending of the Festival:

> So the great Wexford Festival is now no more! The merchant princes have discovered that their short excursion into 'culture' is less rewarding than the more prosaic commerce. Must everything in this little country be judged and valued on its monetary return? Among our small but fabulously wealthy merchants is there not one who could be influenced by something other than the profit motive? When I think over the early years of the Wexford Festival – with the first nights, the mink stoles, the long cigars and the midnight parties – what hypocrisy it all was! The merchants and their glamorous ladies were there only to see and be seen – not a genuine lover of the arts among the lot. Goodbye Wexford. For a few short years you had us fooled. Get back

to your trade and commerce and build up those big bank balances with the consolation that, one day, your graveyards will hold some of the wealthiest merchants in the country.[3]

At the eleventh hour, Guinness entered the scene. Guinness had actually taken an interest in Wexford Festival Opera as far back as 1957, donating a cheque for £100 towards the liquidation of the Festival debt. The successful brewing company stepped in with an offer of sponsorship for three years, securing the 1964 Festival and saving the Festival as a whole from this type of criticism. It could not have come at a better time for the Festival or indeed for Guinness, who were making concerted efforts to become involved at grass-roots level with ventures that they sponsored. It was a novel idea for Guinness to send their front man, Guy Jackson, to converse with Walsh on how the sponsorship scheme would work to the advantage of both parties.[4]

Jackson contacted the Wexford Festival Council in March 1964 to inform them that the company was prepared to make a gift of £2,500 each year for three years, on condition that the 1964 Festival was 'a success artistically and financially'. The terms of the agreement were straightforward. Guinness requested that the 'old level and standard of the Festival' be maintained and that Guinness should receive publicity in 'a dignified way'. The objective of Guinness was naturally the promotion of its company but it stipulated that it was extremely anxious to assure the continuation of Wexford Festival Opera. It required no say in the choice of operatic productions. Interestingly, the contract stated that:

> it is essential that the Director and Council agree on all these points and that the Festival will carry on as usual under the control of Dr Walsh as Director, and Council combined.

And so Walsh made the vital decision to accept this offer, given that the financial burden of the Festival had been eased considerably. For Walsh, too, it was a significant event, because it ensured that he would remain with the Festival at least until 1966. Walsh's alliance with Guinness essentially placed the authority over Festival proceedings back into his hands.

It was a strong indication that Walsh had assumed control again when an agreement was drawn up between himself and the Executive Council for his continuation as artistic director. It was stipulated that he would be appointed Director of Wexford Festival Opera for a period of three years and that the Festival would be renamed the 'Wexford Festival'. Walsh was also to be appointed manager of the Theatre Royal for three years, with the responsibility for theatre maintenance. Press releases for the Festival would in future be released by Walsh to the public relations officer, James O'Connor, and all operatic publications were to be prepared by Walsh. It was the task of the Council to draw up the budget allowance for the operas, and Walsh was requested not to exceed this amount.[5]

For the 1964 season, Walsh himself devised *Corno di Bassetto,* an entertainment based on the musical criticism of Bernard Shaw. Singers for this included Bernadette Greevy and Franco Ventriglia, along with pianist Jeannie Reddin. Walsh's own brother, John Welsh, had a spoken part.[6] The main stage operas the same year were Donizetti's *Lucia di Lammermoor,* Rossini's *II Conte Ory* and *Much Ado about Nothing* by Charles Stanford.[7]

Having informed the press that he was not willing to accept any lowering of standards by the Council for the coming Festival, Walsh again explained to the Council that he would not have as much time to devote to the Festival in 1965, compared to previous years. He therefore requested the assistance of a personal secretary and permission to make Festival calls from outside the Festival office. These calls would naturally be recorded for payment.[8] It was clear at this stage that Walsh continued his retreat from the frontal position he had held with the Festival. Following the intervention of Guinness however, financial matters no longer monopolized the agenda at Council meetings.

Walsh appeared to be searching for a new challenge, and in June he reported to the Council that he had been in contact with the Northern Ireland Arts Council, who had requested that the Wexford Festival perform two operas in Belfast in October 1966. The idea was agreed in principle, but discussion on the matter was deferred[9] and the venture never reached fruition.

Walsh informed Beit in June 1965 that he would retire after the 1966 season, concluding that:

> the Festival, which for many years has taken up all my spare time I now find, perhaps, due to the fact that I have less time to spare, is completely monopolizing my life, and so I must withdraw when our three year agreement ends ... I naturally will miss the Festival very much as it has been so much a part of my life for so many years.[10]

Carl Ebert and
Ivana Mixova,
Don Quichotte,
1965

The Executive Council was notified of this on 9 August 1965, but it was hardly a surprise to anyone present at the meeting.[11]

The 1965 season successfully produced Massenet's *Don Quichotte*, Verdi's *La traviata* and Mozart's *La finta giardiniera*.[12] Three generations of the Ebert family took part in the production and design of this year's Festival. Carl Ebert had made a huge impression on audiences at the Glyndebourne Festival with his operatic productions, and it served Wexford well that he agreed to produce opera at the Wexford Festival.

A memorandum from Walsh to Guy Jackson in December 1965, however, indicated that Walsh now had more respect for the Guinness contingent than he did for his own Council. In this confidential document, intended to outline the future of the Festival, Walsh began by saying that he had 'little enthusiasm'

Birgit Nordin, Ugo Benelli and Stefania Malagù in *La finta giardiniera*, 1965

for another Festival year that would compare with the 1965 season. He made reference to the fact that the financial situation of the Festival would be a serious one again in 1966, believing that the Festival owed the bank between £2,300 and £2,500. With regard to the 1967 Festival season and subsequent years, Walsh emphatically declared that he 'would not be happy to continue acting as Director of Wexford Festival Opera under the Festival Council as presently constituted, though I should be very content to be responsible to Guinness'.[13]

On 8 January 1966, Beit wrote to Walsh to clear up an issue that had been discussed between Walsh and Guy Jackson. Beit was incensed at the fact that Walsh had indicated to Jackson his disagreement with the Festival Council's decision to incorporate only two operas in the 1966 Festival instead of the, by now, regular three. Beit was of the opinion that Walsh had agreed to concur with the wishes of the Council.[14] Jackson told Beit that the opera that Walsh had wanted to include was Johann Strauss' operetta *Wiener Blut.* Beit was obviously uncomfortable about the fact that Walsh had turned to Jackson with his proposed policy rather than to Beit himself, and he continued:

> I am surprised that you raised this matter with him since we had a long and free discussion on the subject at our meeting on 30 December last. Several members of the Council participated in this discussion and one or two were in favour of a third opera at the beginning. However, I thought I had convinced the Council that for financial reasons and also because we were going to get the orchestra one day late it would be better to stick to the two main operas. Your opinion was asked and in my clear recollection you stated that you would fall in with the wishes of the majority, and consequently the decision only to do two operas was taken. You never said a word about the Strauss operetta.[15]

Beit went on to say that even Walsh himself had been in agreement that the chorus could not undertake three operas, if a chorus was required for *Wiener Blut* at all. Beit again stressed that an extra opera for the coming season would put more financial strain on the make-up of the Festival, bearing in mind that full opera prices could not be charged to see 'lesser works' such as operettas, or works where 'full blown opera singers' were not engaged.[16]

Beit had sent a copy of his letter to Guy Jackson, and two days later Walsh replied to him, hastily correcting his many errors, as Walsh saw it. First Walsh explained his reasons for not mentioning the production of *Wiener Blut* as the third opera for 1966 at the last Council meeting. He declared that he

> realized that the feeling of the Council was entirely against the third opera and I had no wish to be out-voted twelve to one. The decision to do two operas *only* was not taken either because the Orchestra was coming a day late, or because I fell in with the wishes of the majority, but because the Council decided it.[17]

He explained further that *Wiener Blut* would incorporate a very short chorus. Although Beit had accused Walsh of agreeing that three operas in one season was too much for the chorus to undertake, Walsh denied this, citing that they had mounted three with chorus in 1963. Walsh ended his discussion with Beit by emphatically concluding:

> I do not think that the financial problem should be added to the many others that I have to solve, but I am satisfied that it could be solved.[18]

Walsh was astute enough to realize that if he could work under the aegis of the Guinness group, rather than as part of the Festival Council, money and financial considerations should no longer be a contentious issue. He was clearly uneasy about the notion that his Festival had come under the increasing influence of a rich, individual patron. Beit and Walsh conflicted on a number of issues regarding Festival policy.

The minutes of the early July 1966 meetings were taken up with discussions about the future of the Festival. A replacement for Walsh was the most significant issue. There were no viable alternatives presented at this stage, for the Festival's budget would not stretch to employing a really first-class artistic director to replace him. Guinness and Bord Fáilte were involved in the discussion, in an attempt to ascertain whether or not they would be prepared to pay for the engagement of a professional artistic director. Both parties declined to comment at this point.

Walsh was at the forefront of the discussion regarding his replacement, but, ultimately, it would depend on the financial situation of the Festival. Peter Ebert's name was put forward again. He had served as producer for a number of seasons at Wexford. As Walsh then divulged,

Dr Tom Walsh and the cast in *La finta giardiniera*, 1965

there was the question of prestige and there really was nothing to offer
a Producer of repute who would consider coming to Wexford ... The
qualities required were a knowledge of singers and an administrative
ability ...[19]

No decision was reached at this point, however, as the most pressing issue was
the oncoming 1966 Festival. Walsh continued with his duties as artistic director
and in April 1966 travelled to Paris to find singers for the new productions.[20]

On 17 August, a special meeting of the Wexford members of the Executive
Council was held in White's Hotel to discuss the dilemma of Walsh's imminent
departure. Walsh had asked to be excused from this meeting. Des Ffrench,
incoming chairman of the Council, opened the discussion by reading a letter
that he had received from a Council member, indicating that it would be more
desirable for the Festival to 'end on a high note' in 1966, 'rather than to continue
on a lower level until we fade out unmissed and unmourned'.

The question was posed whether or not the donors and guarantors who
were listed for the 1966 Festival would continue in their support if the Festival

Antonio Boyer and Anna Reynolds in *Fra Diavolo*, 1966

came under new direction and chairmanship. It was generally assumed that support would still be forthcoming if such changes were implemented. It was also stipulated that the unsecured debt of £1,700 would have to be taken care of before a new council was put in place.

A very significant question was posed by John Small, Council member and owner of White's Hotel, at the meeting – 'Does Wexford want to continue the Festival?' This was promptly put to a vote at the Council meeting. One Council member indicated that he did not wish for the Festival to continue without Walsh as its artistic director. David Price stated that he 'was not prepared to go back to "square one"', but added that he 'would support the continuance of the Festival if the standard was maintained'. James O'Connor was indecisive about how he wished the Council to proceed, but was disappointed to hear the reservations of Price, whom he considered to be a key figure associated with the Festival Council.

Not all the Council members were pessimistic about the future of the Festival, however. John Small, for example, said that he was

> extremely sad to hear the despondency of the foregoing Members of the Council. First of all he said he would like to declare his commercial interest in the Festival. He added, however, that the town of Wexford needed the Festival, which as an institution of 15 years standing had brought great prestige to the town quite apart from the commercial side, and that without the Festival Wexford would fade off the map. He would give his all-out support to continue the Festival.

The chairman, Des Ffrench, then spoke on behalf of Sean Scallan, who agreed to support the Festival in the future. The chairman's own outlook was quite pessimistic, however:

> Ffrench said that he was one of the original tribe at the instigation of the Festival in 1951 and his feeling was that the Festival had come to the end of the road [even] without the resignation of Dr Walsh. He felt that costs had risen to such an extent that the maintenance of the alleged high standard would be impossible in any event. He felt that Wexford was too small to support the kind of Festival with which it had made its name, and for which all credit must go to Dr Walsh.

The meeting ended with the realization that unless the Council could raise substantial extra funding for the employment of an artistic director and to pay any remaining debt, the future of the Festival was again in doubt. It was also noted that the citizens and firms of Wexford would have to be prepared to contribute substantially to the maintenance of the Festival.[21]

A sub-committee was formed to investigate how much money could be obtained through a local Wexford appeal. On 23 September, it was reported at an Executive Council meeting that an appeal had proved quite successful and the sub-committee had managed to obtain pledges of £1,250.[22] On 10 October, an urgent meeting was held at the Guinness headquarters in Dublin with representatives from Guinness, Bord Fáilte, RTÉ and the Wexford Festival Executive Council. The points that were agreed upon were critical to the continuation of the Festival. Significantly, RTÉ was expected to reduce the cost of providing the orchestra for productions from £2,400 to £1,500. Guinness agreed to renew its donation of £2,500 for the next three years and also agreed to provide £250 annually for a Festival party. Although the Arts Council was not represented at the meeting, it was expected that it would contribute £1,000 towards costs. The final stipulation that was laid down at the meeting was that 'the existing high standard of Wexford Festival, set by Dr Walsh, must be maintained'.[23]

Amid the growing concern for the future, the 1966 Festival got underway with two productions at the Theatre Royal. The Council's decision to present only two operas this year ensured that there was no place for Walsh's proposed Strauss operetta. Instead, Daniel Auber's *Fra Diavolo* and Donizetti's *Lucrezia Borgia* were produced.[24] The costumes for *Lucrezia Borgia* were obtained from Covent Garden and those for *Fra Diavolo* from Paris.[25]

The professionalization of the Wexford Festival was highlighted in the number of executive committees, sub-committees and special committees that were springing from the original Festival Council. In November, another level of the Executive Council, the Opera Management Committee, was set up to oversee the appointment of an artistic director. Beit was naturally part of this sub-committee. An advertisement for the position was placed in the *Irish Times*, the *Irish Independent*, the *Irish Press*, the *Daily Telegraph*, the *Times* and *Opera* magazine. A stipulation for appointment was that the suitable candidate would have 'two-thirds musical qualifications and one-third business qualifications'.

It was obvious that, with the transition from amateur to professional values, the Council would continue to play an integral part in policy-making, much to Walsh's disgust. It would not have been an exaggeration to say that, where opera was concerned, Walsh knew best. His first priority was the operatic productions at Wexford and although Beit was also a knowledgeable man in the field of opera, his motives were largely linked to financial viability where policy-making was concerned. Walsh's reign was coming to an end after his three-year contract with Guinness concluded and with it threatened the end of Compton Mackenzie's very significant presidential role with the Festival. In May 1967, Mackenzie had written to Walsh to explain that:

> between ourselves, I think I ought to make this a farewell Presidential occasion and hand over to Alfred Beit. It will never be the same for me without you.[26]

This change had been suggested by Mackenzie when Beit first appeared on the Wexford scene, but Walsh obviously managed to convince him to reconsider.[27] It must be noted too that all the voluntary backstage workers, including Seamus O'Dwyer, agreed to resign with Walsh, although in the event, some were persuaded to reconsider.[28] This was a massive indication that Walsh was hugely respected and his insight as founder and as artistic director of the Wexford Festival was duly noted.

Walsh had agreed to remain on the Executive Council for the foreseeable future and he got assurance from Mackenzie that he would also stay on as president. Walsh was incidentally absent from a meeting in November 1966 when the future of the Festival was yet again considered. This time the discussion was largely taken up with Walsh's resignation and the uncertainty of the Festival as a result. The chairman read a letter from Michael O'Mahony, a subscriber to the Festival, urging the Council to engage a paid administrator to ease the burden of Walsh's former post, so that he could be persuaded to remain with the Festival as artistic director. Many of the Council members were in agreement with this request and all seemed to be of the opinion that Walsh should be offered £1,500 to employ an assistant, so that he personally could 'run the Festival as he so wished'. It was even suggested that the Executive Council should be divided into four committees, the first of these being a Wexford Festival Opera Committee, under the chairmanship of Walsh himself, who would be free to choose his own committee members. Five applications had been received for the position of artistic director, as advertised, but it was generally felt that Walsh should be approached in the first instance. As the Council reported:

> it was also agreed that without Dr Walsh it would be almost impossible to maintain his high standard, since the Festival had revolved around him alone since its inception.[29]

But Walsh was not for turning. He subsequently cited his own personal reasons for retiring as artistic director from the Wexford Festival:

> I recognized that there were other reasons. I would be retiring at the age of 55 – time to leave the strenuous job which directing the Festival had become, but still time to find another role in the opera world.

When I resigned, I had no clear idea what I wanted to do. Vaguely I thought about writing, vaguely I thought perhaps I could retire temporarily and later return to the Festival.

In retrospect I realize now that I had grown tired and that what I really needed was a sabbatical period away from the Festival, just to think.[30]

Describing it fondly as 'the festival for the man who is tired of festivals', Desmond Shawe-Taylor indicated in an article in the *Sunday Times* in 1967 that the spirit and atmosphere of Wexford could be retained for the future:

True, it arrives at the fag end of the year, when the travel-stained journalist may be forgiven if he hankers after a few nights at home with a good book and an autumn fire and a stack of not the very latest records. What, cross the sea and sand down through Wicklow to hear a couple of forgotten operas in a converted cinema! It sounds mad.

Once there, however, the magic works. Nor is it all a confidence trick made up of Irish geniality, festoons of coloured lights along the narrow streets, and non-existent licensing hours. Wexford can offer a novel and genuine musical experience: the fun of exploration, the chance of encountering, in surroundings so intimate and pleasant, a fine new singer from Italy or Ireland, France or America, in one of those operas that our grandfathers loved and that we have always wanted to hear.[31]

But because Walsh was such an integral part of the Festival, it was unclear if the magic would remain once Walsh himself had departed, as Brian Quinn wrote in *Hibernia* in 1967:

Walsh and Wexford, Antony and Cleopatra, Napoleon and Josephine, bacon and eggs, these things just went together and that was the end of it …[32]

Press criticism, on a relatively small scale, of Walsh's ability to work as part of a team, particularly from Fanny Feehan, appeared also in the *Hibernia* magazine much later on.[33] Walsh retorted:

On behalf of many hundreds of voluntary workers, several now dead,

Virginia Gordoni
and Ayhan Baran
in *Lucrezia Borgia*,
1966

who over sixteen years gave so generously of their time and effort to
the Wexford Festival and their loyalty to me, I challenge Miss Fanny
Feehan's 'doubt' that I 'could have secured the team-work which
[others] have in recent years …'[34]

But Feehan was determined not to let Walsh have the final say, and concluded
her personal attack by reporting that she 'shall continue to have doubts about
co-operation in the early days … Dr Walsh's loyalty to his old friends is admirable
and only to be expected'.[35] Feehan had praised Walsh at length in her article,

but the comment about non-cooperation had hit him hard. She softened her criticism, however, by stating that:

> Walsh infuriated many people, but I don't think there is an artistic director anywhere in the world worth a damn who does not do so. If they didn't have that extra amount of arrogance they couldn't get on with the job any more than a nice, easy-going man can get the best out of an orchestra. Walsh fought many battles, and his most successful was in preventing this marvellous festival from being run as a souped-up Fleadh Ceoil. A lesser man would have been swamped by those who can never see beyond the end of their immediate bank over-draft.[36]

Even Brian Dickie, who was to become Walsh's successor, recognized Walsh's unique musical ability and intense knowledge of his subject:

> Dr T.J. Walsh ... probably knows more about the history of opera in Ireland and Irish opera than anyone else alive.[37]

Perhaps the most significant story appeared in a newspaper, the *Free Press* (a cutting of which Walsh kept), quite possibly written by a friend of Walsh's. Some articles that he kept in his files were anonymous letters to the editors of various newspapers, to which he had added names of those he believed to have written them. The article implied that Walsh was ousted from his position with the Festival, partly by those who believed they knew best and partly by the inevitable professionalization of the venture. The story took the form of an old-type children's story:

THE DWARFS WITHOUT SNOW WHITE

Once upon a time in a land far away there were seven little dwarfs, none of whom at that time had even heard of Snow White (or any other detergent) for that matter, and the names of the seven were Grumpy, Dopey, Sleepy, Sneezy, Happy, Bashful and Doc.

At one time the seven little dwarfs decided to hold an annual celebration and to organize and arrange that celebration the six, by unanimous choice, selected Doc [Walsh]; for you can see by their very names, which were appropriate, that only Doc had any qualifications.

Under Doc's guidance, the annual celebration became a great success and in time the celebration became known all over Fairyland. However, one year all the dwarfs, with the exception of Doc of course, decided Doc was getting a bit old for the job, and decided to appoint a successor to him.

Later they heard of Dick Whittington [Brian Dickie] who was making a wonderful name for himself, and so they appointed him.

Now Dick proved such a success at the job that he won applause from all the folk of fairyland and the six little dwarfs were very pleased with him ...

About that time the six dwarfs became the owners of a wonderful mirror which could foretell the future and could also speak. It was known as the Flattering Mirror, for each day the six little dwarfs would individually and secretly go to the mirror and say: 'Mirror, mirror, on the wall, which of us is best of all?' And the mirror would reply: 'You dear Dopey (or whoever it might be) are the best; you're a better man than all the rest'.

Having made such a grand success of his first year, Dick was invited back again to organize the merriment and fun. The next year, when he was busily arranging all the events, the six little dwarfs came to him and said, 'We have appointed six others to help you next year'.

Now Dick didn't know what to say, because he thought he was doing very well on his own, but as the statement of the dwarfs implied that he would be appointed again next year he decided that it would be best to be discreet.

'Why should six be selected to help me?' he asked.

'We thought it was a good idea', said the six vaguely. Dick could do nothing but agree, but the next year there were seven organizing the fun and merriment and a strange thing happened: the Magic Mirror never spoke again. It did not know what to say anymore.[38]

The implication of the story was clear enough. The magic of the original Wexford Festival had been extinguished. Needless to say, fingers were crossed for the future.

CHAPTER 6

THE PROFESSIONAL AMATEURS

1967–73

As Walsh stepped down from his pivotal role, the rift between him and the Executive Council dragged on as the planning began for the 1967 Festival. Walsh had refused to return to Council meetings until certain conditions laid down by him were met. Dr James Ffrench, chairman of the Executive Council at this point, had had a meeting with Walsh in the Theatre Royal and an inventory of the furniture that Walsh owned was recorded. At an Executive Council meeting in January 1967, it was agreed that tapes of performances should be presented to Walsh. Copies of these tapes could be made at the Council's expense. It was further agreed at the meeting that Colonel Price would approach Walsh in an attempt to encourage him to resume his position as an integral part of the Executive Council.

The appointment of Brian Dickie as artistic director of Wexford Festival Opera marked a decisive shift from the amateur charm that the Festival had under Walsh. Following the recruitment campaign, it was in fact Walter Legge who was offered and had accepted the position of artistic director. He was head of Artists and Repertoire at EMI as well as the founder of London's Philharmonia Orchestra. It was not to be, however, as he suffered a heart attack and had to withdraw just weeks after accepting the position. Brian Dickie was delighted to be offered the role, having been interviewed by Beit. Dickie's salary was set at £1,200 plus foreign travel expenses of £200 and £100 to cover domestic travel. The link between Glyndebourne and Wexford was further strengthened during Dickie's term as artistic director. His associations with Glyndebourne were well known, and as early as February he suggested that even the Glyndebourne contract form for artists should be adapted to suit Wexford. Further, Glyndebourne now offered Wexford its 'members mailing list' which ran to 4,000 names. There was also the possibility of a visit of a BBC camera team to the Festival.[1]

Meanwhile the relationship between the Executive Council and Walsh reached its lowest point. In a letter to the chairman in June 1967, Walsh made his feelings clear:

> I should be obliged if you would tender my resignation as a member of the Wexford Festival Council at your next Council meeting. As I am writing I should also like to suggest that it would be better that Council members did not discuss Wexford Festival Opera with me in future on social occasions.[2]

Walsh was incensed by the fact that he had been asked by the Council to return the keys of the office to the Executive Council and two files that had been removed from the office. Furthermore, the chairman had undertaken to ask Walsh to return all property belonging to the Council that was in the possession of Walsh at his home.[3] Walsh was by this stage becoming more involved with Ulster Opera, and for its 1967 season he was its Honorary Opera Advisor.

But surprisingly, by 16 August Walsh had again withdrawn his resignation from the Council. The Council was relieved that relations had once again been restored.[4] Walsh clearly did not want to jeopardize the success of the forthcoming Festival.

Two operas were performed in 1967 – Rossini's *Otello* and Charles Gounod's *Roméo et Juliette*. Albert Rosen conducted the RTÉ Symphony Orchestra for the performances of *Otello*, and David Lloyd-Jones, conducting for the first time in

Ugo Benelli, 1970

Wexford, conducted *Roméo et Juliette*. The Festival performances began on 21 October and continued until 29 October. The *Sunday Independent* reported that Compton Mackenzie had expressed his desire to 'keep the Festival intimate' and he added that he 'wouldn't like to see the Festival become too expanded and thus become perhaps a financial burden'.[5] There was indeed a recurring concern that the Festival was moving away from the intimacy of its early days.

It was not long before Walsh again aired his discontent to the Executive Council and explained that the withdrawal of his resignation from the Council was only a temporary measure. In a letter that was read by the chairman at an Executive Council meeting in November 1967, he stipulated that he did not wish for any plaque or 'demonstration of appreciation' to be considered for him (he had read in the local paper that this was under consideration at the time).[6] Walsh went on to say that:

> when we have arranged affairs in the Theatre next December I intend to resign from the Council. My reason for allowing my name to remain among the list of members this first year of my retirement was

Christiane Eda-Pierre and chorus in *Lakmé*, 1970

to keep private the fact that a serious rift exists between us, which had it become known to the Press could, I believe, have done the Festival harm. The absence of my name from the list of members in future years, will, I feel, pass unnoticed.

Walsh had never been so infuriated. He added:

Finally, may I suggest that the ending of the pretence that I still have any interest in or connection with the Wexford Festival will save us both a considerable amount of pointless correspondence.[7]

On 23 January 1968, Walsh's letter of resignation was finally accepted by the Executive Council. He had again listed reasons for his decision to resign, this time his main reason being:

the defamatory remarks made by Mr Dickie to the Press during the 1967 Festival concerning [Walsh's work] as Director of the Festival and the fact that the Council had condoned these remarks by making no protest whatsoever.[8]

Walsh's departure passed as an unmarked event, as he had indicated he would prefer, but his resignation would undoubtedly leave a significant gap. Its founder no longer wished to be associated with the enterprise, a fact that was not made known publicly for fear that it would cause decline in the Festival's popularity.

In addition to the disruption involved in employing a new artistic director for the first time, it was noted at an Executive Council meeting in March 1968 that, aside from hotel contributions in the locality, Wexford local financial support remained poor. It was agreed that letters should once again be sent out to individuals to encourage them to make a contribution towards the pending 1968 Festival.[9] It was also decided to raise the price of seats and membership subscriptions.

The growing concern about financial uncertainty was compounded in June 1968 when an article appeared in the *Irish Times*, indicating that 'Organizers of Festivals need more help'. The report went on to comment how festivals, the Wexford Festival in particular, had a positive influence on its surrounding county:

> Tourism officials have for a considerable time recognized that festivals are an ideal way of extending the tourism season in any given area, and also that they are responsible for bringing local people together, hopefully – in harmony ... Festivals which can be cited as outstanding successes are the Wexford Opera Festival and the Kilkenny Beer Festival, both of which are rated among the best of their kind in Europe.[10]

The outstanding success of the Wexford Festival was reflected in a critically acclaimed season in 1968. With performances of Mozart's *La clemenza di Tito*, Bizet's *La jolie fille de Perth* and Rossini's *L'equivoco stravagante* the season extended from 25 October to 3 November. The Taoiseach, Jack Lynch, was reported in the *Evening Press* as saying that 'Wexford is Tops' and that:

> the Festival was clearly in the class that had gained its international reputation. Its prestige was in no small measure due to a special quality of thoroughness which was typical of all good Wexford products including their hurling teams.[11]

When evaluating the success of the 1968 Festival, Brian Dickie's commitment to Wexford came into question. The then chairman of the Executive Council, Des Ffrench, had decided to write to Dickie to enquire as to why he had spent so little time in Wexford and why there was an apparent lack of control of stage staff and budgets. Dickie had aired his own grievances previously, and these were put before the Council in January. Dickie replied that he could not guarantee that the figures for the coming year would not also exceed the budget as long as he was presented with what he described as a 'shoe-string budget'.[12] The Council had made it clear to Dickie that he must keep within the budget that had been put in place. In Walsh's time, Walsh himself would have set about finding the extra money required to maintain performance standards. Dickie, as a professional employee of the Wexford Festival, however, felt no need to concern himself with such financial matters.

The increased reliance on help from Glyndebourne was apparent again in early 1969 when the Glyndebourne Festival requested that the Wexford Festival Council increase the amount paid to Glyndebourne in administration costs by £50 per annum. The Wexford Council had no option but to agree.[13] Relations with Glyndebourne had always been amicable and were of huge importance for the successful continuation of opera at Wexford.

By May 1969, tentative discussions had begun about the 1970 season. Council members were particularly concerned for the season ahead, due to the fact that all contracts between the Wexford Festival and its sponsors ceased at the end of the 1969 Festival. An additional £4,000 was necessary if the Festival was to continue. It was agreed that the acquisition of another sponsor was desirable and the Council decided to discuss the matter with Guy Jackson of Guinness following a press conference that was due to take place in Dublin.[14]

The Guinness conference proved to be very successful from the Wexford Festival's point of view. The Executive Council was represented at the conference by Brian Dickie, Bernard Doyle, John Small and the chairman, Des Ffrench. Guy Jackson represented Arthur Guinness, T. O'Gorman was present on behalf of Bord Fáilte, Mervyn Wall represented the Arts Council, and Gerard Victory was present from RTÉ. There was unanimous agreement that the Wexford Festival should continue and that, in order to make this possible, sponsors of the Festival would increase their subsidies. But this came at a price. It was inevitable that the sponsors would want to become more involved in policy-making. Both Mervyn Wall of the Arts Council and Gerard Victory of RTÉ suggested that the Wexford Festival should consider producing modern opera in English.[15]

In the end, Haydn's *L'infedeltà delusa* and Verdi's *Luisa Miller* were performed in 1969. Bernadette Greevy was a member of the cast in *Luisa Miller*, but the newspaper reports were far from kind. An *Evening Press* reviewer commented:

> On the whole I am afraid, this has been a most disappointing festival. It has taken almost 20 years to build up the highly international reputation of Wexford Opera, and I think the time has come for those in charge of the Festival to consider very seriously whether these standards are being maintained. For this year at any rate they are not.[16]

The Festival Executive Council correctly pointed out that 'the Irish critics had given us very adverse notices but on the other hand the English papers had been more favourable'.[17] Dickie certainly had a difficult relationship with the Irish press, with some Irish reporters believing that he was engaging with international media about opera choices, before communicating them to the Irish media. When asked by one Irish music critic to 'conceal your contempt for us', Dickie retorted:

> You must know very well that I despise neither Ireland nor its press. What I do *not* show is an unstinting admiration for everything Irish, because it *is* Irish, but rather hope to judge each and everything without reference to creed or nationality. In this I may well fail, but surely it can hardly be an approach to deplore. I am concerned to help Wexford achieve the best artistic standards under the circumstances, physical and financial, which exist. I am as aware as you of our limitations, but not enough Irishness is not one of them. Not enough quality? – that is another matter.[18]

Looking ahead to the following year, it was agreed that the main production in 1970 'must be excellent'.[19] Irish press criticism in 1969 was compounded by dissatisfaction with Wexford's apparent growing reliance on Glyndebourne support. The Festival Council, however, was certain that this was not the case:

> Regarding the press criticism of the growing influence of Glyndebourne, Mr Dickie informed the Council that he had done a random check

The chorus in *La rondine*, 1971

on the number and, with the exception of the technical staff, there were less people employed now who had Glyndebourne connections than there had been before 1967.[20]

The financial strain on Council affairs had not eased by the time the 1970 Festival was about to begin. £4,000 was needed to supplement the increased costs of the artists, the conductors and the producers. At an Executive Council meeting in September 1970, Dickie aired some of his views about how to meet rising costs. First of all, he pointed out that an extra £8,000 was needed – £4,000 to cover rising costs of 1970 and £4,000 for the following year. He suggested that the Wexford Festival should produce only two operas in 1971 and that the price of seats should be increased. He argued that more money could be collected locally by voluntary efforts. This last suggestion must have particularly aggravated Council members who had been making concerted efforts each year to raise money for the Festival. The entire discussion was then turned back on Dickie and he was criticized for his inability to stay within the allocated budget for the pending 1971 season:

> It was pointed out to [Dickie] that at the moment, the problem was where we would get the money for this year. Mr Scallan stressed the fact that the Budget had been drawn up in November [1970] and that Mr Dickie had said that he was quite happy with it. Since that date he and the secretary had amended it frequently according as events warranted it. They had had no indication until late July that the fees would go so far astray. [It was] felt that it was just a farce for the committee to waste [its] time drawing up a budget when no attention was paid to it ...[21]

The Council was in agreement that money needed to be found to ensure that the forthcoming Festival was not sub-standard.

On the eve of the 1970 Festival which presented a double bill of Rossini's *L'inganno felice* and Donizetti's *Il giovedì grasso*, as well as Delibes' *Lakmé* and Britten's *Albert Herring*, the *Enniscorthy Echo* was positive about the overseas support, even if local support was less impressive. It reported that overseas bookings had trebled and, when asked to comment on the slowness of Wexford bookings, a spokesperson for the Festival had responded:

I think our people are inclined to leave it to the last minute. However, this is Wexford's own festival and it is a festival of far greater prestige than any other in this country and many in Europe. I would be sorry to see any Festival audience with a minority of Wexford people in it. With a steady stream of bookings daily from outside, our concern is that when Wexford people go to book them they may not be there.[22]

It became apparent in early 1971 that a large Festival was planned in Ulster and that it would include operatic performances. Ulster 71, as it was known, aimed to celebrate and promote Northern Ireland on the 50th anniversary of the foundation of the state of Northern Ireland. The Wexford Festival Executive Council acted quickly to contact the Arts Council of Northern Ireland to enquire as to when this Ulster Festival would take place. It would most definitely have impinged upon the audience at Wexford had the dates of the Festivals coincided. However, they had little cause to worry about the impact. Ulster 71 ran from May to September and it did not have any material bearing on the Wexford Festival.

Christopher Fitz-Simon of the Executive Council was perturbed when he heard what he deemed to be a 'most unusual complaint' from Bord Fáilte 'that the Festival was attracting too many overseas visitors and that maybe we would lose our Irishness'.[23] This was a recurring observation in media circles and the Executive Council no doubt feared that this type of publicity would affect its efforts to gain financial support locally.

As had become the norm, three operas were performed in 1971; Bizet's *Les pêcheurs de perles*, Puccini's *La rondine* and Mozart's *Il re pastore*. The Festival lasted for ten nights, from 21 October to 31 October. The critics were satisfied with the standard that had been achieved, commenting that 'opera succeeds with zest and conviction'[24] at Wexford. It was further noted that 'Wexford is not so much a festival as a way of life. What other festival is so incongruous and so intimate, so friendly and so fantastical?'[25]

Harold Rosenthal, editor of *Opera* magazine, contributed an article to the newspaper *Hibernia* to coincide with the Festival. Interestingly, he divulged that he:

fail[ed] to discern any real shape or artistic purpose in the way the Festival is planned. But then perhaps that is the peculiar charm of

Wexford, which appeals to so many of its regular visitors, and which I find so baffling.[26]

Anthony Lewis of the *New York Times* described the sheer experience of the Festival:

> The romantic quality that we outsiders find so attractive in the Irish, the ability to escape one way or another from the hard world of fact, is gloriously illustrated by the opera Festival.[27]

Dickie's dedication had again come under scrutiny in June 1971, however. Beit was the first to pose the question whether or not Dickie was devoting enough 'time, drive and energy' to his work at Wexford. Des Ffrench felt that Dickie's first allegiance was to Glyndebourne. Beit was further concerned because few 'exciting new discoveries' had been made in recent years with regard to singers.[28] It was unfair to compare Dickie to the local doctor whom he had replaced, but the fact that a professional artistic director had been appointed clearly did not rest easy with the Council. It would take time for the Council members to learn the new director's way of working.

There was a growing concern among the Council members that there was perhaps too little work being done between meetings. The intentions of the group were clear, yet the group was relatively large in size and decisions were becoming more difficult to reach. The Council seemed to lack leadership – something that Walsh had provided from the outset. As instigator of the Festival, Walsh had been the dominant figure at Council meetings and the most valued member in decision-making. It was decided in November 1971, then, that a sub-group of five members of the Executive Council should be elected with the power to make quick and decisive decisions on behalf of the Council.[29] This, it was felt, would ensure that the Council could in future work more effectively. The growing professionalism of the organization demanded this type of efficiency.

The decision on the successor for the role of chairman of the Executive Council was another important matter that had the potential to impinge on the effectiveness of the Council as a working body. It was proposed that Sean Scallan be elected as chairman. He himself believed that the term of office should only last for one year and that more Council members should be given the opportunity to act as chairperson for a period of time. According to Scallan, if more Council members were involved,

> it would overcome (1) the lack of overall knowledge of the workings of the Festival amongst the Council members and (2) that if the chairman stays too long in office he is likely to part on bad terms with the Council.[30]

Scallan's final comment was surely a reminder for the Council members present that relations with Walsh remained particularly tense since his departure from Festival affairs. It was noted, however, that the sponsors of the Festival would not be satisfied to see a new chairman appointed every year.[31] This point again highlighted the control that the Festival's sponsors now had over policy.

It was further proposed that at least two deputy chairmen should be appointed to assist the chairman and to learn, from a practical point of view, how best to carry on the position in the future. This method would ensure continuity for the Wexford Festival. Beit suggested retiring as vice-chairman but was persuaded to retain the position 'as his help and guidance were of great assistance'.[32]

It became apparent in 1972 that Derek Bailey from London Weekend Television had spent some time in Wexford and had expressed an interest in preparing a feature on the Festival.[33] The publicity was invaluable yet it doubtless fuelled the argument that the Festival was attracting foreign visitors rather than Irish opera lovers. A discussion took place on the problems of the acoustics in the Theatre Royal – a solution to this was urgent if London Weekend Television was going to publicize opera at Wexford.[34] Talks continued in 1972 about the importance of the Festival looking 'to the future' rather than taking one Festival at a time.[35] Dickie's comments on the Festival were again captured in print and what he had to say certainly had a positive effect on the critical acclaim of the Festival locally:

> What does the festival do for Wexford? Mr D. [Dickie] sees it in terms of a cosy family hobby in which everybody co-operates to produce something enjoyable, something that improves the quality of life for the local people. That is the important part of it.[36]

The 1972 opera season began with von Weber's *Oberon* and also produced

John Stewart and
Marco Bakker in
Les pêcheurs de perles,
1971

Bellini's *Il pirata* and Janáček's *Kát'a Kabanová*. Dickie indicated to the Council that he simply could not afford to remain with Wexford on the current salary. At the same time, the Council could not afford to absorb any more debt on the artistic side. 'I believe you realize quite as clearly as we do that gross overspending on the 1972 operas, as in the previous years, had led us into very grave difficulties', Scallan wrote in exasperation. He added:

> It would be very nice if we could all afford to adopt an airy and casual approach to finance and budgets, but there simply is no room in this organization for waste of money. This is precisely what has resulted from overspending by producers and designers, and it is what I am not prepared, as chairman of the Festival or as a director of Wexford Festival Limited, to tolerate again this year.[37]

Following this season, advertisements appeared in English and Irish newspapers and *Opera* magazine for a new artistic director.[38] This change in artistic leadership would mark a further turning point in the Festival's history.

In an attempt to involve more young people in the Festival, the Festival Council had started to make dress rehearsal tickets available to senior students in all of the secondary schools in the town and had initiated an essay competition to generate interest. In 1972, the title of the essay was 'Wexford Festival – Vanity or Prestige'. From the many worthy entries, the four prize winners were chosen. Second prize that year was awarded to a local boy, an aspiring writer from St Peter's College, Wexford – a young Colm Tóibín, who would become a world-renowned author, shortlisted three times for the Man Booker Prize and recipient of the Hawthornden Prize.

Probably one of the most poignant events in the history of the Festival was the announcement of the death of Sir Compton Mackenzie in 1972. As Walsh had written to Mackenzie's third wife on the death of her husband, the Festival was completely indebted to the man:

> Monty's influence on my life has been enormous – as his influence was on so many lives. Not alone in the twenty odd years before when I was searching like so many other young men for a broader and fuller life he gave it to me through the pages of *The Gramophone* and through many of his novels which told me much about the world before I had discovered those things for myself.
>
> I need not go into what he did for Wexford and the Festival except to say that had it not his tremendous prestige and backing in the beginning it never would have happened. It exists today as one of the many lost causes in which he believed, but which because he believed in them somehow took root and flourished.[39]

Mackenzie's death marked the end of the old guard at Wexford. He had threatened to leave before when Walsh resigned but had been persuaded to retain his position. He was the remaining link to the memories of how the Festival had come about. The presidential position was now vacant for the first time since the inception of the Festival.

Mackenzie was the first man to understand the financial burden of events such as opera festivals and had commented to Walsh in the beginning about how the Edinburgh Festival had similar financial concerns. Things had not changed by 1973, and financing the next season was again the burning issue. The Governor of the Bank of Ireland was approached to lend financial support. Interestingly, one of the questions he put to the Festival Council was what kind of support was available from local firms. It was further decided to approach the government and to notify them of the future plans of the Festival.[40]

By February 1973, applications had been received for the position of artistic director, although notably not one of the applicants was Irish.[41] It was unanimously agreed at an Executive Council meeting that Thomson Smillie be appointed. His contract would initially be for one year, to be extended to a two-yearly contract and his first season would be 1974. According to the chairman of the Executive Council, Sean Scallan, 'he has been in Wexford and is aware of our *special situation*'. The Council was generally satisfied with the high standard of applications that they had received for the position.[42] This was a positive sign that Wexford had managed to retain its international standing on the opera scene.

The growing professionalism of the Executive Council was again apparent with the establishment of a fringe group, the Wexford Festival Development Council. It was set up to look at the future of the Festival. Clearly the work of the existing Executive Council centred on the daily organization of affairs, and policies for the future were not being explored to their full potential. The first decision taken by this new council was to agree a sum of £300 to send John Boyle, a Council member, on a fundraising trip to America. As early as 1973, there was talk of trying to raise funds in America to build a new theatre in Wexford and Boyle was keen to progress this. The Theatre Royal was costing money in more frequent renovations. It was in the legal ownership of Loc Garmain Enterprises Limited, and there was an informal arrangement whereby Wexford Festival Limited occupied the building and was responsible for all outgoings of rent, rates, insurances and maintenance. The present Council members controlled less than 25 per cent of the total ownership. In the end, the decision was taken to spend the money on the existing Theatre, as the funds coming from America had not transpired and so there was little point in imagining grand plans for any future development.

The increased professionalism could further be seen in the discussion that took place regarding the safekeeping of the minutes book and also the press cuttings that were housed in the theatre.[43] This had never arisen as an issue before. It was agreed thereafter that this material would be stored in a fireproof location.[44]

Up to such time as a safe was built, the material would be stored in the bank. It seemed that, suddenly, the Executive Council had begun to take notice of the importance of the whole enterprise and of the archiving of its history.

A further discussion at this meeting concluded with the agreement that 'Wexford Festival policy regarding opera selection was "no policy".'[45] The Executive Council was obviously reiterating the point that it wished to maintain complete control over the operas that were performed at Wexford. Yet publicity and press relations were not in the hands of the Executive Council, a fact that became obvious at a meeting that took place between the major publicity agents involved, in March 1973. Bord Fáilte and Guinness were among the bodies that were represented at the meeting; the publicity aims of each body were discussed and 'a policy of full information exchange between the various groups was determined upon for future festivals'.[46]

The financial situation seemed somewhat healthier in June of 1973 with the agreement of Guinness to provide an extra £1,500 towards the Festival. Bord Fáilte agreed to provide £1,400 and the Arts Council pledged an additional £1,000. Discussions were ongoing about the possibility of approaching the government for a direct contribution towards running costs.[47] Matters had come to a head in November when it was suggested that 'a direct attack should be made on the government for funds'.[48]

In July 1973, the chairman of the Executive Council approached Walsh to ask him if he would agree to become the next president of the Wexford Festival, but Walsh declined the offer.[49] He clearly had no desire to have any further part in Festival proceedings. The 1973 Festival which produced Glinka's *Ivan Susanin*, Prokofiev's *The Gambler* and Donizetti's *L'ajo nell'imbarazzo* was another remarkable success. It was Dickie's last year at Wexford and journalists were fully supportive of the high standards, which served as invaluable publicity for the healthy state of the Festival. The *Sunday Times* reported of the 'constant charms' of Wexford:

> So much for Wexford's initial attraction. Once he is there, the visitor's curiosity gives way to admiration at the general standard of performance and artistic involvement which extends to every facet of the productions. Moreover, one is almost certain to be hearing, also for the first time, some vocal talent soon likely to be heard elsewhere, in grander houses. So Wexford draws the talent-scouts as well.[50]

The Minister for Labour, Michael O'Leary, too, was kind in his words on Wexford's contribution, in a press interview:

> O'Leary said that the excellent standard of the Festival was attested by its record over the years and this standard, he believed, was much higher than in other important opera centres in Europe, if not in the world. He hoped that elsewhere in the country opera companies might emulate what was done in Wexford.[51]

Again, the overseas press was first to congratulate Wexford on its success. The *Glasgow Herald* reported that 'it could happen only in Ireland' and went on to observe that:

the Irish are noted for being contradictory – or is it that they have a logic of their own that escapes others? ... To some extent the Festival's opera reflects the same attitude, since the Theatre Royal, where the performances take place, is the sort of building that no-one in his right senses would dream of using as an opera house.[52]

By December 1973, the Wexford Festival Development Council, just over a year in existence, drew up a report to highlight causes for concern. The first item raised in the report was the theatre itself, an aging building that was densely surrounded by other property which would naturally prevent any type of major expansion to the building. Recent improvements and repairs had been carried out, but it was an ongoing process to keep the theatre in a suitable condition.

As usual, money matters took up much of the report. It was pointed out that any money that was accumulated was being used to repair the Theatre and to maintain operatic standards. This left little scope for expansion or improvement. In some ways the Council felt that they had reached a type of plateau, and where they should aspire to go next was unclear:

> The Festival Council is conscious of a continuing responsibility to the town and county in which it exists. It would like to contribute more to the life of the area and the nation than simply two weeks of opera – however internationally acclaimed – and mollify the eternal if misguided criticism that the essential steep prices create an elitist and exclusive entertainment monopoly for the enjoyment of a few.[53]

It was a promising sign for the future that the Development Council had realized that the Festival must continue to expand its vision; there was no question about standing still. The report also took note of the general environment in which the Festival was trying to survive and improve. According to the report, Wexford was

> exceptionally well placed for the future. Accepting that the troubles in the North are going to pass in the next few years and that we have now entered the Common Market, the importance of the town as a communications centre with Europe and England cannot really be over-emphasized. New links are being established with the

Continent and it is obviously confidently expected that Rosslare will build itself into the most important gateway to Ireland after Dublin itself. Industrial and commercial interests press for the expansion of the port's facilities and it is noticeable, when the majority of our English friends have for a time abandoned us, that the visitors from the Continent are in fact increasing in numbers.[54]

The Development Council had recognized the need to promote the Festival as a cultural catalyst that could draw visitors to the town. The tourist industry in the region would benefit as a result.

Proposals put forward by the Development Council centred on the possibility of extending the Theatre Royal or constructing a new building to house fringe Festival activities. An earlier suggestion of transferring the entire operatic proceedings to a new theatre was met with stern opposition. It was not disputed, however, that the theatre was in need of modernization. The expansion and updating of the theatre would naturally require less financial assistance than building a new theatre. This was a huge consideration for the Wexford Festival Executive Council and also for the Development Council. No decision was reached about how to proceed; the report was presented to the Executive Council for consideration.

Thomson Smillie now entered the scene as Wexford's artistic director. He was born in Glasgow in 1942 and studied at Glasgow University, where he was president of the opera club. In March 1966, he began full-time employment with Scottish Opera as publicity officer, a position he held until his move to Wexford.

Following the tremendous loss of Compton Mackenzie, Lauder Greenway came in as President in 1974. Greenway, an American, had already given much help and support to the Festival. He had been chairman of the Metropolitan Opera in New York from 1956 to 1970 and had valuable musical connections all over the world. His kindness and generosity to the Wexford Festival was noted on many occasions. Taking up his position at Wexford, he declared that 'I feel like a "Johnny come lately" American that the Wexford Festival is something so much to be treasured, the world should know of the honour it is to be invited to take a serious part in these October festivities'.[55]

CHAPTER 7

NOT SO MUCH A FESTIVAL AS A WAY OF LIFE

1974–85

It was apparent by early 1974 that the Executive Council was aware of the magnitude of the annual cultural event, when it was decided that the history of the Festival should be written. It stipulated that 'the history of the Festival should be written in a convivial style rather than exposing the many ups and downs it has seen'.[1] The Council recognized that in order to generate enthusiasm for the Festival, which might translate into sponsorship, it was important not to emphasize its difficulties, in particular its financial concerns.

In making a subvention in June 1974, the Arts Council reiterated that it was more than satisfied with the standard of each Festival and that it wanted to see it continue.[2] The chairman of the Executive Council, Scallan, stressed that 'the Festival must expand and diversify if it is to maintain its present status and support'.[3]

The *New Ross Standard*, although complimentary of Wexford's cultural enterprise, noted that local support was still particularly poor in 1974. In the year that produced Mayr's *Medea in Corinto*, Massenet's *Thaïs* and Cornelius' *Der Barbier von Bagdad*, Tony O'Brien reported how 'live music is dead in Wexford':

> Wexford is known throughout Britain and Ireland and indeed the world as a centre of art and culture. This comes about principally (or solely depending on your point of view) through the presentation each year of the Wexford Festival Opera. This annual Festival is a grandiose auspicious affair which appears to mean a lot to the world of opera but other than being the reason for extended drinking hours it holds little or no interest for those of other music persuasions, particularly the young. Yet this is the only major music event in Wexford's social calendar.[4]

There were a number of disgruntled members on the Council by 1975, all articulating the same grievances. The chairman read out letters that he had received, airing discontent. In his letter, Sean Mitten expressed his dissatisfaction with 'the artistic trends of the Festival'. Ted Collins mirrored this concern, noting also that he was disappointed with 'the current artistic standards of the Festival'. Marie Fane, upon offering her resignation to the Council, mentioned what was by now becoming a common concern – that she too was dissatisfied with the artistic development of the Festival. This outpouring of discontent was a positive sign that the Executive Council members were active in their attempt to ensure that the Festival progressed and maintained its high international standards. To aggravate an already tense situation, however, it was reported that an application to the Taoiseach for financial support had not been successful.[5] The Taoiseach intimated that any funding request would have to be made directly to the Arts Council.

The 1975 season delivered remarkably well in terms of high standard of opera. Between 22 October and 2 November, performances took place of Lalo's *Le roi d'Ys*, Cavalli's *Eritrea* and Rossini's *La pietra del paragone*. The press noted how Wexford took on a 'Festival face' at this time of the year and how private sponsors had ensured its successful continuance to date:

> The Festival has had its good and lean years. Many times its survival has been in doubt and that it has been able to build up an immunity

Richard McKee in *Der Barbier von Bagdad*, 1974

to the viruses that have killed so many other artistic endeavours is due
in large measure to frequent expensive injections paid for by powerful
friends.[6]

In an attempt to show that opera was not an essentially 'Anglo-Saxon' hobby,
Nicholas Furlong wrote of student interest that had been aroused in the Festival:

The rare opera lovers which we find coming annually to Wexford do
not belong to a decaying Anglo-Saxon or old ascendancy remnant.
Nor are they aged. Over a hundred students were involved in our half-

price offer and a like number worked like demons backstage, front of house and all over the town in dozens of events as volunteers.[7]

New ways of obtaining further financial support was of vital importance for the continuation of the Festival, and offering these half-price tickets to students was one way of increasing ticket sales. Local fundraising, coupled with fundraising in America, did little to alleviate the large debt that had been accumulated. Barbara Wallace, chairperson of fundraising at the time, intimated that she felt that more Council members should share the responsibility of raising these much-needed funds, rather than leaving the task to a select few.[8] This was a contentious issue that Walsh had raised many times in the first decade of the Festival. He felt that the fundraising responsibilities had rested with him alone and he had remarked on various occasions how he had hated this particular burden.

Beit had also been called upon many times to provide personal donations towards the Festival. He too was growing tired of the endless cycle of fundraising, without a sustained and appropriate level of support from either the government or the Arts Council. He wrote to Scallan and outlined his views on the matter:

> I think that it would be true to say that no one is more devoted to the Wexford Festival than I am. True, I leave the mechanics to others, but I am heart and soul engaged in the operatic side to the extent that Thomson Smillie and I keep up a regular correspondence about our future activities and we have sketched out tentative programmes up to 1978, all of which will naturally have to be agreed by the opera committee and the Council. However, all of this seems to be rather academic in view of our short and long term financial situation. To me, the ending of the Festival would be a dagger in the heart, but how can we continue, against eternally rising costs, when we can get no additional subsidies and, apart from the existing ones, the government, not to mention the municipality or Wexford County Council, show absolutely no interest in our activities.[9]

Again the changing dynamics of the Festival were noted, especially the difficulty in obtaining voluntary workers.[10] From the start, the availability of these volunteers had been a feature of the Festival's distinct private and amateur nature. The suggestion now that more of these workers would have to be paid for their services marked the changing of the Festival to a more public, professional organization.

Even the newspaper articles of 1976 looked back with fondness to the early days of the Festival and tried to link the old school with the new. Rodney Milnes reported how he believed that those involved in running the Festival in its present form had not changed its direction, but had successfully continued it in Walsh's mould:

> The whole issue of neglected masterpieces is fairly bogus: an opera is worth performing or it is not. The only way to find out is to perform it and this Wexford has been doing since those heady days when Dr Tom Walsh started to explore *bel canto* long before anyone else and his successors have maintained both his enterprise and his canny way with casting. Around fifteen good operas have found their way back into the repertory from beginnings at Wexford, and dozens of singers, conductors, designers and producers have cut their teeth there.[11]

The *Wexford People* made the point that many of those who had been involved from its inception were still integral to the make-up of the Festival in its present form.

> The folk that operate the Festival in the Theatre Royal are seasoned campaigners, many wearing the coveted badge of 25 years' service and as such have weathered upsets and catastrophes like the Rosslare lifeboat crew have tasted saltwater.[12]

Although with the absence of Walsh and Mackenzie from Festival affairs, a new guard had emerged.

The year 1976 saw the production of Verdi's *Giovanna d'Arco*, Nicolai's *The Merry Wives of Windsor* and Britten's *The Turn of the Screw* and the season was reportedly as successful as ever. President Ó Dálaigh's last official act before his resignation as President of Ireland was to open the 25th Wexford Festival Opera.

It was perhaps a sign that the Council had failed to remain in control of the financial situation, coupled with the spiralling cost of producing opera, when the decision was taken in 1977 to employ a professional fundraiser. Ian Fox accepted the position and agreed to work towards a target of £300,000

Sandra Browne in *La pietra del paragone*, 1975

to be used primarily for capital expenditure and also for running costs.[13] This decision left the Council free to concentrate on productions for 1977. Barbara Wallace, chairperson of fundraising, took an alarmist approach in the 1977 Festival programme book, in an article entitled 'Will You Let Wexford Die?' She outlined the continuous problems that the theatre building faced, including the age-old problem of lack of space backstage. Dressing-room plans for the development of the Theatre Royal were being put in place. A sum of £350,000 was put forward as the target amount to be collected to ensure the survival and development of the Festival. This work was due to commence after the 1978 season. This was Richard Jefferies' first year as chairman of the Council, a position he retained until 1979.

In 1977, Massenet's *Hérodiade* and Gluck's *Orfeo ed Euridice* were produced, along with a triple bill of Cimarosa's *Il maestro di cappella*, Ricci's *La serva e l'ussero* and *La serva padrona* by Pergolesi. As a way of ensuring local involvement in the Festival, the Wexford Children's Choir took part in *Hérodiade*. To add to the national participation, members of the Irish Ballet Company under its artistic director, Joan Denise Moriarty, performed in Gluck's *Orfeo ed Euridice*. Moriarty had participated in the very first opera that took place at Wexford, Balfe's *Rose of Castile*, and it was fitting that she should return with the Irish Ballet Company in 1977.

Wexford's artistic director, Thomson Smillie, told the *Sunday Independent* that Wexford had done remarkably well in ensuring that it could attract talented artists within a limited budget year after year:

> Our policy in Wexford is to engage young opera talents, for Wexford just would not be able to afford the top commodity. I think we have done very well on the small resources at our disposal.[14]

But the artistic spending continued to plague operations at Wexford. In a letter to the chairman, F.X. Butler, the Finance Officer of Wexford Festival at the time, requested to be relieved of his financial responsibilities:

> Having witnessed the amount of imprudent spending in the artistic budget during the past twelve months, I am strongly of the opinion that I should no longer waste my time and Festival funds on this futile function. In effect I am asking to be relieved of the function of Finance Officer so that Council will not be under the illusion that I am in a position to control expenditure through that office.[15]

This was Alfred Beit's first year as president of Wexford Festival, Lauder Greenway having been forced to retire through illness. In his opening address, Beit commented on the incessant financial turmoil of the Festival:

> The financial position of the performing arts in Ireland is even more critical than it is in other western European countries and the United States. Countries such as Great Britain, France and Germany are in the happy position of being able to enjoy enormous grants from their respective governments; even so most of them want more. In America no such money is available but its place is taken by lavish private benefactors and by charitable or educational trusts.
>
> In England some of the principal banks and business houses have made valuable contributions to the performing arts over and above

government subsidies through similar Trusts which they have set up.

Ireland probably has only about one-twentieth of the population of some of these western European countries but how happy we would be if we could get anything like one-twentieth of the subsidies they enjoy. This is not to disparage the invaluable help given over the years by the Irish Tourist Board, the Arts Council, Guinness and other sponsors, but there is a limit to the amount these can give and many more sponsors are needed.

Unfortunately the type of Trust referred to above simply does not exist in Ireland, at any rate as far as the Arts are concerned, so we struggle on year after year with ever present inflation, a declining pound, and an uncertain future. Even so I hope we continue to give pleasure.[16]

By August 1978, the potential for further funding of the Festival was a distinct possibility. Barbara Wallace reported at a Council meeting that negotiations had begun with Heinz Food Company. Allied Irish Banks had agreed to give £5,000. Beit was responsible for contact being made with the Lombard and Ulster Bank.[17]

Smillie went on a promotional tour of the United States to publicize the 1978 opera season. There was no doubt that the Executive Council was willing to try any promotional activity to ensure that tickets would be sold for the coming season. Eugen d'Albert's *Tiefland* was a feature of this year's Festival, along with Haydn's *Il mondo della luna* and Smetana's *The Two Widows*.

At this point, having raised £150,000 of the proposed £350,000 needed for the theatre renovations, Wallace thanked the new Friends of the Festival who had lent their valuable support at this time. Further, she made special mention to local people and companies in the Wexford area, noting that 'this is another tribute to local involvement in the Festival'.[18] She was acutely aware that it was vital to encourage the support of local businesses and individuals to ensure the Festival's success and she paid tribute to the major contributors to this fund – the Arts Council, the Bank of Ireland and Allied Irish Banks.

As the 1979 season approached, the Festival benefited greatly from the volume of publicity that it received from the very beginning of the year. Television and radio programmes produced reports on the Festival, and newspapers carried stories that provided valuable early publicity. It was estimated that the publicity had saved the Festival Council £150,000 in advertising expenses.[19]

Another matter had arisen in early 1979 to cause further concern over funding. Questions were raised over the legal status of the Festival as a profit-making organization. Barbara Wallace, who had brought this concern to the attention of the Executive Council, stressed that the Council 'must be *seen* to be using the money raised. To this end, she was keen to start work on the Theatre as soon as possible.[20]

It was the Arts Council that came to the rescue of the Festival in 1979. In May of that year, it intimated that unless it was satisfied with the long term plans of the Festival, it could not guarantee financial support for the next three years. However, following a specific subvention in its budget, the Arts Council could now provide a grant of £25,000 to go towards current debt and a further £25,000 to be used specifically to strengthen the theatre development programme. It was stipulated however that the funding would be provided only on condition that the Festival would incur no further debt through production costs. The total amount to be awarded by the Arts Council had naturally exceeded the Executive Council's expectations; nevertheless the Executive Council was adamant that each member must remain as proactive as ever in identifying funding for the future.[21] Furthermore, following discussions between Bord Fáilte and the Arts Council, it was agreed that in future the Arts Council would be responsible for the total state allocation towards production costs to Wexford Festival Opera, and the Festival's funding relationship with Bord Fáilte came to an end.[22]

In November 1979, music critic Charles Acton made a public plea for financial aid on behalf of the Festival, and reported the views of the then artistic director, Thomson Smillie, as well as the incoming director, Adrian Slack:

> If anyone in a position to write a cheque for £22,500 would do so within the next week or so, the Wexford Festival could be saved a continuing expenditure and could actually be given an income-producing asset, and a load could be taken off their communal minds ... To return, however, to fees, Thomson Smillie, when asked how he would spend extra money if he had it he replied, without hesitation 'on more expensive singers'. Adrian Slack seemed to have a more perceptive attitude. He denied that he would spend any extra money he got on singers because already singers were willing to come to Wexford for about a quarter of their going fee and paying more to other singers would only 'destabilize' the entire operation.[23]

Adrian Slack had been Director of Productions at the State Opera of South Australia. Having completed an apprenticeship at the London Opera Centre and Sadler's Wells Opera, he joined Glyndebourne Opera. Slack remained with the Wexford Festival Opera for three seasons.

The 1979 Festival produced Montemezzi's *L'amore dei tre re*, Spontini's *La vestale* and Luigi and Federico Ricci's *Crispino e la comare*. The Wexford Children's Choir again took part in Montemezzi's creation. At the end of the Festival, it was brought to the attention of the Council that Slack was not satisfied with the short-term policy of the Festival. Permission for the engagement of artists was generally granted less than a year before they were due to perform, but this was often too late to book many of the artists that Slack would require. He stipulated that ideally he would rather be in a position to employ artists two or three years in advance. This request marked a further step on the road to professionalization.[24]

Following a very generous donation from Lauder Greenway, the Festival was in a position to purchase No. 31, High Street, a property that ran behind the back wall of the Theatre. For the first time, the Wexford Festival Council had the scope to tackle the backstage issues that had plagued the Festival up to now. In the Festival programme book of 1979, Albert Lennon, the consultant architect to the Theatre Royal, gave an update on work that was being carried out to the theatre. He noted his amazement at the backstage conditions:

> Visitors to the Festival over the years may occasionally have remarked the somewhat shoddy appearance of the Auditorium, seating etc. However when the curtain goes up this is quickly lost in the elegance and often sheer brilliance of the many fine sets which have graced the stage over the past twenty-eight years, not to mention the quality of the stars, orchestras and choruses which enthralled us. What they will not have realized, is the appalling backstage conditions which produced such beauty. There was literally no sets workshop, except already undersized stage, a props workshop which doubled as a canteen, dressing rooms hardly fit for rugby players, an attic wardrobe reminiscent of Hong Kong sweat shops, and sub-standard toilet accommodation. One watched with wonderment this magical use of such a small stage, but if familiar with the backstage conditions this wonderment must turn to awe. A debt is owed to the many professional

Dr Tom Walsh receiving the Freedom of Wexford

stars, on and off stage, and indeed to the 'Professional Amateurs' who have produced such beauty from such an impossible base.[25]

Lennon went on to make his justification for spending in excess of £300,000 to renovate this theatre rather than building a new one. Although the building was old, it was structurally sound. If a new building was planned, it was very possible that the costs would spiral out of control. He concluded by saying that 'whatever its shortcomings, and it will still have many, Wexford's Theatre Royal has and, we hope will retain, that indefinable and unrepeatable thing we call "character".'

The matter of the 'Irishness' of the Festival surfaced once more. It was decided that for the 1980 Festival:

> where possible Irish people should be employed, Irish goods should be used and sets should be made in Ireland, provided the highest standards could be maintained, and costs would not be increased.[26]

This again was a sign of the times and was a sign of a renewed awareness about

Sesto Bruscantini, David Beavan and Gianni Socci in *Crispino e la comare*, 1979

the potential of the Festival to give employment to young Irish musicians. Slack was notified that he should abide by this preliminary policy for the 1980 season.

The Festival Council remained concerned about artistic over-spending, with financial difficulties again threatening to mar the continuation of the Festival in 1980. RTÉ was at the centre of the discontent when an invoice received from them for the 1979 Festival amounted to £16,892. Budget estimates had presumed that RTÉ's fee would be £9,500. Concerns arising from the grave financial situation prompted a discussion on RTÉ's involvement in the Festival. Only once before had the future of the orchestra's involvement been questioned, and this was during Walsh's time as artistic director. At this stage, it was intimated that the Ulster Orchestra would charge a more reasonable rate for its services. Ian Fox, a member of the Festival Council, was wary of the discontinuation of the RTÉ Symphony Orchestra as the main orchestral body of the Festival, pointing out that any hostility between RTÉ and Wexford might cause difficulty with the future of RTÉ recordings. Still, he was more than willing to work with the Ulster Orchestra in place of the RTÉ Symphony Orchestra.[27]

Further difficulties arose with the decrease in the Arts Council grant for the 1980 season. It was stipulated at a Festival Council meeting in March 1980 that there would be substantial cutbacks in government aid for the arts. The Arts Council said that they would continue to provide 'a minimum grant' to all major festivals; the amount provided in 1980 would be £46,000, instead of an estimated £50,000 that had been calculated in the budget figures. The Executive Council made clear however, that it 'must not lose sight of artistic standards but must try to balance artistic standards with financial constraints'.[28]

This renewed concern about artistic standards came to the fore with the beginning of Jim Golden's term as chairman of the Council. Golden had worked with the Festival for many years and watched it progress to the stage it was now at. Not only was he aware that artistic standards had to be maintained, he knew what the costs associated with this could be. Fundraising, then, was one of the main items on the agenda of each Festival Council meeting. Local fundraising was proving particularly difficult, even though many small businesses and local people had expressed an interest in lending their support. The problems with fundraising, at a local and national level, were a direct result of the worldwide recession.[29] In the United States the fundraising situation was reported to be 'promising', although no money had yet been received for 1980. To compound concerns about the future difficulty of maintaining a high standard of opera at Wexford, Bank of Ireland had turned down an application for an interest-free loan of £40,000.[30]

The newspapers were full of articles relating to the acute financial difficulties and the sponsorship that had been promised thus far. According to the reporter Brian Quinn,

> The Irish America Fund under the auspices of Dr A.J.F. O'Reilly came to the rescue [of the Festival]. Some £80,000 must be still found for the building and there is £30,000 outstanding for this year's festival. But as [Barbara] Wallace put it: 'We still believe in miracles in Wexford'.[31]

The Festival produced another three critically acclaimed operas in 1980 despite the financial strain. Giacomo Puccini's *Edgar* was presented; Handel's *Orlando* was performed on four of the nights, and living composer Carlisle Floyd's *Of Mice and Men* was the third choice for the season. The American composer, Floyd, travelled to Wexford to hear the performance of his opera, which added to the excitement of the occasion. Ultimately the RTÉ Symphony Orchestra was retained to support the productions, along with the Wexford Festival Chorus, and the Bride Street Boys Choir also took part, constituting local participation in the Festival proceedings.

The growing professionalism by now expected from the Executive Council was again apparent when the Council experienced a further reshuffle to leave each member of the fourteen-body group with a specific responsibility. Marion Creely was named as the Arts Council observer on the Council, a practice that continued for a number of years.[32]

Press acclaim for the achievements of the Wexford Festival Opera was substantial again in 1981. Performances of Wolf-Ferrari's *I gioielli della Madonna*, Mozart's *Zaïde* and Verdi's *Un giorno di regno* were popular among the patrons. Kenneth Loveland, in the *South Wales Argus*, praised the success and uniqueness of the Wexford annual event:

> Wexford is the festival you just have to love. There is the picturesque town itself, a unique atmosphere of tradition and spontaneous welcome and a sense of community involvement rivalled by only a few.[33]

Following what was agreed to have been a very successful Festival, the Executive Council received much correspondence praising the standard of performance. The chairman read aloud a letter from the Mayor of Wexford, 'thanking him for a most enjoyable Festival'. Mark Hely-Hutchinson, Director of Guinness Ireland Limited, had also contacted the Council to express the enjoyment he had experienced during the 1981 Festival. The Director of Music at RTÉ, Gerard Victory, too, voiced his congratulations on the success of the annual venture. However, his praise was followed by the sobering account of RTÉ's plans 'to recoup the total direct costs in connection with the orchestra on a rising scale over the next four years' (up to 1981, Wexford had been responsible for only fifty per cent of the direct costs). This delivered yet another financial blow. Following a discussion at an Executive Council meeting in December, it was suggested that the Council request that RTÉ would postpone the proposed increase for 1982 as the budget for the season had already been agreed. RTÉ could open discussions regarding an increase for subsequent festivals.[34]

In December 1981, the Wexford Festival Executive Council received a very interesting offer. An individual, who wished to remain anonymous, offered to

Alvaro Malta in
L'amore dei tre re,
1979

donate the sum of £31,000 'if certain conditions were met'. The first condition was that the opera *Médée* by Luigi Cherubini should be presented during
its 1983 season. The second condition was that Helen Lawrence should be
selected for the leading role. The Council agreed immediately that the artistic
director should decide on the artistic merits of both opera and singer and that
the financial offer should not be the deciding factor. The offer was indeed
a fascinating one as it posed a difficult dilemma for the Executive Council.
The money of course was badly needed but perhaps not at the expense of
relinquishing control over operatic standards and performance choices at
Wexford.[35] The offer was eventually declined, perhaps strengthening the notion
that the Executive Council was now responsible for a professional enterprise
and could not afford to let the standard of opera deteriorate as a result of an
innovative funding opportunity.[36]

Cast and chorus of *I gioielli della Madonna*, 1980

This was Slack's last year as artistic director at Wexford. Intimating to Beit and Golden that he 'was not certain as to whether [he] was properly suited to the job of artistic director', he favoured directing his own productions one at a time rather than overseeing the work of others.[37]

Elaine Padmore joined Wexford Festival Opera for the 1982 season. She was Wexford's first female artistic director. She had studied music at Birmingham University, where she occupied leading roles in university opera productions. She lectured in opera at the Royal Academy of Music and gave broadcast talks. Before taking up her position at Wexford, Padmore had become a full-time radio producer, in charge of planning and producing opera broadcasts. She was to have a hugely successful career at Wexford, lasting thirteen years.

In preparation for the 1982 Festival, Barbara Wallace, in her final report as chair of fundraising, set out the points that needed to be stressed so that individuals and businesses alike could identify the very significance of the Festival for the town of Wexford:

Wexford Festival, in a very positive way, creates a good impression of Ireland abroad thereby helping to counteract the bad publicity generated by Northern Ireland news. The fostering of good music, in particular, Opera, the opportunity which this affords to young Irish artists and the educational aspects for the Wexford community, both young and old, with offshoots such as the Arts Centre, School of Music, Wexford Singers all justify supporting the Opera Festival.[38]

But, in a sense, Wallace was preaching to the converted and the difficult task would be the communication of these ideas throughout the town.

The professional contract between the Festival Council and RTÉ remained unclear as could be seen from a letter sent by John Kinsella of RTÉ, questioning dates for the 1983 Festival and future Festivals. The letter implied that RTÉ was less than enthusiastic about any future arrangement with Wexford Festival Opera.[39] Although the Executive Council had discussed on occasion the possibility of employing a different orchestra at a lower cost, in reality much of Wexford's success had depended on a good working relationship with RTÉ. The orchestra, however, played as usual for the 1982 season of Alfano's *Sakùntala*, Haydn's *L'isola disabitata* and Massenet's *Grisélidis*.

A situation arose early in 1983 concerning Elaine Padmore's control over artistic direction. Up to this point, the artistic director had been assigned virtually complete control over the choice of operas. However, because of differences between Padmore's choice of operas and the Executive Council's view on the matter, or more specifically the views of the Repertory sub-committee, a decision was taken that, for future festivals, the artistic director would no longer have complete control over opera choice.[40] The following report emerged in January of 1983:

It is the principal responsibility of the artistic director to choose and mount successfully the Festival's operas and recitals. This is to be achieved in association with the Repertory committee. The Council expects that the committee will contribute to the discussions concerning the selection of the operas and recitals. In the unlikely event of a real disagreement the committee can make a separate report and the matter will be resolved by Council.[41]

Christian du Plessis and Sergei Leiferkus in *Le jongleur de Notre-Dame*, 1984

The age-old complaint that Wexford Festival Opera had lost its appeal of earlier days resurfaced, not for the first time, in February 1983. The Repertory committee reportedly had long discussions about the possibility of re-introducing 'a few more late night events and a bit of "sparkle" back in the Festival'.[42] The early tradition of opera singers singing in the Wexford pubs after performances had been stamped out by Walsh himself in the early days, for fear that the singers might strain their voices. This late-night entertainment, it was felt, might interfere with performances in the Theatre Royal.

The issue of renewing the early excitement of the Festival was picked up by more than one of the local and national newspapers, and, as the *Enniscorthy Echo* reported:

> at the first meeting of the Council in 1983 an enthusiastic Council gave considerable thought and discussion to ways and means of injecting

new vitality into the event ... A most welcome note of strong local co-operation was introduced when it was reported that many local people ... have decided to raise modest amounts to help the Festival's financial problems.[43]

It was enough to offer hope for the future of the Festival and yet evasive enough not to identify any of the areas that this 'modest' financial aid might come from. At least the issue of the discontinuance of the RTÉ Symphony Orchestra's role as an integral part of the Festival seemed to have subsided, as they once again took part in Wexford's operatic treats – Marschner's *Hans Heiling*, Wolf-Ferrari's *La vedova scaltra* and Donizetti's *Linda di Chamounix*. This year's Festival lasted from 20 to 31 October.

In the wake of a successful Festival, not surprisingly, the budget was again the main item on the agenda at the beginning of 1984. It was noted that the financial outlook for the country as a whole was bleak, and this was reflected in the increased difficulties that the Executive Council was experiencing in its quest for funds. The Council also realized that 1984 would see significant expenditure cuts throughout the industry and commerce sectors. The fee for the employment of the RTÉ Symphony Orchestra had risen – an added expense that the Festival Council could not afford. Padmore made reference to the fact that the Festival could not sustain its current standard of performance within the proposed budget, especially with the added pressure of media and television interest in the Festival.[44]

'I really would love to be able to give you enough money to do the bloody job properly but I suppose it's the times we live in', Golden wrote to Padmore in exasperation in January of this year. 'Council does realize, as I do, how well you spend the money, how careful you are, what good value for money you get and how you make a profit on recitals but still money is hard to come by'.[45] By March, Padmore's frustration was manifesting itself as she was requested to cut spending for the coming season. She registered her discontent in a letter to the Council members:

Our small excesses, such as they were, were occasioned 1) by anomalies in the budget categories that are only now becoming clear, 2) by the proven impossibility of trying to pin some costs as low as those imposed on us, 3) the necessity of hiring additional male choristers when the promised local amateurs failed to materialize. Privately, members of Council have commended what we achieved financially. Collectively, you write to us 'demanding an explanation' for our over-spending. You cannot in fairness adopt a laissez-faire attitude throughout the year and then put on a collective face of stern correction and start baying for blood when suddenly hit by panic at the thought of the growing deficit … If I can save more, I will: but be warned – it is money that buys excellence and if I am to exercise the brief of high artistic standards that you so recently hired me to operate, there are areas of budget which you cut at your peril: the artistic budget buys what our ever-critical customers pay to enjoy.[46]

At the same time, the Council penned a letter to the Minister of State responsible for the Arts, Ted Nealon, urging him to engage with RTÉ on behalf of Wexford Festival, seeking the use of the RTÉ Symphony Orchestra free of all subsistence costs and fees for concerts. The subsistence costs for the orchestra was a considerable overhead at £30,000. The letter outlined that Wexford Festival should be entitled to the same rights to the National Orchestra as organizations in the capital that did not have to pay subsistence rates. The Minister forwarded on the response he received from the Director General of RTÉ on the matter, which simply concluded with the statement 'I intend to help them'.[47]

Amid the financial worry which never seemed to go away, the 1984 Festival opened with a flourish and, despite the bad weather, a large crowd turned out to witness its opening by Pat Kenny, who was beginning to make a name for himself in RTÉ.[48] The opera crowd was treated to Massenet's *Le jongleur de Notre-Dame*, Cimarosa's *Le astuzie femminili* and Smetana's *The Kiss*. The press was full of praise for the 1984 season. Charles Acton in the *Irish Times* recalled:

'This is Wexford as it used to be' was a sentence that I heard there often this year, which nostalgia being what it is, means that it is better than it ever was, habitually that is. That, fundamentally, is the highest praise that can be given to Elaine Padmore, the artistic director, since it reflects people's views of the three operas and their presentation as well as the general pattern of the Festival. The Council carry the can (and its chairman, Jim Golden, was one of the many who expressed that quotation) but it is the artistic director, who makes the plans.[49]

Not only could Wexford Festival Opera be distinguished for its operatic performances, it was steadily growing a reputation for its distinctive Festival atmosphere throughout the town which could be attributed to the fringe events. Perhaps the most important aspect of these events was the fact that they instilled a feeling of local participation in the Opera Festival. Although many local Wexford people did not attend the actual opera performances, the streets were thronged daily with people admiring decorated shop windows and attending various art exhibitions and concerts. Padmore had worked hard to create a daytime Festival, as well as the evening one, in particular with regard to the lunchtime concerts. Cyril Murphy, local organist and Executive Council member, assisted with the management and organization of these concerts which grew to become an integral part of the Festival. Notwithstanding the known high standard of the lunchtime concerts, it was no surprise that the Executive Council began to take special note of the standard of other annual fringe events taking place in the town.

In January 1985, a letter from Medb Ruane, Visual Arts Officer of the Arts Council, was read aloud to the Executive Council, commenting on the standard of the exhibitions that were held in Wexford in recent years. The chairman had requested this report from the Arts Council as a means of gaining advice on how to raise the current standard. There had been a reported drop in standard of fringe events, including exhibitions, the reason cited being a lack of suitable venues and a lack of finance.[50]

Meanwhile, RTÉ continued to provide its Symphony Orchestra for operatic performances, and the 1985 season saw the production of Catalani's *La Wally*, Handel's *Ariodante* and Weill's *The Rise and Fall of the City of Mahagonny*. The *Enniscorthy Guardian* reinforced the point that the support of Guinness was imperative to the continuation of the Festival.

There was some relief in 1985 with the announcement that Wexford Festival had succeeded in securing exemption under Section 32 of the 1984 Finance Act. In essence, it was now possible for individuals to claim back full taxes on personal donations. Now seemed like an opportune time to renew emphasis on the fundraising drive.

CHAPTER 8

WALSH'S FINAL FAREWELL

1986–8

Despite huge efforts to achieve a 'no-deficit' situation by the end of the 1985 season, the 1986 preliminary Council meetings opened with a report from the chairman that 'a serious financial problem' was predicted again for 1986. To add to this, Padmore requested an increase of £14,000 for the season.[1] It was amid this tumultuous period that the chairmanship of the Executive Council passed from Golden to Barbara Wallace. Golden's parting message as chairman resonated with all its members. 'The Festival is bigger than all of us', he began, 'and I will certainly be available to give what help I can to anybody who wants it. The Festival must survive and flourish'.[2]

The worst was yet to come: in February of 1986 a letter was circulated to the Council members from Patricia Quinn, Music and Opera Officer of the Arts Council, indicating that the Arts Council had taken a decision to suspend its grant aid to the Festival in 1986. Quinn attended the Executive Council meeting where she pointed out that the Arts Council had only taken the final decision in February and that the Festival Council had been notified as soon as possible. She explained that the decision had been taken to defer assistance to festivals across all disciplines until 1987. Quinn requested that Wexford keep the Arts Council informed of its plans for the 1987 season, although funds could not be guaranteed.[3]

The Executive Council was naturally incensed by this decision, which left the deficit for 1986 at £101,250. Immediately, fundraising, local and national, was discussed with a proposed target of £120,000.[4] Quinn was faced with a very angry and desperate Council. They wanted to know first of all where the money received by the Arts Council for 1985 and 1986 had been spent, requesting to see a list of those who were supported. They demanded to know who the members of the Arts Council were; what organizations they were representing; whether any members were political appointees; and whether any organization received more money this year than it had in the past. The session ended with the sarcastic question as to whether the 'Arts Council [is] saving some of the money for administration or to buy guns?'

The situation was a grave one for the Festival's future, if indeed it had any future at all, causing one Council member to declare disdainfully:

> I am very surprised that the [Arts] Council members who would not support [Wexford] have not resigned because it is obvious to the whole country that the members of the Arts Council are not capable of making a reasonable and logical decision … It is obvious that there is no use in requesting anything from the Arts Council and they are of no further use to this country and as a matter of fact they would be a hindrance ... As we see things tonight there is no hope of mounting a festival for 1986.[5]

The Council concluded by passing a resolution deploring what it described as the Arts Council's 'grossly irresponsible action'.[6]

The Arts Council had reportedly only received half of the funding it had requested from government, and although denying that it had used Wexford as a means of embarrassing the government, Arts Minister Nealon was emphatic in his response that neither he, nor his department, had been consulted in this 'unilateral and surprising decision' to cut funding of festivals.[7] This indeed was a difficult period for the new chairperson, Wallace, who had pioneered the fundraising cause with great energy up to this point. Given that £90,000 was expected from the Arts Council, and Wexford Festival Council had committed to raising £30,000 from private fundraising, it was now in the impossible position of trying to identify ways to raise the full £120,000. Immediately a document entitled 'Save the Wexford Festival' appeared and formed part of the national and local fundraising initiative that was ongoing to maintain the Opera Festival.[8] Ted Howlin, member of the Executive Council, managed to convince Tom Walsh to give two lectures on the Festival, one in Wexford and a second one in the Royal Hospital, Kilmainham, Dublin. The aim of the lectures was to publicize the Festival, and Jim Golden was also instrumental in encouraging Walsh to participate in Festival affairs at this stage.

Wallace wrote to Tony O'Reilly, who she knew personally, on 20 February, setting out what she had communicated to the Arts Council and to the government directly, and seeking financial support from him. O'Reilly was chairman of the Ireland Funds, a philanthropic, non-political, non-sectarian organization whose function was to channel funds raised in the United States and elsewhere to the causes of peace, culture and charity in Ireland – north and south. Within two weeks of making contact with O'Reilly, the Ireland Funds made a pledge of £50,000, which was transferred immediately into Wexford Festival's bank account. Locally then, the plea for funds had accumulated a further £15,000 from the Wexford community. Beit wrote to Wallace, pledging £10,000 following the sale of a painting and a further £10,000 from another fund. His wife, Clementine, also made a donation to the Wexford Festival fund. Bank of Ireland agreed to provide a one-off subscription of £10,000 to the Festival as a result of the particularly difficult situation it faced.[9]

With the much-needed outpouring of support, the decision was taken at the beginning of March to go ahead with the Festival in 1986. The artists had already been contracted and Patricia Quinn wrote to Wallace confirming that the Arts Council would make available the sum of £30,000 for essential expenditure, including administration, salaries and expenses, insurance and a portion of light and heating costs.

The dire financial situation that had unfolded before the Executive Council had one positive effect on proceedings. Innovative ideas for the improvement of the annual event were discussed at length. This uncovered many viable options for the successful progress of the Festival into the future. In May 1986, Wallace reported on 'a major new plan to strengthen the financial base of the Festival'. The introduction of 120 new seats in the extension of the theatre was discussed which would benefit box office income. The cost of such an extension was debated among Council members, although all appeared to see this as one realistic solution to a deteriorating financial situation. According to the chairperson, this expansion would give Wexford Festival something to sell to new sponsors ahead of the 1987 season.

Wallace had also met with Padmore in London in order to further discuss and develop revenue generating ideas. Their discussions centred on the idea of an opera for children, bursaries for young Irish singers and a proposed Wexford Festival summer school.[10] Wallace discussed these ideas with Máirtín McCullough, former Festival Council member and now chairman of the Arts Council, who had remained a confidante. 'Experience has taught me to have some certainty of success before inviting public discussion', she confided in McCullough, as an explanation as to why she had not discussed her plans as yet with the Festival Council.[11]

Wallace was confident that if correct programmes were put forward, the Department of Education or even the Arts Council might, in the future, provide some funds for their successful implementation.

By 27 August, the crisis was over. Wallace reported that the 1986 Festival would now safely proceed as planned – 'by the grace of God and the generosity of many'.[12] Furthermore 100 per cent seat occupancy was now expected.[13] At the Guinness Press Conference in June, Wallace paid tribute to the many individuals and organizations that came to the rescue of Wexford Festival:

> The help and support came pouring in – the anonymous donations, the offers of help in kind from Glyndebourne, Covent Garden, Royal Hospital Kilmainham, Wexford School of Music and Festival Singers. From France, the UK, Belgium, the US, words of encouragement, donations large and small were made. Many at great sacrifice to the donors and here I include Wexford County Council – all were prepared to suffer so that Wexford could survive. And the result, well another £17,500 will allow us to come out of the 1986 Festival without a deficit and we are going forward in 1987 with hope, courage, confidence and some promises.[14]

Wallace also introduced a new programme – *Opera for Youth*. Scottish Opera's Educational Unit was commissioned to visit Wexford for two weeks. A team of four music and drama specialists visited a number of primary schools in the

Pauline Tinsley and Daniela Bechly in *Königskinder*, 1986

town where about one hundred pupils in each school had the opportunity to be involved in performance projects, including costumes. It was a new departure for Wexford and the schools that had the chance to take part were extremely appreciative of this opportunity. Furthermore, Wallace announced ten bursaries to Irish students who were on a path to professional singing careers. Wallace and the Executive Council were hopeful that these new initiatives would attract new commercial sponsors at a critical time for the organization.

The Festival opened with Humperdinck's *Königskinder,* accompanied by the RTÉ Symphony Orchestra and the Wexford Festival Chorus, under chorus master Ian Reid. Rossini's *Tancredi* followed on 23 October and was performed with the aid of the Wexford Festival Male Chorus. Ambroise Thomas' creation, *Mignon,* was the final selection for the season. The press realized how fortunate the town was, this year in particular, that the Festival had survived into its thirty-fifth year:

The 35th Wexford Festival got underway this week having overcome the financial problems which had earlier threatened to sink the event without trace. For weeks during the spring it looked as if there would never be a 35th Wexford Festival but the determination which has helped it through so many crises in the past, saw it through what was possibly its most serious problem ever.[15]

Wallace must have been particularly relieved and proud to have steered the Wexford Festival through its most turbulent time. Straight away however, the focus moved to raising extra funds to build seating capacity in the Theatre Royal.

Wexford Festival Executive Council decided that the time had come to appoint a managing director to support the running of the Festival. Sean Scallan inferred that the need for such a position had arisen out of the realization that the Executive Council, as presently constituted, was 'too weak'.[16] Costs for running an Opera Festival in Wexford had by now exceeded £500,000. It was no longer going to be possible to raise this sort of money on a voluntary basis.

The 1987 Festival was indeed another successful event, with the productions of Bellini's *La straniera* and Giordano's *La cena delle beffe*. The third choice for 1987 was *Cendrillon*, a fairytale in four acts by Jules Massenet. Members of the Dublin City Ballet participated in this novel piece. The unveiling of the refurbished Theatre Royal, with the President of Ireland, Patrick Hillery, as the guest of honour, helped to create a high public profile for the Festival this year.

In the aftermath of the Festival, Wallace reported to the Council that the Festival had reached 'an all-time high'. This, she added, was a new concept for the Opera Festival that had struggled to overcome a myriad of difficulties since its inception. The continued success of the Festival, however, was heavily dependent on the availability of the orchestra; on being viable financially; and on selling the extra seats.[17] The participation of the RTÉ Symphony Orchestra was never assured from one year to the next, and this was a significant concern. Wallace, however, was satisfied with the progress that had been made, particularly since she had taken up her role as chairperson. This could be seen in a letter she wrote to Alfred Beit following the 1987 Festival. She told him of her delight in negotiating a £30,000 grant from the Irish National Lottery for work on the theatre, and a further £13,000 from the Arts Council for the 1987 season. A successful application had also been made to Bord Fáilte for £10,000 to put towards theatre costs. Moreover, Guinness had renewed its contract for a further three years at £35,000 a year. 'I hope to present a four-year plan to Festival Council sometime early in the New Year,' Wallace said, 'showing all the exciting things which we hope to try to do, not least improving the standard even more'.[18]

The growing confidence of the Festival Council was beginning to show and John Small requested permission to employ Professor John O'Hagan to conduct a study on the 'Economic and Social Impact of the Wexford Festival on a Local and National Level'. The cost of the proposed report was £4,000 and O'Hagan was due to visit Wexford in April to carry out a preliminary examination of Festival proceedings.[19]

Jerome Hynes joined Wexford Festival Opera as its new Managing Director. Although he was very young to be taking on this role, he brought significant experience that he had acquired as general manager of another successful cultural institution – the Druid Theatre Company. He had been responsible for the management of that company during a time of significant growth, aiding its transformation from a small regional company to a significant national one, whose reputation was steadily growing, due to its tours in the United Kingdom, the United States and Australia. With his appointment came another significant shift towards professionalism.

The 1988 Festival witnessed an ambitious programme. The Festival opened with Dvořák's *The Devil and Kate*, and was followed by Mercadante's *Elisa e Claudio*. There was a double bill again this year with Gazzaniga's *Don Giovanni Tenorio* and Busoni's *Turandot*. The Wexford Festival Chorus and the RTÉ Symphony Orchestra played their respective vital parts as usual.

Tom Walsh died after the 1988 Festival. A poignant obituary appeared in the *Times* on 14 November 1988, written by Bernard Levin. Levin, who religiously attended the Wexford Festival, had dedicated the final chapter of his 1981 book *Conducted Tour* to the Festival, describing it as one of his favourite festivals. It was fitting that he should write about Walsh's legacy:

> We laid Tom Walsh in the earth on Friday, under a glorious Indian-summer sun, in the Barntown cemetery outside the town; that way he can sleep amid the soft green hills of his native County Wexford which he loved so much.
>
> After the requiem mass in his home church, the cortège formed

Cast and chorus of *Mignon*, 1986

up; we filled the street from side to side and end to end. Solemn robed figures walked immediately behind the hearse; easily mistaken for members of the Guild of Mastersingers, they turned out to be the entire borough council, in full fig.

The town band wasn't there; perhaps it had been wrongly thought insufficiently reverent for such an occasion. The Taoiseach, though, had sent a telegram. The flowers, piled up, made an Everest of beauty and farewell; the church was heady with their scents. We sang 'Abide with Me', and meant it.

Well, your man had done a lot for the place ... His worth and achievements were recognized; the University of Dublin made him first an honorary MA, then a Doctor of Philosophy, then Doctor of Literature. He was an honorary fellow of the Faculty of Anaesthetists of Ireland, a fellow of the Royal Historical Society, a Knight of Malta, a freeman of Wexford (well I should think so). He wrote a series of scholarly books on the history of opera; he was twice married and widowed; he is survived by his daughter and sister ...

Tom died smiling. At least, I assume he did; he was certainly smiling when I saw him in Wexford Hospital a few days before the end. As a doctor, he could not deceive himself about his condition, and his colleagues did not try to bluff him. But there were no solemn farewells; solemn farewells were not much in his line, except, to be sure, operatic ones.

Wexford know him as 'Doctor Tom', and would call him nothing else. I often wish I had been living in Wexford at the time; I would have loved to watch the scene as he went about the town telling people of his plan, while the news went much faster about the town that Doctor Tom had gone mad. For consider: Wexford in 1951 was not only a quiet place, unheard of outside Ireland and hardly heard of even inside; it was also savagely poor. The Theatre hadn't been used as such for a century (some say two); moreover it would hold only 400 people, and anyway it was now a furniture repository.

The very Muses wrung their hands and wept at so forlorn a hope, but they didn't know Doctor Tom; the iron-clad principles of rectitude and honour that guarded his life were translated into an irresistible inclination to see his dream realized. The Wexford Opera Festival, with the weeping Muses engaged for the Chorus as a token of forgiveness, opened its doors on time; that was 37 years ago, and they haven't shut yet ...

He sought no fame, no fortune. He had got hold of the notion that he was on earth to tend the sick and spread the love of music, and he pursued both vocations with great diligence and no fuss. It pleased him, as it pleased all of us, that over the years Wexford had become noticeably better off; his festival brought a good deal of money into the town ...

We returned, en masse, to the hospital, to see him for the last time.

He fought on for another week; death would not have dared approach his bedside until the 1988 Festival was over. Last Tuesday afternoon, he fell asleep, and in sleep he left us. We who knew him will keep his memory bright, forever in his debt for the joy and friendship he and his festival have given us. We are even more blessed by having known and loved a man of such goodness, wisdom, generosity and laughter. Doubt not that he feasts in Heaven this night, with Mozart on one side of him and Hippocrates on the other, and a glass of good red wine in his good right hand.[20]

The *Guardian* wrote of a man who would be remembered in Wexford for what he had brought to the town, trying in some way to explain why he had not been an integral part of the Festival for some years now:

After the 1966 Festival which had a very 'Walshish' programme, Dr Tom ... had a disagreement with the festival board. He was replaced by an Englishman, Brian Dickie, who was later to become General Administrator at Glyndebourne. Walsh was not pleased with the change in the festival which artistically he had managed to run almost single-handedly right down to the editing of the programme in which his own face never appeared. For some time he went back only reluctantly to the theatre where once he attended every performance.

But Dickie continued the policy of Wexford much in the Walsh mould, as does the current festival director Elaine Padmore, in going for little-known operas cast with singers on their way up.

The Wexford wounds had healed and he came back to the festival he had created although usually avoiding first nights. The door of his house, five minutes' walk from the Theatre Royal, was ever open both to singers and the critics whom he realized had helped turn Wexford into an international affair.[21]

A minute's silence was observed at the meeting of the Wexford Festival Council

Peter Lightfoot and the chorus in *The Devil and Kate*, 1988

in his memory. Wallace, as chairperson, spoke about his contribution, stating:

> Wexford Festival was deeply indebted to Dr Walsh. His courage and
> vision as a founding member was instrumental in taking the Festival
> and making it truly international. His deep interest in the future of
> the Festival was evident from his ideas for its development, right up
> to his death.[22]

Somehow this did not even seem sufficient.

CHAPTER 9

WE STILL BELIEVE
IN MIRACLES AT WEXFORD

1989–2003

One year after the idea for an economic study was discussed, the O'Hagan Report was officially launched in Wexford and Dublin. Albert Reynolds, Minister for Finance, attended its launch in Dublin, where he 'praised the Festival for its excellent efforts and agreed to bring the report to the attention of the Taoiseach'. As stipulated at a Council meeting in September 1989, the findings of the report would be used in the pursuit of more state-aid sponsorship, while all the time conveying the Festival's worth for Wexford.[1]

Marschner's *Der Templer und die Jüdin* was the first choice for the 1989 season. Mozart's *Mitridate, re di Ponto* was performed for five of the festival nights, and Sergei Prokofiev's *The Duenna* (Betrothal in a monastery) was the third opera chosen. The Dr Tom Walsh lecture series was initiated this year and would become an integral part of the Festival from this year on. It was an opportunity to invite distinguished guests to Wexford to relay their personal

Gary Harger and Christopher Trakas in *Gli equivoci*, 1992

stories of the Wexford Festival. Rodney Milnes, English music critic and musicologist was the first such guest to be invited.

Despite the perceived stability of the Festival as it moved towards its fortieth year, below the surface, particularly at the Executive Council level, the situation was never far from crisis. Scallan remained concerned that the deficit being carried was too high, estimating that the deficit by the end of the 1989 Festival would be £184,000. He added that he did not believe that the 1989 Festival could be mounted as planned, unless there was the possibility of a cash injection of at least £100,000. He suggested too, that information was being withheld from the Council. Wallace addressed these criticisms in a letter to Scallan:

Prior to the arrival of our Managing Director, and as I mentioned at the last Council meeting, I, as the current 'caretaker' and acting not just as a chairman but as an executive chairman/chief executive, found it unwieldy to try to run the affairs of the Festival with such a large Council. I tended to seek the advice of a small group which included the Finance Officer, Fundraising Chairman, the two Vice-Chairmen, Administrator and Managing Director. This group have held 40 meetings since the evening when news of the Arts Council 'cut' was received in 1986. Again I would like to say that in so far as I have been remiss in not consulting with other members of the Council in advance, I apologize. I tried to make every hour of the time which I gave to the cause, be effective and productive.[2]

Scallan commented that 'it is many years since I saw the morale of the Festival Council so low'.[3] With the engagement of a managing director at Wexford, the role of the Executive Council had inevitably changed. Council members found themselves in the uneasy position of having less power over decisions than before.

As alluded to by Wallace, the Council now had reached a membership of between 25 and 30, and was obviously too large to deal sufficiently with urgent matters. In line with the changing management structure, Wallace brought forward a document to Council for discussion. This document centred on the issues of structure and change. She made reference to the fact that it was the general assumption of those outside the Festival Council that there was 'an inability to accept new ideas or blood'. She was keen to dispel this notion and essentially welcomed change to the Council as presently constituted while also welcoming new ideas:

May I leave you with a thought? To remain as we are, we must change. We cannot stand still; if we try to stand still we will lose ground. Let us display the same courage and determination as did the founders. Let us hand the Wexford Festival Opera over to our successors as we were 'handed it', strong and vibrant.[4]

Wallace challenged each Council member to consider what they had to offer the future of Wexford Festival Opera:

Perhaps we should examine what and who is needed to run the Wexford Festival as opposed to trying to make what we have fit, or to try to effect change for change's sake. I suggest that this should be the basis for a discussion by the Council.

My reason for suggesting a holocaust leaving only YOU was not in an effort to be dramatic but simply to try to get everyone to be objective, and to stop thinking in terms of how change might affect any one of us who are involved at present.

She reinforced her statement by saying that she believed the structure of the Festival to be, by and large, a good one, but that was no reason for not exploring possibilities for the future advancement of opera at Wexford. She highlighted the importance of the chairperson's role, the role of the managing director and the role of the artistic director: none of these should rule with a dictatorial hand.

The work of the volunteers at Wexford and the importance of their continued presence at the Festival was never far from Wallace's mind. Her document relayed just how important the voluntary workers were to Wexford:

Wexford Festival's success is due in no small measure to the atmosphere in the town. This is partly due to the goodwill and influence of the voluntary workforce. I believe that it is not just important but it is essential that local voluntary workers know, understand and are willing to run as many departments of the total Festival as is possible. It has been proven that they are capable once they are trained. That is why I have frequently exhorted the heads of departments to nominate a deputy to bring on stream new people in their areas, not just because of the financial implications but to ensure continuity of local knowledge and to avoid having the existing people over-burdened as the Festival extended. These might work for short periods on a regular basis, e.g., there are many, many people in Wexford who are willing, able and anxious to be involved at this level.[5]

Any tension that existed in the Council over the maintenance of high standards of the Festival was not reflected in the successful 1990 season. The newly named National Symphony Orchestra and the Wexford School of Ballet and Modern Dance played an integral part of Leoncavallo's *Zazà*. The Wexford Festival Chorus

John O'Connor, Jerome Hynes and Ted Howlin

and the Loch Garman (Wexford) Silver Band took part in Maw's *The Rising of the Moon*. And Boieldieu's *La dame blanche* was performed, again with the aid of the Wexford Festival Chorus, conducted by Emmanuel Joel. Eleanor White, as local liaison within the Executive Council, was in charge of co-ordinating the organizations taking part in the parade for the Festival's opening. A brochure was also produced, in association with the Junior Chamber of Commerce, to publicize all events and exhibitions during the Festival, outlining times and venues.[6]

The rising orchestral costs remained a concern for the Festival Council. The figure for the 1990 season represented a 35 per cent increase – to £88,000 – on the costs for the 1989 season, and no breakdown was given by RTÉ as to what the increase related. The matter was raised with the Director General of RTÉ, who relented and agreed to charge £70,000 for the 1990 Festival, due to the unreasonable increase and the lateness in advising Wexford Festival of same.[7]

Patricia Quinn of the Arts Council wrote to the Executive Council following the 1990 season, to ask if Wexford would consider putting on the work of a

(*above*) Cornelia Helfricht in *Die Königin von Saba*, 1999; (*opposite*) Jacek Janiszewski, Elizabeth Woods and Dariusz Stachura in *Straszny dwór*, 1999

contemporary Irish composer during its 1991 season. Padmore was emphatic in her response to this request:

> We have no plans to either present or commission anything in this sphere in 1991. Although we would not positively rule it out in the future, were there to be an obvious and outstanding candidate, we do not see any reason to change from what we do best.
>
> Our special place in the world of international opera has been won by the championing of neglected or forgotten works of the 19th century: that is Wexford's hallmark, and we have a loyal audience who support us very solidly in our explorations of the operatic past (and even, less willingly, support us when we drag them into more modern times, as this year). We believe that what we do already is extremely

valid, and highly valued by our audience – but this audience we have built comes here for opera, not for contemporary music, and would be unlikely to support us if we changed tack.

... I would be interested to receive lists from the Arts Council of <u>which</u> Irish operas or composers you think we should be supporting. There may be people working in this area that we know nothing about and would at least like to be aware of.[8]

The pressure to review its strategy around operatic choices was set to continue and the Arts Council, as principal sponsor of the Festival, was keen to ensure that its own agenda was being met.

It was reported at a Festival Council meeting in December that the 1991 Festival had been 'one of the easiest to date' – much to the relief of the Council members.[9] It was no easy task trying to maintain a professional standard of opera year after year in a very uncertain environment. Financing each consecutive year was an onerous task and the Festival Council had worked extremely hard

Dario Volonté in *Siberia*, 1999

to ease the financial burden. John O'Connor was the Council member called upon to report on the financial situation. Within a short space of time, both the Finance Officer and the Administrator had left the company and the Council was grappling with deficits and trying to get to grips with the full financial picture. Wallace requested that Paul Hennessy, a partner in Coopers and Lybrand, be co-opted to the Council. Part of his brief was to fulfil the role of Finance Officer, and to put a structure in place, between fundraising and the Finance Committee, to ensure that controls were in place for the future.[10]

But the theatre was in constant need of renovation and the sum needed to ensure that it would remain a suitable venue was significant. In June 1991 a special meeting of the members of the Council was held to specifically deal with the issue of the Theatre Royal. As Wallace pointed out, phase one would involve moving the location of the box office and providing a new cloakroom. Funding of £50,000 for these improvements was forthcoming from Guinness, and Bord Fáilte had pledged a grant of £65,000 from the European Structural Fund in respect of phase one – front-of-house developments. Plans were already in place to move offices to a new location in 21 High Street, beside the Theatre Royal.

This was still only phase one of the proposed project, which was estimated to cost £250,000 in total. Facilities for patrons and artists remained a concern and a solution needed to be found. There remained, however, one property between the offices and the foyer that was not in the possession of Wexford Festival Trust. This, and the fact that the entire project was estimated at £1 million, were two substantial stumbling blocks.[11] The Arts Council was reportedly concerned at this stage about the viability of such enhancements and requested to be kept informed of the proposed cost of such extensive work.[12]

The 1991 Festival season extended from 24 October to 10 November. Donizetti's *L'assedio di Calais* was performed on the opening night, followed by Gluck's *La rencontre imprévue* and Goetz's *Der Widerspänstigen Zähmung*. All operas were very well received. Scottish Opera's *Opera for Youth* programme did not take place in Wexford in 1991, much to the disappointment of the local schools. It simply was not financially viable to run the programme this year.

Wallace's time as chairperson of the Council was coming to a close and she presented the group with a report in March 1992. It consisted of recommendations for the future about how the Festival could strengthen relationships, its image and its fundraising position. She noted that relations with RTÉ, that had on many occasions been strained, had improved considerably. She recognized RTÉ's contribution to the Festival from the very start and hoped that RTÉ was aware of this appreciation. Relations with Guinness, although also at times fragile, were in a healthy state by 1992. She emphasized the importance of showing gratitude for support received from the Wexford community, both commercial and individual: this continued support was seen as key to a successful future. The Arts Council had had an uneasy relationship with the Festival Council since the decision not to make the 1986 grant available; nevertheless Wallace knew the importance of the Arts Council's long-term contribution. Furthermore, Patricia Quinn continued to attend Festival Council meetings as an observer.

By now, the professional structures were well embedded at Wexford Festival Opera. Its new Finance Officer, Paul Hennessy, provided the Council with a report on Corporate Affairs and Statutory Compliance in August 1992. The report took note of the legal entities that Wexford Festival Opera consisted of: Wexford Festival Trust; Wexford Festival Ltd; Loc Garmain Enterprises Ltd; Wexford Festival Trust (UK); and the American Friends of Wexford Festival Inc. Hennessy set out the professional obligations of the enterprise – to ensure that Wexford Festival Opera complied at all times with statutory and legislative requirements relating to its corporate affairs; and to put in place a corporate structure appropriate to the needs of the organization.[13]

The Wexford Festival went on to purchase No. 32 High Street, a property across the road from the Theatre Royal. The Executive Council then managed to secure an agreement with the occupants of No. 25, next door to the theatre, to swap the properties. A subsidy from Guinness was going some way towards meeting these costs but a general plea went out to Wexford patrons in the 1992 Festival programme book, seeking support to enable Wexford Festival Opera to achieve its objectives:

> Any members of our audience who feel that they, or someone they know, could assist us in this development should contact our Managing Director, Jerome Hynes who would be happy to provide further details concerning our plans for development. We would be grateful for any donations patrons may wish to make towards this development.[14]

The Festival was opened on 22 October by the Taoiseach, Albert Reynolds. Mascagni's *Il piccolo Marat* was the first opera to be performed this year. The National Symphony Orchestra, formerly the RTÉ Symphony Orchestra, was conducted by Albert Rosen. Storace's *Gli equivoci* was performed on six nights also and the Festival closed with an acclaimed performance of Marschner's *Der Vampyr*. It had been a frustrating year for Padmore however. She had written to Hynes early in the year, expressing her utter dismay at the request to achieve savings on the artistic side:

> I've spent hours wrestling with the budget today and have agonizingly scraped an additional £13,000 off it. Please tell John [O'Connor], Paul [Hennessy] and any other interested parties that this is finally and

Lada Biriucov in *Orleanskaya deva*, 2000

definitively *it* as far as I'm concerned and no amount of staring at the
figures is going to produce any more cuts.[15]

The press was impressed nonetheless with what Padmore was able to achieve
within the constraints:

> In these difficult times when six, or even seven, figure production
> budgets for opera are becoming the norm, and similarly deficits
> for major opera houses increasingly common, the little fishing port

(*above*) Joseph Calleja and Iwona Hossa in *Si j'etais roi*, 2000; (*opposite*) Emma Martin and Dara Pierce in *Si j'etais roi*, 2000

of Wexford in the south-eastern corner of Ireland shines out like a beacon … Not only that, but in some uncanny way the Wexford Festival, even today, contrives to achieve its successes on a shoe-string. Singers will almost always be young and on their way up, and such is Wexford's reputation that many promising international singers will be prepared to sing there for a fraction of their normal fee. The same goes for producers and designers. Elaine Padmore's eagle eye permits not a penny to be wasted, yet under her skillful artistic direction the Festival has gone from strength to strength. She was able to tell me, with some pride, that the total production budget for the scenery and costumes of the three operas staged this year was just over £45,000. If the stagings had been skeletal and rudimentary that figure would still have been creditable, but they were nothing of the kind.[16]

Furthermore, Padmore continued to have a difficult working relationship with the Repertory Committee and felt that her work was undermined by constant

questioning of her operatic choices. 'I know of no other opera house or Festival which allows its artistic director to be subjected to this kind of frankly insulting treatment', Padmore claimed,

> Nor can I think of any likely successor to myself who would put up with it. It is precisely the sort of negative confrontational situation that committees of amateur enthusiasts versus a professional will produce, and for which frankly you will not get much support from the Arts Council if you allow to persist. In my opinion this committee is obstructive, is much too narrow in its musical tasks, has little spirit of adventure and is very thin on real expertise and on imagination. I have suffered – all too politely – at their hands for more than 10 years. That is quite long enough.[17]

In support of Padmore, the Festival Council agreed to disband the Repertory Committee as presently constituted, and left the way open for a new Artistic Committee that would be developed in due course.[18]

Sir Alfred Beit notified the Festival Council that he wished to step down as President at the end of the 1992 season. He had served on the Council since

Declan Kelly, František Zahradníček, Ekaterina Morozova and Stefano Costa in *Alessandro Stradella*, 2001

1957, as chairman from 1962 to 1966, and then as president from 1977 to 1992. His departure was significant because he had left an indelible mark on the fortune of the Festival: he was its first significant benefactor.

Sir Anthony O'Reilly accepted the role of President following Beit's departure. As former CEO of the Heinz Company, and having led Independent News and Media Group since 1973, O'Reilly was an impressive asset to Wexford's cause. He was active in many cultural and charitable organizations and held the position of global chairman of the Ireland Funds, spanning more than ten international entities.

John O'Connor was an obvious successor to Wallace and he duly took up the role of chairman in 1993. O'Connor had assumed a leadership role in the Council, lending his expertise on financial matters in recent years. The 1993 Festival got underway with Tchaikovsky's *Cherevichki*. This well-received work was followed by Paisiello's *Il barbiere di Siviglia* and Hérold's *Zampa*. It was a very successful season in what turned out to be Padmore's penultimate Festival with Wexford.

As soon as the Festival ended, Jerome Hynes set about preparing for the future, with a new President at the helm. A briefing document was drawn up by him for O'Reilly, to update him on developments at Wexford Festival Opera, and was to form the basis of an agenda for the meeting between O'Reilly and members of Wexford Festival Opera at O'Reilly's home at Castlemartin in mid-December. The document outlined that the work undertaken on the structures of the organization were now completed, and membership of both a newly constituted Board – replacing the Executive Council – and the Festival Council had been established. Guinness and the Arts Council were both invited to nominate a representative. The document outlined that, where decisions had to be made between meetings, an Executive Committee consisting of the Chairman, Chief Executive (formerly Managing Director), Vice Chairman, and Finance Officer, and where possible the Artistic Director, could be called together. The document also outlined how the Council – 'the upper house' – would meet between one and three times per year. O'Reilly was a member of the Council, as was Sir Alfred Beit, Bishop Willoughby and Bishop Comiskey. Liam Lynch was elected chairman. The newly formed Council had a fundraising function on behalf of the organization. Furthermore, networking for the Festival would be an important part of its function.

Sir Alfred Beit died in 1994. His extraordinary interest for and knowledge in all forms of art and culture was noted by the Festival Council as they paid tribute to the man whose help and financial support were inestimable. His presence in Wexford was unique, and the amount of energy he bestowed on the Festival was such that it truly would not have survived without him; and it was a tribute to him that it should survive after him.

Elaine Padmore directed her last opera at Wexford in 1994. She held a special place in the history of the Festival, serving in her role for thirteen years. Only Walsh himself had directed for a longer period. A fitting tribute was paid to the talented director in the Festival programme book:

> Wexford's standing, both nationally and internationally, has never been higher. The numbers of foreign visitors who now visit us and the massive media coverage the Festival receives bear witness to this.

Under Elaine's aegis it has become a truly international Festival.

We are richer for her years with us and we are in her debt. Traditionally after the final performance of the Festival 'Auld Lang Syne' is sung. In 1994 the words 'should old acquaintance be forgot' will have a very special meaning. Elaine Padmore will certainly not be forgotten in Wexford.[19]

Padmore's final season of opera at Wexford included Rubinstein's *The Demon*, Leoncavallo's *La bohème* and Richard Wagner's *Das Liebesverbot.* The standard of the Wexford Festival Chorus continued to progress, this year under the leadership of chorus master, Gregory Rose. Padmore had indeed ended her term on a high note. More voluntary workers than ever before participated, and the operatic standard of this year's Festival was highly praised. The new Board of Directors had been appointed and the inaugural meeting of the new advisory body, the Council, had taken place. It was further noted that 'the company spirit throughout the Festival was excellent'.

Against the backdrop of such enthusiastic praise, and following a recruitment campaign that yielded forty national and international applications, Luigi Ferrari entered the scene as the new artistic director of Wexford Festival Opera.

Luigi Ferrari was already well known in international opera circles when he accepted the position at Wexford. He was born in Milan in 1951 and had received degrees in both composition and musical analysis from the Verdi Conservatory in Milan. He worked as assistant to the director of the International Festival of Contemporary Music at Venice and had recently taken over the position of artistic director of the Rossini Opera Festival in Pesaro, Italy. He had also been a member of the jury at several international singing competitions in Italy and Spain and at the BBC's Cardiff *Singer of the World* competition in 1991 and 1993.[20] Ferrari's unique style was evident from the beginning, with a strong emphasis on the Italian and late Romantic operas.[21] He himself admitted that crucial policy decisions had been taken by the Festival Council before he arrived at Wexford. These decisions made it possible for him to extend the repertoire of the Festival to include his own distinct choices.

One of these decisions received an immense amount of press criticism. It was decided that the Festival could no longer rely on its local chorus to constitute the majority of the singers on the stage. The reason for this decision was that the local people involved in the chorus were often in full-time employment and

Children's Chorus in *Jakobin*, 2001

could therefore only dedicate Saturdays to rehearsals. Furthermore, there was the additional irritation of people dropping out in the weeks before the Festival was due to commence (sometimes they received offers to sing elsewhere and were paid to do so). This made planning and rehearsing increasingly difficult, as the Festival strived to become a more professional organization. It was a reasonable solution to employ professional singers who would come to Wexford for an extended period before the Festival and who could dedicate substantial time to rehearsals. Ferrari argued that the availability of a chorus that had already worked together, and that was attending rehearsals at Wexford with the preparatory work already done, was of huge benefit to him. Ferrari thus employed twenty-four professional singers from the Prague Chamber Choir along with their chorus master, and sixteen additional singers were also chosen through auditions.

It was interesting to note that, at the same time, the Arts Council initiated a feasibility study to investigate the opportunity of developing a chorus to serve Irish opera. An initial meeting took place and all of the potential stakeholders, including the Arts Council, Wexford Festival Opera, RTÉ, Dublin Grand

Opera Society, Opera Ireland, Opera Northern Ireland and Opera Theatre Company, were present. The total cost of the proposed chorus was £600,000, approximately double what companies were currently paying for a chorus (Wexford Festival Opera was paying £85,700 for six weeks of chorus time). The logistics, too, were difficult to agree, with overlapping seasons and with the rehearsal period for one company overlapping with the performances of another. Wexford Festival Opera took part in the discussions but it did not hold out much hope that an optimal solution would be found.

Another issue that Ferrari was keen to solve in his first few months at Wexford was the inadequacy of the orchestral pit in the Theatre Royal. Ferrari had come to Wexford for the first time in 1994 during the Opera Festival. On this visit, he had noticed that the orchestral pit was absolutely inadequate to house the number of musicians needed for many of the productions that Wexford had the potential to stage. As a result, music regularly had to be orchestrated to suit the number of musicians that could actually fit in the space. As Ferrari attended his first Festival Council meeting, he produced a drawing, sketched by himself, to highlight his proposed solution to extend the pit under the stage. The Board was puzzled by his drawing that suggested knocking down one of the original walls under the stage and putting up a pillar in its place. The viability of the plan was nevertheless scrutinized and subsequently the pit was extended to cater for eight extra players. As Ferrari admitted, this gave the orchestral repertoire significant scope for extension. It was not particularly unusual that Ferrari's first efforts to provide a solution to the inadequate orchestral pit were successful, considering the fact that he had a degree in Architecture from the Milan Polytechnic.

The new artistic director was agitated by the length of rehearsal time that was available to him before the season began. He succeeded in persuading the Board to arrange the extension of this rehearsal time from three weeks to four weeks, adding to the cost of festival preparations. He also persuaded the orchestra to extend its rehearsal schedule.

Ferrari's incremental progress allowed him to pursue an artistic policy that differed from that of his predecessors. His main focus during his tenure at Wexford was threefold. First, he re-evaluated the repertoire of Eastern Europe, including Czechoslovakia and Poland. Further, he explored early Italian repertoire and also the music of composers between the First and Second World Wars who did not belong to the second Viennese School.

It was a relief to the Festival Board that the Arts Council reconsidered its award to the Festival and decided upon issuing a further £40,000 ahead of the 1994 season. This brought the total amount of grant aid to £230,000, an increase of £50,000 on the 1993 season. Jerome Hynes was congratulated for his part in securing this increase.[22] Hynes also opened up a conversation with the newly constituted Board about the necessity to reorganize the UK Trust operation. He suggested a move away from the focus on high risk, low return fundraisers, towards a greater emphasis on the potential to raise significant amounts in the corporate and personal sectors in the UK.[23] The Board of Directors was supportive of Hynes' suggested change in focus for UK fundraising.

Furthermore, having initiated a very successful funding scheme in 1991 called the Wexford Festival Opera Ruby Circle, which raised a surplus of £24,000, Hynes set his sights on a new scheme in 1995, called the Wexford Festival Opera Circle 2000. This was to be operated on the same basic principles as the Ruby Circle and would guarantee participants tickets for each of the fifteen operas between 1996 and 2000. It was proposed to charge £2000 for each unit. The Board was naturally delighted with the proposed solutions being put forward by Hynes, and provided its support.

Ferrari's first season opened on 19 October with Pacini's *Saffo*. This year also witnessed the production of Rimsky-Korsakov's *Mayskaya noch'* and Mascagni's *Iris*. Each opera utilized the Prague Chorus. The Festival Board paid tribute to Ferrari for his 'extraordinary achievements' over the previous few months.[24] His influence on Festival affairs ensured that international recognition was growing steadily for the Festival.

Much to the relief of the Festival Board, it was becoming increasingly obvious that matters were well under control by 1995. As the chairman indicated in a statement to the Board, 1995 was a real turning point. On the financial side, the elimination of the working capital deficit was achieved, and for the first time in many years the balance showed a surplus on the working capital account. A policy of 'strict budgetary control' was in place and this was appropriate for an organization that now had a budget of £1.2 million. Moreover, Ferrari had built a reputation for himself of being able to manage the artistic budget very well, his work at the Pesaro Festival standing him in good stead in this regard. O'Connor further intimated that, by 1995, the number of voluntary workers had reached its highest level – a vital factor for the successful continuation of opera at Wexford.[25]

Ermonela Jaho and Brandon Jovanovich in *Sapho*, 2001

A small Opera Development Group was formed by the Arts Council to consider future opera policy. Wexford Festival Opera was invited to make a submission to inform the process. Hynes took the opportunity to reiterate that a number of its core policies – extending back to the foundation of the Festival – remained the same. These included the fact that co-productions were not seen as a viable option at Wexford, given the unique nature of its artistic policy regarding the production of rare and forgotten operas. It was also noted that commissioning of new operas was not a priority for Wexford within its existing policy. This must have come as a disappointment to the Arts Council. Nevertheless, Wexford Festival was adamant that its success to date was dependent on a complex set of factors, not least its artistic policy.

In 1996 the conversations began in earnest about the possibility of developing a new Theatre – either on the existing site in High Street or on a greenfield site, possibly across the bridge at Ferrybank, Wexford. Hynes, Paul Hennessy and Ted Howlin had organized an away-day to Tinakilly House to examine a report that Hynes had put together, which documented decisions that Wexford

Festival Opera would need to make to ensure future growth and expansion. Hynes was astute enough to realize that a significant infrastructural project might garner the interest of the Festival's President, Tony O'Reilly. An initial discussion with O'Reilly did not generate the interest they had hoped for and O'Reilly expressed his reservations of Wexford's financial ability to take on such a significant project. However, they remained dogged in their convictions and wrote to O'Reilly again outlining the context within which they believed that a new building was ultimately the right way forward for Wexford Festival Opera:

> We are planning our future with confidence. We can do so because over the past decade we have steered the organization through a significant period of change. We are proud of those achievements … The development of our thoughts on the future of the Festival has been deliberate and extensive. We are certain that we have a responsibility to grow the organization in this way and are convinced by the merits of our proposals. That is not to say that we do not approach the idea with a degree of trepidation. We do and with downright fear at times. But the easiest option is always to do nothing and to do nothing would, in the medium and long term, lead to a stagnation and decline in the importance of the Wexford Festival. Crucially we will not proceed to commit to these plans until we have secured the commitment of adequate funding to ensure their completion.
>
> We have been entrusted with an important responsibility in being given stewardship of an organization as important as the Wexford Festival. We commit ourselves to the nurtured, planned and positive development of the organization and in this regard we see the proposal before you as essential. I hope that the above convinces you of the seriousness of our intent.[26]

Hynes left O'Reilly in no doubt that the Festival was intent on purchasing the property adjacent to the Theatre Royal, owned by Independent News and Media. A feasibility study was commissioned even, confidentially and at no cost, to understand what the possibilities might be if the property was to be part of the future development. Significantly, these conversations were taking place at a time – the first time – when the organization was operating without a deficit.[27] This undoubtedly gave the Festival Board the confidence to plan for the future.

It was disappointing then, that the age-old complaint that Wexford favoured international singers over Irish counterparts surfaced again in 1996. A report appeared in the *Wexford People* in October entitled 'Quality before passport the criterion'. This statement had apparently been made by the Festival's chairman. It was a recurring criticism over the years at Wexford that foreign singers were utilized and, as the Dublin-based tenor Brian Hoey pointed out,

> there were plenty of young Irish singers well capable of playing roles in the operas and various fringe events, but were not being given the chance to do so. If an Irish director was working in Italy he would be expected to fill over half of his cast and chorus from native Italian singers.[28]

Hynes penned a memo to the Board, reminding the members why it was important to be resolute on the matter:

> Wexford Festival Opera is, of course, committed to providing Irish artists every opportunity at Wexford and this policy has been clearly accepted by both the current and previous artistic directors. In order to keep up to date on the talent available in Ireland we participate jointly with the Dublin Grand Opera Society and Opera Theatre Company annually in a series of auditions in Dublin. On occasion, where required, we will also hold separate auditions for particular singers where the artistic director feels there may be a role or a position available for the singer or singers concerned. Even if a particular Irish singer is successful at audition this in itself may not lead to his or her employment:
>
> - There may not be a suitable role for them in the next festival
> - The dates offered may not suit
> - The role offered may not suit
> - The fee offered may not be acceptable to them.
>
> One of the things we must be quite firm about is the absolute right of our artistic director to cast the operas. It is his right to do so and while we can have many discussions with him about particular singers the final decision on casting must remain with him. We must

also acknowledge that Wexford is an *international* festival. It has an international reputation to uphold and the productions we present are unique. Finally on this matter, to put it bluntly, in casting we check the talent first and the nationality later. In a situation where two artists are of equal standing and one is Irish the artistic director has no problem in deciding at that point to favour the Irish artist.

Wexford had invested much energy into producing a world-class event and from the very early days when Walsh was artistic director, public comment, good or bad, was not allowed to affect artistic decisions taken. Other comments, however, were more positive about artistic decision-making, and one report carried the story that Wexford Festival Opera managed to uphold its 'cosmopolitan image' by attracting artists from fifteen different countries to perform at Wexford.[29]

Amid these doubts about how international the Festival should be, the 1996 Festival moved ahead, extending from 17 October to 3 November. Donizetti's *Parisina* was the first opera to be performed, followed by Meyerbeer's *L'étoile du nord* and Fibich's *Šárka*.

The year 1997 was very positive with regard to the financial situation for Wexford Festival Opera. Paul Hennessy was delighted and relieved to report at a meeting in February that the financial position had never been stronger. In particular, both box office income and sponsorship had performed extremely well. He referenced the significant impact of the Circle 2000 initiative, noting that the Festival was now producing 75 per cent of its income itself, with 25 per cent coming from grant aid.[30] Hynes was delighted to report, too, that Wexford Festival had managed to finalize the purchase of the Independent News property next door. This significant purchase was the catalyst to a new and exciting adventure.[31] 'So we are now busy planning a development and will shortly begin raising money, determined however not to lose a festival in the process', Hynes reported excitedly in an email to one of Wexford's former artistic directors, Thomson Smillie.[32]

Ferrari's distinct choice was again apparent in 1997 with the production of Respighi's *La fiamma*, Dargomïzhsky's *Rusalka* and Mercadante's *Elena da Feltre*. It was an encouraging sign that journalists and opera critics were flocking to Wexford. 'May God preserve you from all importunate journalists save this one', the well-known journalist, Kevin Myers, wrote to Hynes immediately before the Festival opened:

Davide Damiani, Manrico Tedeschi, Hadar Halevy and chorus in *Il giuramento*, 2002

Seeing you briefly the other day at Heuston reminded me that the Festival is at our throats, and I have done nothing to flatter, cajole or wheedle tickets from you. I would be beside myself with gratitude if you could fit my body, and my wife's, into little seats somewhere, the roof even. I know I made a grave mistake in not going last year. Life is limited – one day it will end, and it would be an awful shame if I missed any more good Wexford opera. Of course I understand if you can't manage anything. It is after all very late; and I will merely push you under a train the next time we meet at Kingsbridge.[33]

As far as the Festival fringe events were concerned, Ferrari was keen to reinstate the popular opera scenes which took place in White's Hotel. They had been cut from the programme in 1996 much to the dismay of the Festival patrons. The idea was first introduced by Elaine Padmore, where operatic repertoire was reduced significantly and performed during the Festival, first at the Arts Centre in the town and later at the hotel. Ferrari began to use this platform as a type of training ground for young singers. The idea was that they would come to Wexford to sing in the opera scenes, and if they were deemed to be of high quality they could be invited back to sing in one of the mainstage operas at the Theatre Royal. The opera scenes were also used to give young directors an opportunity to work at Wexford.

Ferrari was conscious of the growing number of musical events during the Festival that were not related in any way to opera. He was intent on shifting the focus back to singing. After all, it was incumbent on the Festival Board to give singers the opportunity to make money when they arrived in Wexford by performing extra concerts. They were still agreeing to come for a fraction of the fee they could receive elsewhere. The singers were, in effect, making an investment in Wexford in the hope that their exposure there would lead to international opportunities.

Ted Howlin assumed the position of chairman of the Festival in 1998. He was formerly Mayor of Wexford Borough Council, having been a member of the Borough Council in Wexford for some time. He had also been an integral part of the Festival organization for many years and had assumed the role of box office manager along the way. The transition from O'Connor to Howlin was therefore a smooth one. The Festival Board continued to support the distinct flavour of Ferrari's taste, and year after year his choice of operas was acclaimed. In 1998 he put on Gomes' *Fosca* and Haas' *Šarlatán*. The length of the season did not change and Zandonai's *I cavalieri di Ekebù* rounded off another highly successful season.

By 1999, the Arts Council grant to the Festival had reached £450,000, an amount that was warmly welcomed by the Festival Council.[34] The 1980s had proved such a struggle financially that it was a relief to be able to deal with other matters, including strategy for the future. Ferrari had proved to be a huge success and his choice of operas continued to bring acclaim for Wexford Festival Opera.

The President of Ireland, Mary McAleese, opened the Festival in 1999. Ferrari had chosen Goldmark's *Die Königin von Saba*, Moniuszko's *Straszny dwór* and Giordano's *Siberia*. There was a noticeable enthusiasm about the Festival this year, generated by both the Board and the audiences that had attended the performances. All operas had achieved 100 per cent occupancy, with 53 of the 57 fringe events also booked out. Wexford Festival Opera had received an additional allocation of £150,000 from Ireland's Millennium Festival fund to stage a spectacular opening to the Festival in 1999. Events organizer Rupert Murray was engaged to develop and oversee the opening, which included a Ghost Train that made its way along the quay and down to Rosslare. The extravagant fireworks display that opened the Festival amazed and entertained the many thousands that packed onto Wexford's quayfront.

A vision for the redevelopment of the Theatre Royal was agonizingly close, with the announcement that Wexford Festival had managed to purchase No. 23 High Street, completing the Festival's ownership of houses from 15 to 31 High Street.[35] The National Building Agency was commissioned to report on the options for Wexford Festival. Its chief executive was Matt O'Connor, a Wexford man, who would play an important role in the development of the project from this point on. The concept of the Wexford Festival Foundation was also brought to life at this time. This would be a fundraising group, and Wexford Festival sought the support of Liam Healy, CE with Independent News and Media, to fulfil the role as chair. This new entity would be charged with the task of identifying areas of potential private funding and using the money raised for capital development. Healy and his wife, Eithne, had been introduced to the Wexford Festival years before, when Hynes sought Healy's help with a printing matter at the People printing house at Wexford. The People Newspapers building, beside the Theatre Royal, printed its paper on an old-fashioned, noisy printer. With opera in full swing in the Theatre, at ten o'clock at night, the paper would start rolling, resulting in loud thumping noises inside the Theatre. Believing this to be wholly unacceptable for patrons attending the opera, Hynes invited Healy to Wexford to witness the disruption for himself. Healy concurred with Hynes that the situation was unsatisfactory, and subsequently changed the printing time to 11p.m. to accommodate the performances. Both Healy and Eithne would become long-term friends and supporters of Wexford Festival Opera.

The 2000 season saw the reintroduction of the composer Zandonai; this time the opera was *Conchita*. Tchaikovsky's *Orleanskaya deva* was performed on opening night and was followed by Adam's *Si j'étais roi*.

The fiftieth anniversary celebrations of the Festival in 2001 then were indeed spectacular. The fireworks scene on the opening night was more impressive than ever. The magnitude of the event did not pass unnoticed by the President of Ireland, Mary McAleese. She commended the Festival for its wonderful achievement, commenting that it 'has long since enjoyed an international reputation for excellence and this year will be no exception, providing a feast of glorious music which will be enjoyed by Irish and international visitors alike'.[36] The operatic choices for 2001 did not disappoint either. Flotow's *Alessandro Stradella* opened the season on 18 October and was followed by Dvořák's *Jakobín* and Massenet's *Sapho*.

Silvia Vazquez, Vicenç Esteve, Ana Maria García Pérez (Dancer) and Festival Chorus in *María del Carmen*, 2003

The Taoiseach, Bertie Ahern, summed it up most accurately in his message in the Festival programme book:

> In Wexford, what began fifty years ago as the humble aspiration of a small number of local people has grown into a world-renowned festival. In the world of opera, every October, Wexford becomes the shining city on the hill, the beacon that draws people, time and time again, from all over the world.
>
> It is the people of Wexford who founded the Festival and whose continuing welcome and hospitality make it so special.
>
> Wexford Festival Opera has a proud history. I have no doubt that it also has a bright future. The Festival is a focal point of the Irish cultural and social calendar. It makes Wexford the essential meeting place for people who enjoy opera and enjoy life.[37]

For only the second time in the Festival's history, the National Symphony Orchestra was not engaged. It was an unusual and potentially damaging decision to employ the National Philharmonic Orchestra of Belarus for this, the Festival's fiftieth anniversary. The Festival had been supported by RTÉ since its inception and the decision to move away from the country's national orchestra was no less difficult in 2001 than it had been for Walsh in 1961 when he employed the Royal Liverpool Philharmonic Orchestra.

Negotiations with RTÉ had reached a stalemate over terms and conditions of the contract as well as fees. As Ferrari pointed out, the problem was not artistic but financial: the Festival Board ended its lengthy relationship with RTÉ because it could no longer afford to bring the orchestra to Wexford. He further commented that the National Symphony Orchestra was essentially a symphony orchestra, not an operatic one, and as such was used to performing *on* the stage rather than *under* it. The regimented schedule of the orchestra no longer suited the needs of those trying to stage an opera. Furthermore, the orchestra was travelling up and down from Dublin between rehearsals – a most inflexible arrangement. Ferrari recalled an occasion where he needed to switch the order of the opera rehearsal because of a set problem. When he notified RTÉ about the schedule change, he was duly told that RTÉ could only accept emergency changes. 'But this is an emergency,' Ferrari told the broadcasting station in exasperation, only to be told that fifteen days' notice was needed for 'emergency changes'.[38]

The National Philharmonic Orchestra of Belarus was thus selected as a replacement to the National Symphony Orchestra when there was no hope of reaching an agreement with the broadcasting station. The following year further attempts were made to reconcile the differences between the professionals in Dublin and the 'amateur professionals' in Wexford. But these attempts failed, and once more the Belarus Orchestra returned to Wexford for the entire period of rehearsals leading up to the 2002 Festival.

In 2002, Mercadante's *Il giuramento* was performed, along with Martinů's *Mirandolina* and Auber's *Manon Lescaut*. The performances raised quite a stir that year and, as the *Guardian* exclaimed,

> there is plenty of sex on offer at the Wexford Festival this year. The three operas have, it would seem, been chosen for their erotic content, and weave complementary variations on the theme of female self-assertion and masculine responses to it.[39]

This season was a particularly joyous one following the announcement at the Fianna Fáil Party Conference by the Taoiseach, Bertie Ahern, that the plans for the redevelopment of the Theatre Royal would be supported by the government. The unforgettable image of Ted Howlin, chairman of the Festival Council, jumping for joy outside the Theatre building was enough to evoke the sense of excitement that was now felt about the future of the Festival. 'It represents a clear milestone in the development of Wexford Festival Opera and of the arts in the region and further afield,' Hynes said with an air of satisfaction.[40]

An incident that threatened to mar the festivities of the 2003 season was the presence of members of the Musicians Union of Ireland protesting outside the Theatre Royal. The demonstration drew attention to the fact that the Belarussian Orchestra was still being employed at Wexford. As Hynes pointed out, however, 'the Festival's new partnership underlines the international nature of the event, and presents exciting new opportunities for both the orchestra and the Festival, which we look forward to developing'.[41] In fact, the Festival Council had tried each year to repair the relations with its once professional allies in Dublin but to no avail.

The 2003 Festival saw performances of Mahler's *Die drei Pintos*,[42] Granados' *María del Carmen* and Jaromir Weinberger's *Švanda dudák*. Wexford was particularly pleased to win the Opera of the Year award at the annual Irish Times/ESB Irish Theatre Awards for its production of *Švanda dudák*.

Matjaz Robavs and
Tatiana Monogarova
in *Švanda dudák*, 2003

2004 was Ferrari's last year at Wexford. He was philosophical about Wexford's future. He noted that the Festival would begin to be affected by developments in the wider operatic world, where other opera houses had begun to present rare operas as part of their repertoire. In essence, this was Wexford's legacy: it had led the way in demonstrating that it was possible to successfully mount little-known and rare works that were worthy of production. 'Many opera houses now have one title each season which is unknown or rare, and this affects the uniqueness of a place like Wexford,' Ferrari regretfully admitted.[43]

While preparing for his final curtain, Ferrari openly admitted that the 'budget is still ridiculous', referring to the artistic budget at his disposal. Yet he disclosed that many prestigious artistic directors were keen to take up his position when he stepped down. This continued interest in working at Wexford Festival Opera, Ferrari deduced, was because 'despite logistical difficulties, financial and location difficulties, the prestige of the Festival is at a high point'. He noted that he had seen operas on the stage in Wexford that he never imagined he would see performed anywhere. 'It's probably the one place in the world which still has a mission in opera', he divulged.[44] When asked why he had chosen to take the position in the first place, without hesitating he said,

> being an artistic director is not a career but a vocation. In Wexford, all they ask you is to dream. Wexford is the only place that will allow you to realize your dreams.[45]

CHAPTER 10

THE BEST OF TIMES, THE WORST OF TIMES

2004–5

By 2004, Wexford could report a record of eight consistent years of 100 per cent capacity, bringing in an estimated €25 million annually to the local economy. The future was exciting and there was a feeling of anticipation and confidence about what was to come.

Also in 2004 – the year that Poland joined the European Union – Wexford welcomed one of Poland's major orchestras to join the company for the upcoming Festival. Having partnered with the Belarus Philharmonic for the previous three years, the Cracow Philharmonic took up the position of orchestral partner for the 2004 season. The orchestra performed in all three of the operas, the Symphony Concert and the Choral Concert. Ferrari's decision in 2001 to replace the RTÉ National Symphony Orchestra was still not a popular one and was seen to impact on the standard of orchestral playing at Wexford. At the 2004 Festival Press Conference, Paul Hennessy, incoming chair of the

Board, responded to criticism that orchestral standards had dropped since the link with the National Symphony Orchestra was severed. He cited Wexford's 'fiscal responsibilities' as being the primary reason why the national orchestra was no longer contracted to play at Wexford. This assertion was supported by Jerome Hynes, who pointed out that it had proven impossible to find an Irish-based orchestra: the National Symphony Orchestra was far too expensive and the Ulster Orchestra, who had also been approached, was engaged in other commitments. Hynes added that the Board had a responsibility to consider the long-term future of the Festival, and that this informed its decision-making at all times. Ferrari added that, from his immense experience, he was aware that developing an orchestra from nothing would be enormous work, in terms of commitment and also the availability of players. He pointed out that when the National Symphony Orchestra was first established in Ireland, many of its players came from abroad, and that it remained difficult to identify sufficient high-quality professional musicians in the country. He further clarified that within the expanding European Union there was a freedom of movement of workers in and out of Ireland and the Festival could apply the same rights to a Polish orchestra as it could to other orchestras in Europe. 'There is no cheap exploitation of workers', he concluded.[1]

Wexford Festival Opera had to defend its position because the Arts Council, as a condition of its funding in 2004, instructed Wexford to 'respond with vigour' to address the criticism that there was a neglect of Irish singers, directors, designers and répétiteurs for its productions, noting again its concern that Wexford had failed to nurture Irish opera artists and practitioners.

Having successfully acquired the People Newspaper property and the five houses adjoining the Theatre Royal, Wexford Festival Opera announced that it was applying for planning permission for a major development, at a cost in the order of €20 million. Given the Taoiseach's address at the Fianna Fáil party conference as early as 2002, where he included this infrastructural project at Wexford in future priorities, executives and the Board at Wexford Festival Opera were quietly confident of progress in this regard. Wexford was very clear that it needed financial support from the government to realize its ambition and used all opportunities to publicize the importance of this development for nurturing the careers of opera practitioners and professional musicians across Ireland.[2] The Office of Public Works had drawn up plans detailing an expanded 750-seat auditorium where the operas would be staged, plus a second 180-seat space for

Ladislav Elgr, Andrea Patucelli, Davide Damiani, Dante Alcalá, Agata Bienkowska, Doriana Milazzo, Danna Glaser and Festival Chorus in *La vestale*, 2004

events like the popular Opera Scenes.[3] The front and backstage facilities would be state-of-the-art – in sharp contrast to the facilities at the Theatre Royal.

This was for certain the most complex and significant development that the Wexford Festival Board had been tasked with delivering. Amid the excitement of what was to come, the 2004 Festival was the most immediate consideration.

The town experienced the worst flooding in living memory during this Festival. Members of the emergency services played their part in rescuing the Wednesday night performance of *Eva*, by carrying members of the orchestra on

David Agler

their shoulders through the flood waters from their quay front apartments to the Theatre Royal in time for the performance.[4] Nevertheless, the weather did not deter the patrons from dressing up and taking their places in the Theatre Royal. One reporter recalled standing on the platform at Pearse Station, eagerly awaiting the opera train to Wexford:

> At 3.45 last Thursday afternoon, dressed in a bow tie, I was standing on the platform sipping a glass of champagne. Fortunately, I didn't stand out from the crowd. There were dozens and dozens of similarly dressed men, and as many women looking even more *soigné* in cocktail dresses and evening gowns. We were all waiting to board the Wexford Festival Opera Train, to my mind one of the great train journeys in the world. Further down the line, in Dun Laoghaire and Bray, other similarly garbed opera fans were gathering waiting to be picked up by the train. The Opera Train is one of the long-standing traditions attached to what's been called 'the friendliest opera festival in the world'. The Festival has 100% seat occupancy every year, with

a waiting list of hundreds for the very few returned tickets. The whole town will be *en fête*.[5]

Despite the weather, it was a great year for Wexford Festival Opera. The Festival opened with *La vestale* by Mercadante. Foerster's *Eva* and Braunfels' *Prinzessin Brambilla* were the other operas chosen by Ferrari. The company members were jubilant, having been informed during the Festival that planning permission was granted for the new Opera House. The news was announced to the audience as the curtain fell on the last night in the Theatre Royal, the sign of a new beginning for Wexford and one that had been in the making for many years.

'How many British opera companies have the nerve to do what the Irish do?' was the question posed by British journalist Roderic Dunnett.

> One man set the pattern: since Tom Walsh launched Wexford Festival Opera in 1951, its penchant for rare or neglected operas has led to one of the boldest programming policies in Europe. The mainstream gets relegated to the spare stage. Yet the punters come, in colourful, chattering droves. At the Theatre Royal, the boss greets you at the door, legends abound and names are made.[6]

Wexford lost one of its most avid supporters that year. Bernard Levin, a long-time friend and supporter of the Festival, died following a long illness. Levin had famously written about Wexford many times and his words helped to create a sense of mystery and intrigue about the Festival, which encouraged others to visit to witness the atmosphere for themselves. He was hugely supportive of Dr Tom Walsh, recognizing his immense contribution to what was, by now, an internationally renowned Festival.

With the ending of the Festival this year, Ferrari's time in Wexford also came to an end. Having served as artistic director for ten years, Ferrari was well placed to outline the task facing his successor. He described how confidence needed to be restored in Wexford as an event which had a 'relationship of respect' with musicians and the musical profession in Ireland.

Michael Dervan, a reviewer with the *Irish Times*, also set out the challenge as he saw it for the incoming artistic director – that of creating an Irish orchestra contracted to service the needs of Irish opera companies, not just Wexford Festival Opera. If it succeeded, it would enable freelance musicians to make a living in Ireland and would satisfy the Arts Council requirement to provide opportunities to Irish artists.[7] In fact, the Arts Council awarded Wexford Festival Opera €950,000 towards the 2005 Festival, which represented an increase of €150,000 on the grant for 2004. The Arts Council had stipulated in the award letter that the additional funding would go towards the increased costs of engaging an Irish orchestra for 2005 and subsequent years.

Following an international search and selection process, the role of artistic director was offered to David Agler, a North American conductor who had already amassed significant experience. He held the positions of music director of the Vancouver Opera; principal conductor of the Australian Opera; resident conductor of the San Francisco Opera; principal guest conductor of the Oper der Stadt Köln; conductor and administrator of the Spoleto Festival; artistic director of the Opera Festival of New Jersey; and music director of the Syracuse Opera. Agler had travelled to Wexford in 1996 to conduct Zdeněk Fibich's *Šárka* in the Theatre Royal, the same season that Maurizio Benini and a very young Vladimir Jurowski appeared at Wexford.[8] Agler was the seventh artistic director at Wexford, the first from North America. Upon taking up his new role, he commented that 'I understand what is peculiar to Wexford; there is the sense that everyone in town is part of this and has an interest in its success'.[9]

He was aware from the start that there was an expectation that he would bring a fresh perspective and that he would at least attempt to deal with some of the issues that were perceived to be affecting Wexford. He also knew that his strategy for choosing operas would differ from that of his predecessor. While giving due regard to the fundamental principle at Wexford of producing little-known works, Agler decided that he would concentrate less on the obscurity and rarity, and more on the concept of neglected operas. 'I'm not running a seminar on operatic history,' he declared when questioned about his strategy by Michael Dervan in an early interview. Further, he was acutely aware of the importance of Wexford Festival Opera on the world stage and not just on the national one; 'Wexford Festival is a beloved thing for opera lovers all over the world,' he reminded Dervan:[10]

> It has made an important contribution to operatic history. Ireland is small. You know how it can be. All nations and communities can dwell so much on ourselves that we forget this. Wexford Festival is one of Ireland's great gifts to the cultural life of the world.

Constructing the set of *Pénélope*, 2005

The criticism of Wexford's perceived lack of use of Irish musicians and artists remained. Straight away, Agler set out his perspective on 'the Irish question', as he called it.[11] In discussions with Paul Hennessy, Agler outlined that, in principle, he was predisposed towards having an Irish orchestra, but not at any cost. He believed that the Belarus Orchestra that had performed at Wexford from 2001 to 2003 was not of the standard that Wexford had come to expect. However, he was full of praise for the Cracow Orchestra, and believed that it had made an important contribution to the success of the Festival overall. Agler certainly had reservations about forming a Wexford Festival Orchestra. He was aware that it would be a huge undertaking for the Festival, with little guarantee

Jerome Hynes

that it would have the desired impact. While not disputing the fact that there were excellent freelance musicians in Ireland, he doubted if they were sufficient in number to meet the needs of the Festival. Incidentally, the same point had been made by Luigi Ferrari on many occasions.

As Agler worked through his plans for his first season, he found himself defending Wexford's position regarding contracting Irish musicians time and time again. He reiterated the point that, even if constructing an orchestra was desirable, it was certainly not possible in his first year. The complexities of marketing the opportunity, the audition process, the time required to make offers and develop individual contracts, along with contingency planning when musicians turned down offers and the financial considerations of this entire process needed to be carefully measured. In an early memo to Hennessy, Agler set out his position:

> If, in the end, it is agreed the Festival should proceed with building an orchestra I will participate enthusiastically. However, I want to be clear about an essential principle. I am not interested in giving into parochial and provincial demands. I sincerely desire to participate in and to build up everything that is *authentically* Irish about Wexford Festival. Still, I am mindful of my <u>and</u> the Board's responsibility to maintain the historically international flavour, content, and reputation of Wexford. How we can have both, is the question I am struggling with.[12]

To assist Agler, Hynes was busy gathering information on other national orchestras. He approached the Ulster Orchestra, the Irish Chamber Orchestra, and the Irish Film Orchestra, detailing the list of requirements for orchestral services at Wexford. He sought, from these bodies, an expression of interest, and a detailed financial proposal. However, Hynes was not optimistic, even at this stage, that the Ulster Orchestra *or* the Irish Chamber Orchestra would be available to play at Wexford, given their long-standing patterns of planning and performance.

In the end, there was no Irish orchestra in 2005, despite the Arts Council's request in its grant award letter for the year, but much had been learned about how it might be possible to address this issue in the near future. 'I'm happy to say that all the sets and costumes for this year's operas have been made in Ireland,' declared Agler in an interview with the local press, in an attempt to stem any further criticism:

> Every worthy Irish person should have a right to work in this festival. The nature of the festival, however, and the kind of operas we do are such that no nation could supply everything that is needed to carry it off. The kind of work we do is so specialized here that you have to go everywhere to attract the right people to sing the roles. And this has been the case from the very beginning. To be honest, I think the whole issue is a bit of a red herring.[13]

The orchestra was not the only 'Irish question' that required Agler's attention. He was aware that the question of Irish singers was also a long-standing bone of contention in some quarters, not least with the Arts Council. Following extensive auditions, Agler noted that the 2005 season would certainly include Irish singers, but not in principal roles:

> Sometimes, it seems to me, that the Arts Council think that singers will crawl on their knees, Fatima style, to Wexford in order to take up a role at the Festival. There are many less gifted singers who might well do so. However, I have learned that some Irish singers are just too busy, too prominent, too interested in the size of fees, or just indifferent about Wexford. Even for an Irish artist, the Royal Opera, Paris and America will be irresistible temptations.[14]

Wexford made a very important decision in 2005 to launch its first ever series of masterclasses under a new Artists' Development Programme. Hennessy

Eglise Gutiérrez in
Maria di Rohan, 2005

engaged Dennis O'Neill – one of the world's leading tenors – to direct the programme and Ian Rosenblatt, OBE, provided the funding in its first year. Following an audition process, twenty-two participants were invited to take part in these masterclasses. Although the majority were Irish – twelve in total – there were singers from further afield, including Russia and South Korea. The public was invited to the Presbyterian church to observe some of the classes, while the remainder were held in private at St Iberius' Church and the Theatre Royal. The tutors included a distinguished international team of vocal teachers, coming from renowned homes of opera such as Covent Garden and the Bayerische Staatsoper in Munich. Ireland was represented by the venerable Veronica Dunne. The eleven-day blitz of coaching sessions, masterclasses and lectures (illustrated evening lectures by Norman White, consultant to Nimbus records' Prima Voce series of early vocal recordings), many of which were open to the public, concluded in a gala concert at the Theatre Royal in August 2005. This new initiative was widely welcomed as an important step in demonstrating commitment by Wexford Festival Opera to the training of young singers.

Meanwhile, as Agler was finding his feet and putting together his strategy for his tenure at Wexford, Hynes and

Hennessy were also busy strategizing. There was the rather significant matter of the proposed new building for opera in Wexford, which required all of their attention to plot a way forward. It was a remarkable vision, with so many moving parts, that great credit must go to those at the helm that persevered and believed, through the tough days, that the ultimate goal could be achieved.

Hennessy recalled driving, with Jerome Hynes, to Tony O'Reilly's house in Merrion Square in Dublin to ask him to provide financial support to the Festival to the value of €2 million. An architectural model of the proposed new Opera House had been developed and sent to O'Reilly's house in advance of the meeting.[15] They made the pitch for funding to him, highlighting the importance of his support in demonstrating to the government that this new development was a plausible ambition. O'Reilly, who was the President of the Festival at the time, did not respond immediately, but indicated that he would give it some thought. Both Hennessy and Hynes were relying on a positive response from O'Reilly – there were few other options that they could explore. Finally, O'Reilly made contact to indicate that he would agree to make a gift of €1 million to the opera house project and intimated that this would be matched with a gift of €1 million from Independent News and Media.

An intensive political campaign followed. Hennessy and Hynes led the charge and were unwavering in their attempts to influence political opinion and gain support for their venture in Wexford. They were fortunate that the senior civil servants that they were dealing with were sympathetic to the arts and understood that for the venture to be a success, it would need to be a true partnership with the government. Hennessy and Hynes made regular contact with the Department of Arts, Sport and Tourism in order to be kept informed of Minister John O'Donoghue's official functions. They were relentless in their pursuit of O'Donoghue and were more than prepared to attend the various launches and events in the hope of discussing their plans with him.

At one stage, between Hennessy and Hynes, they were attending up to three events each week with the sole purpose of getting into O'Donoghue's company and informing him of their vision for Wexford. Hennessy recalled pursuing the Minister down the stairs of the Guinness Hopstore to his car, where he imparted a pre-prepared speech about the progress for their new venture. According to Hennessy, he felt the tide was turning in their favour when, on one occasion, as Hennessy entered the Concert Hall, he met O'Donoghue on his way out. 'It's OK Paul', O'Donoghue said, 'Jerome is inside. I've heard it all

Nora Sourouzian, Paul Carey Jones, David Curry, Glenn Alamilla, Saran Suebsantiwongse and Robert Gardiner in *Pénélope*, 2005

already'. Hennessy knew at this point that their strategy of relentlessly pursuing political support was paying off.

Hynes took on the role of updating the Department of Arts, Sport and Tourism regularly on progress being made, and he received the full support of the Department each time he entered government buildings. The Office of Public Works (OPW) was also fully invested in the project at this stage, having prepared the initial concept and feasibility study as well as detailed drawings for the planning application. Its initial cost estimate for the project came in at €25 million. Essentially this confirmed that €20 million would have to come from

Emily Pulley, Howard Reddy and Festival Chorus in *Susannah*, 2005

the government, as Wexford Festival Opera could not commit to raising more than €5 million either locally or from its sponsors and donors. In addition, Wexford Festival Opera was anxious to ensure that if government funding was secured, that the OPW would be formally appointed to manage the project.

Satisfied that O'Donoghue was on board with the proposed project, Hennessy and Hynes turned their attention to getting sign-off from the then Taoiseach, Bertie Ahern. They astutely waited for the right moment of approach, which happened to be a function in Wexford. Armed with a set of drawings, they impressed upon the Taoiseach the necessity for an opera house of this magnitude.

The cast and company singing *Auld Lang Syne* for the last time in the Theatre Royal

A meeting was subsequently set up at Government buildings, attended by Tony O'Reilly, Hennessy, Hynes and Liam Healy, chair of the Festival Foundation. Hennessy recalled how they travelled together to the meeting in O'Reilly's Rolls Royce, with Hynes sitting between the seats, as due to a large telephone console in the car, there was barely room for them all to fit. The Taoiseach heard impassioned pleas from both Hennessy and O'Reilly for an investment of €20 million by the state towards Ireland's first purpose-built opera house. The Board of Wexford Festival Opera would raise the remaining €5 million, to include significant leadership donations from both O'Reilly and

The audience leaving the Theatre Royal for the last time

Healy. It was a convincing pitch, where those present managed to persuade the Taoiseach that Ireland needed and deserved this resource and that they were best placed to deliver it. The Taoiseach brought the meeting to a close by declaring that 'we're going to do this'.[16]

Hennessy and Hynes kept very private the news about the generous pledge from O'Reilly, choosing instead to announce it on the official opening night of the 2005 Festival. They were working towards having the government support announced as part of the forthcoming budget in December. In the meantime, preparations were well underway for the opera season about to begin. It was an annual tradition for the chief executive, members of the board and the artistic director to officially welcome the cast and crew of the three operas to Wexford at a Sunday night function in the Theatre Royal. History was unfolding: the beginning of the end for the Theatre Royal, which in four months would be demolished. This sense of optimism for the future was suddenly eclipsed by the most tragic of events. As Hynes concluded his welcoming remarks and turned to introduce Hennessy, he suddenly collapsed to the floor in front of a shocked company. He died shortly after. He was only 45 years of age.

The impact of Hynes' death on the Wexford Festival Opera tight-knit family was profound. He was considered an excellent administrator, and had made a huge impact on the Festival during his time there. It was Hynes' warm and empathetic personality that many credited with his success in the role – he made it his business to integrate himself fully into Wexford life and instinctively knew the importance of engaging with the surrounding community. His death brought into sharp focus his immense contribution and vision for the Festival about to enter into its most exciting and challenging period yet. His Festival colleague and friend, Ted Howlin, wrote of Hynes:

> Possessed of keen organizational and business skills he was meticulous in forward planning, every detail receiving attention; tasks neither too small nor too large to be undertaken; no journey too long to be made. Inconvenience was disregarded in pursuance of Wexford's promotion and advancement.

Described in an ensuing press report as a man who had the capability to articulate, persuasively and clearly, the needs of the arts in Ireland, Hynes was much-admired for what he had achieved;

> His skills as an arts manager were formidable and exemplary – his ability to combine artistic vision with the kind of business acumen that the arts sector often lacks was rare. He was the ideal communicator to win hearts and minds in the cause of culture. Before it became the mantra it is today, he expressed the view that the arts in Ireland had the potential to be of significant economic and social benefit. As general manager of Druid Theatre Company in its formative years in Galway and as a dynamic chief executive of Wexford Festival Opera,

he proved this to be the case. With both organizations, and as a member of the Arts Council, he had faith in the capability of the arts to win international status, and he had the confidence to pursue and achieve this wider acclaim.[17]

Hynes would have been the first to concede that the show must go on, and this sentiment was shared by those who knew him so well. Everyone involved had to muster up the courage to put the finishing touches to the Festival to ensure that it would be of its usual high standard. The 2005 Festival, which cost €2.5 million to stage, opened with *Maria di Rohan*, Wexford's thirteenth opera by Donizetti, followed by *Pénélope* by Fauré and *Susannah* by Floyd. Floyd, who was due to return to Wexford to attend a performance of his opera, had to cancel his trip due to ill health, much to the disappointment of Agler and the cast.[18] The Minister for Enterprise, Micheál Martin, described the announcement of the pledge of €2 million by O'Reilly and Independent News and Media as a 'wonderfully philanthropic act'.[19]

Any sense of optimism that Hennessy felt for the future of the organization was short-lived. At the same time as Wexford Festival Opera was being congratulated in every corner for what it had managed to achieve, the OPW contacted Hennessy to indicate that it had revised the estimates for the proposed building and the new estimates were now in excess of €30 million. Based on these new estimates, the Department confirmed to Hennessy that Wexford would need to provide 20 per cent of the additional costs. It was a lonely and worrying time for Hennessy, who felt it prudent not to share this update until the Festival was over. Nevertheless, he knew that the company itself would never be in a position to raise any more funding, in addition to all that was being raised for the annual operating costs. He pushed back strongly, saying that Wexford simply did not have the capacity to raise any more money for what he described as a piece of national infrastructure. The conversation closed with an impasse where Hennessy again emphasized that, if Wexford was required to provide any funds above the original estimate of €5 million, that there would be no project.

A few days later, Hennessy received word from Phil Furlong from the Department, confirming that another €6 million could be ring-fenced for the Wexford project and the project was back on. The announcement was not made by the Minister on Budget Day in the end, but the €26 million investment was announced the following Thursday. It was indeed a remarkable achievement that Wexford had, once more, managed to push itself to centre stage and, this time, skillfully negotiate to have a state-of-the-art opera house built in the small provincial town. The news came as an immense relief to Hennessy who had invested so much time and expertise in the future vision for Wexford Festival Opera. Conversely, it was of huge sadness and regret to all involved that Jerome Hynes was not alive to see the culmination of all that he had invested in this proposed new venture. Hennessy recalled that the executive members in the Department of Arts, Sport and Tourism were as delighted as those at Wexford Festival Opera that the new opera house project was going ahead. He described it as a public private partnership of the purest kind, where both parties were 'in it together' and both were keen to get the best result possible.[20]

The 2005 Festival came to an end and it was an emotional night for the Festival company and its patrons as they stood side by side to sing 'Auld Lang Syne' for the very last time in the 170-year-old Theatre Royal. The company and the executive were also still reeling over the shock of losing their much-loved chief executive so suddenly and so prematurely. Hennessy, in particular, must have felt the weight of responsibility on his shoulders, with the burden of moving the new opera house proposal forward without the support and drive of Hynes by his side.

CHAPTER 11

ONE HELL OF A RIDE

2006–8

> A day of celebration and relief! Just to confirm the Minister announced a capital funding package for the arts this morning including €26 million for Wexford. The wait is over ... and the critical construction path has just begun. Hold tight – it will be a hell of a ride ...

Hennessy wrote excitedly to Agler in December.[1]

Less than two months after the close of the 2005 Festival, another significant announcement was made about Wexford's future. Even though building work was to begin immediately on the construction of a new Theatre, the Festival would continue, in a changed format, for the following two years, and would return to its newly constructed home in 2008. The 2006 Festival would run for twelve nights, as opposed to eighteen, at the Dun Mhuire Hall in the centre of Wexford town, and the 2007 Festival would move, not only to a new location, but to a new season – May to June – at Johnstown Castle, on the outskirts of Wexford town. Ursula Sinnott had been appointed as acting General Manager

Demolishing the Theatre Royal, 2006

to fill the gap until a new CEO was appointed. Sinnott had worked as the manager of the Talbot Hotel for a number of years.

Wexford Festival Opera was entering into its most challenging period to date. 'We're a very resilient organization with an excellent artistic director in David Agler and a very strong Board' concluded Hennessy in December. 'And the town moved in behind us. The Festival belongs to the town and the town to the Festival'.[2] At this very critical time, Hennessy was keen to review the organization structure which needed a new chief executive. The structure going forward needed to be able to support challenges that would be new and testing for Wexford.[3] Without wasting any time, he engaged a recruitment company to identify suitable candidates for this important role.

There was strong interest in the job from an impressive list of national and international candidates. Finally, as preparations intensified, Michael Hunt was appointed to the role. Hunt was born in London and was well versed in the arts and opera in Ireland. He had directed the Operatic Scenes in the 1980s at Wexford and had worked for Co-Opera and Opera Ireland. Prior to coming to Ireland, he held posts as Director of Performing Arts at Riverside Studios, London, artistic director of the Cheltenham Everyman Theatre; artistic director of the Bloomsbury Festival and artistic director of the Cheltenham Arts Centre; the Queens Theatre, London and the Royal Albert Hall, London.

The second Artists' Development Programme took place in April 2006, with Programme Director and renowned tenor Dennis O'Neill once again at the helm, together with a distinguished panel of tutors. The young singers and répétiteurs who were chosen to participate were put through an intense programme of tuition incorporating lectures, masterclasses and technical instruction. The programme was part-sponsored by Rosenblatt solicitors again this year.

There were other significant matters that needed Agler's attention, one being the decision whether or not to engage an Irish orchestra for the 2006 Festival. The Arts Council continued to express concern regarding the matter and Wexford Festival Opera had committed to reviewing the situation to find a solution that both Wexford and the Arts Council would be satisfied with. In a paper dated May 2006, Wexford Festival Opera set out its current position and outlined the efforts that had been made to source an orchestra in Ireland. The paper outlined its difficult relationship with RTÉ around the engagement of the National Symphony Orchestra and the issues where resolution could not be reached. These issues included cost, broadcasting rights, programming and working conditions. As part of its research into the availability of suitable Irish orchestras, a number of national orchestras had been approached. Along with the Irish Chamber Orchestra, the Ulster Orchestra and the Irish Film Orchestra, approaches were made to the RTÉ Concert Orchestra and the Orchestra of Saint Cecilia.

The findings showed that any Irish-based solution would involve additional cost to Wexford Festival Opera, way beyond its current budgetary resources. While the National Symphony Orchestra remained the preferred choice for Wexford, it had proved impossible to negotiate terms or resume a working relationship with them. The Ulster Orchestra and the RTÉ Concert Orchestra, while interested in principle, were constrained by existing commitments and performance schedules. The review highlighted that the Irish Film Orchestra was the one that might provide a solution. Hennessy engaged with John O'Kane, Arts Programme Director with the Arts Council, and resolved, on behalf of Wexford Festival Opera, that it would not use a foreign provider for orchestral services from 2007, and would endeavour to use Irish orchestras during the transition period, where possible to do so. The Arts Council was naturally relieved that it had come to an agreed position with Wexford.

Following this review, and after the recent years of controversy surrounding the issue, Wexford proceeded to engage an Irish orchestra once again. With players drawn from the Irish Film Orchestra, managed by director Caitriona Walsh, with Agler as the musical director, the orchestra included the very best of Ireland's freelance players, soloists, chamber musicians and leading members of the state-run orchestras. It included Noel Eccles, principal percussionist with RTÉ's National Symphony Orchestra who had amassed an impressive repertoire supporting acts such as U2, Phil Lynott and Van Morrison. Fionnuala Hunt, one of Ireland's most distinguished performers, was its leader and it became known as the Wexford Festival Orchestra.

Early on, Agler was drawn into discussions with the Office of Public Works (OPW) around the design of the new opera house. One of the most immediate queries from Ciarán McGahon, architect with the OPW, was in relation to the development of the orchestra pit, to ensure it was to the exact specifications to suit Wexford Festival's needs. This was an area that Agler was most familiar with. Orchestral players had long suffered in the Theatre Royal from cramped conditions and impossible sightlines. The main question centred on whether columns in the orchestra pit lift were necessary, as had been outlined in the original specification. If columns were not an option, the design would have to revert to a fixed forestage. Although the orchestra pit lift was a requirement for opera production in the proposed new opera house, it was not a requirement for other events that the venue would be used for in the future. The Festival Board needed to be very mindful of creating a venue that was multifunctional, in essence to justify the significant public investment in the enterprise. Hennessy, however, reminded Agler and the Board that there was a primary focus, on which their success or failure would be judged. 'We are constructing an Opera House which will be used for other purposes,' he said.

> However, we must ensure the capacity for excellence in opera performance. If we fail to do this we will regret it forever after and have no real capacity to rectify matters. Certainly, we should ensure as far as possible the facilities are of a very high quality for other uses but this should not compromise our primary objective. If we produce a facility that is not best in class for Opera performance, we will be subject to very justifiable criticism and I think we will have blown it.[4]

Sinéad Campbell and
Glenn Alamilla in
Transformations,
Dun Mhuire Hall, 2006

Aerial photograph of the temporary theatre at Johnstown Castle

Momentum was gathering and by June the contract for building the new opera house was awarded by the OPW to a Wexford-based firm, Cleary & Doyle. Building works started almost immediately. Commenting on the announcement, Minister John O'Donoghue said:

> The reconstruction and refurbishment of the Theatre Royal in Wexford marks an important milestone in the development of the arts in Ireland. The success of Wexford Festival Opera, as a key event in the cultural life of Ireland for over 50 years, is well recognized and I am delighted that my Department has allocated €26 million towards the overall cost of providing Wexford and the country with a world class opera house that will meet the future needs of the Festival.[5]

Much of the planning was consumed with how to raise the funds needed to supplement the government grant to build the opera house. As an aid to the work of the Wexford Festival Board, the work of the fundraising foundation, established in 1999, began in earnest. Chaired by Liam Healy, distinguished members of the Foundation were Loretta Brennan Glucksman, chairperson of the American Ireland Fund, Sir David Davies, Niall Fitzgerald KBE, Peter Sutherland KCMG and Frank Keane of Frank Keane Motors. Davies was a banker and international businessman, who had been attending Wexford Festival Opera for many years. Fitzgerald was former CEO of Unilever and was chair of a range of companies, including Reuters. Sutherland was a European Commissioner and subsequently the Director General of the World Trade Organisation. He was also chairman of Goldman Sachs at the time. Carmel Naughton, philanthropist and former chair of the Board of the National Gallery of Ireland, and Michael Alen-Buckley, CEO and co-founder of RAB Capital Limited, were significant contributors to the Foundation, along with Irish businessman, Dermot Desmond. The Wexford Festival Board had settled on a target of €7 million to raise locally, through sponsors and through private donors. The personal leadership donations of the members of the Foundation were an important factor in demonstrating to the government that Wexford Festival Opera could reach its funding target, therefore building confidence in the overall vision. Their contributions to the Festival and the new Opera House were immense, financially and personally.

A significant fundraising initiative was organized and hosted by Niall Fitzgerald in June, at Reuters Global Headquarters, in London. The guests were treated to a gala dinner, with performances from Cuban-American soprano Eglise Gutiérrez, who drew rave reviews in 2005 for her performance as *Maria di Rohan*; the Mexican tenor Dante Alcalá, who had starred at Wexford in Granados' opera *María del Carmen*; along with the Welsh soprano Laura Parfitt, a recent graduate of the Wexford Festival Opera's Artists Development Programme. Peter Sutherland attended the gala dinner also. Hennessy, Sutherland and Fitzgerald had one chance to impress upon the guests that Wexford's new Opera House was worth investing in. At Sutherland's suggestion, Hennessy made the presentation to the invited guests. Fitzgerald followed up by asking them to consider giving towards the cause, and Sutherland addressed those in attendance at the end, to emphasize the importance of their support.

It was communicated publicly that Wexford Festival Opera needed to target local businesses for 10 per cent of the €7m of private funding required for the development of the new Opera House:

> While the redevelopment will be a significant addition to the national cultural landscape, it is Wexford and the south-east that has most to gain from the investment in this facility,

said Hennessy, speaking at the launch of another fundraising initiative held at White's Hotel in the centre of town. This time the event was hosted by the Wexford Fundraising Committee, chaired by Helen Doyle, of Doyle Solicitors. Companies and individuals were approached over a number of months, with the aim of having €700,000 pledged by the end of 2007. Speaking at the launch in White's Hotel, local accountant, Board member and former chairman John O'Connor said the town was

> getting this incredible facility for less than two per cent of the total investment required. This is an opportunity now for Wexford people to step up to the mark and support Wexford Festival Opera in its endeavours.

'You have told us to sing, and sing we shall', said Hennessy at the launch of the 2006 programme which was held at the Ferrycarrig Hotel in Wexford. Both White's Hotel and the Ferrycarrig Hotel were important local sponsors of the Festival over many years. The function was attended by the local media, sponsors of Wexford Festival Opera and the High Street Residents' Committee, a group that was established to manage relations with the property owners in High Street. The High Street residents would be significantly impacted by the planned construction works for the new theatre over a considerable period of time – it being a narrow, one-way street – hence Wexford Festival Opera made the early decision to engage with these residents and ensure that they were kept up to date on all matters relating to the construction of the new building.[6]

It was a very different Festival in 2006 and a more modest affair by Wexford's usual standards. The well-known Irish designer, Joe Vaněk, was contracted to transform the Dun Mhuire, the parish hall in the centre of town, into an appropriate venue for opera performance in 2006. Vaněk had worked at Wexford previously, making his Festival debut when Elaine Padmore held

Nigel Richards, Simon Gleeson, Anita Dobson and Nina Bernsteiner in *Der Silbersee*, Johnstown Castle, 2007

the position of artistic director. With one successful season behind him, Agler worked diligently and seamlessly with Vaněk to imagine an Opera Festival that was worthy of Wexford's reputation. Although Agler's initial reaction to staging opera at the Dun Mhuire in Wexford had been far from positive, describing it as 'a depressing and unimaginative idea', he certainly embraced the challenge. Vaněk played a critical role in ensuring that the Dun Mhuire Hall was up to the standard that had come to be expected from Wexford's loyal friends, transforming the modest parish hall with skill and imagination.

Alessandro Riga in *Pulcinella*, Johnstown Castle, 2007

The Festival opened on Wednesday 25 October with *Don Gregorio* by Donizetti. The second production this year was *Transformations* by living composer Conrad Susa. Agler took a risk with this one, as it was very different to what the patrons at Wexford might have expected from a Wexford production. It was based on a set of poems by Anne Sexton that reimagined Grimm's Fairy Tales and was premièred at the Minnesota Opera in 1973. The team he assembled however – Gavin Carr as assistant conductor, Michael Barker-Caven as Director, along with Vaněk – cemented it as a laudable choice. The cast was well represented with Irish singers, including Wexford-born soprano Sinéad Campbell. Susa travelled to Wexford to attend a performance of the opera and to give a talk on it to an appreciative audience. The newly constituted Wexford Festival Orchestra played for the first time – a much pared-back ensemble due to the limitations of the Dun Mhuire Hall – nonetheless the playing was commended by patrons. Taking into account these limitations, the patrons were astonished at the transformation of the hall on Wexford's main street. Vaněk had included a big exhibition in the foyer and a canopy out front stretching into the street for maximum effect. The Board and the Festival executives were keen to preserve as many traditions as possible and the opera train rumbled into town much to the delight of the passengers who had managed to secure tickets to this unique Wexford experience. The ticket included full dinner on board during the journey from Dublin's Pearse Station to Wexford, transfer coach from Wexford Rail Station to the Dun Mhuire Hall, opera ticket, transfer coach back to the station and supper on board during the return journey to Dublin. The cost was €290 euros. Minister John O'Donoghue officially opened the Festival and he addressed the crowds on the quay in Wexford as was the usual tradition.

Diageo Ireland was still the principal sponsor of Wexford Festival Opera, spending over €100,000 sponsoring the 55th Festival from 25 October to 5 November. The Ulster Orchestra, celebrating its 40th anniversary, was invited to perform in Wexford for the first time in 2006. It brought the Festival to a spectacular close, with a concert in Rowe Street Church. It was another example of North–South cooperation that Agler had been keen to nurture.

With the announcement that the Arts Council was in receipt of additional funding from the government to the value of €7.5 million, Wexford was delighted to secure €850,000 towards capital funding. It was looking like a really good year for Wexford and the fundraising structures in place were starting to pay off. There was not shared delight for Wexford's good fortune, however, as was evident in an *Irish Independent* article that appeared after the 2006 Festival:

> In Irish national terms it completely staggered the artistic community when Wexford got €26m for a new opera house, large grants for current activity, and a revolutionary undertaking by Wexford Festival Opera itself to keep the new theatre constantly in operation, for the foreseeable future, all year round. But that was only part of it. The normal route was changed. This funding was direct from the Department of Arts, bypassing the omnivorous Arts Council. More

serious by far are the implications for artistic activity elsewhere. As described, it is a death-knell for much expansion or advances in the development of opera generally. By being so restrictive, it freezes development rather than enhancing it.[7]

Notwithstanding this, Wexford was determined to forge ahead, and understood that there was still a mountain to climb to secure the funds needed. 'I feel so sad that we are launching into phase 2 of this adventure without Jerome [Hynes] snapping at our heels', Vaněk wrote to Agler.

> Jerome would be giving us no peace, full of suggestions and support, enthusiasm and cajoling ... It is, for me, sometimes quite hard to constantly be an instigator and I do feel to be in somewhat of a void and despite my seeming confidence, I am anxious that I make the right decisions. I badly need a co-conspirator. Jerome was so much more. It is also a trial wearing 2 hats, trying to resolve this staging and at the same time deliver another successful production. Of course I can do it, but it doesn't take away from the sadness I feel that we are doing all this without the man who was such a driving force.[8]

Vaněk was referring to phase two of the adventure, which was the preparation of Johnstown Castle for the 2007 Opera Festival. This was a mammoth task and a logistical and operational challenge of a new magnitude for Wexford. But the entire process was hugely exciting too. The gigantic temporary structure – 66 metres long, 14 metres high, 22 metres wide and 750 seats – had more seating capacity than the Theatre Royal. Atlantic Enterprises was brought in as the production team, the same company that had produced shows for artists such as Madonna, Michael Jackson, U2 and the Rolling Stones. The interior of the temporary structure was also impressive. The foyer's centrepiece was built around the existing fountain and pond that sat on the lawn at Johnstown Castle. The orchestra pit was fully sunken down to two metres below the stage and could cater for 66 musicians. The spectacular design was attributed to Vaněk who laboured over the detail to ensure that every aspect was just right.[9]

The artistic freedom that Agler and his team had at this time certainly made their efforts worthwhile. Vaněk was in his element. He wrote frequently to Agler about his plans for every corner of the Castle that would be put to use.

Given the shortened time frame for preparations, with the Festival taking place for the first time during the summer months, the pressure on the team was even more acute. 'My days are endlessly exhausting', Vaněk wrote to Agler.

> I seem to be making so many decisions on so many fronts ... I hope
> I have the energy for rehearsals. This is not to say this is still not one
> of the most (if not THE most) challenging and exciting experiences
> of my career.[10]

Agler responded, empathizing with the enormity of the challenges that they faced. 'The technical issues were always going to be next to impossible', he said, 'which is why I counsel a calm, positive problem-solving atmosphere. The crews are doing their best and really only want the best for everybody'.[11] Vaněk was going into this season having been part of the team that had such success with *Transformations*, which won three opera awards for best production, best lighting and best costumes.

With everything going on, it wasn't possible to give the Artist Development Programme the attention it needed to ensure that it was achieving its objectives. This had been viewed as a positive addition to the Festival in recent years. Dennis O'Neill had big plans, including taking one of the concerts to Dublin, but he needed the support of the Board to put a programme together. In principle, the Board was very interested in continuing with the programme, but from a practical perspective, the other elements that had to be taken care of in 2007 were taking precedence. Furthermore, a sponsor had not been found for the programme in 2007. O'Neill did point out that the programme lacked Irish participants and that this was something that should be rectified. It was certainly a difficult decision to cancel the programme altogether for 2007, but Hennessy conceded that the financial cost of the programme and the time needed to develop it in the right way for the Festival was more than they could absorb at this time.[12]

The production costs for the upcoming season were starting to spiral out of control. The new chief executive, Michael Hunt, estimated that the costs would rise to €4.5 million this year. Therefore, news of the special infrastructure grant of €850,000 from the Arts Council was most welcome.[13]

The Wexford Festival Foundation, chaired by Healy, had by now managed to secure over 60 per cent of the total €7 million target from private funding through a number of leadership donations and was confident that more financial support was on its way. The members of the Foundation had suggested the idea of launching a seat-endowment campaign through which Friends of the Festival would be given the opportunity to name a seat in support of fundraising efforts for the new Wexford Opera House. The 750 seats in the main auditorium of the new Opera House would be made available for naming by individuals or families.[14]

Finally, the opening night arrived and friends and visitors to Wexford donned their black tie attire and detoured to Johnstown Castle. In all, there were an impressive 18 days of Festival performances, which ran from 31 May to 17 June, including a performance by the Prague Chamber Choir. The operas chosen for this experimental season were Dvořák's *Rusalka*, Weill's *Der Silbersee* and a double bill of Stravinsky's *Pulcinella* and Busoni's *Arlecchino*. The double bill was a co-production with Teatro Comunale Bologna, Italy. It was a wonderful event, and although spectacularly different to the Theatre Royal experience, it managed to preserve the coveted Wexford Festival Opera atmosphere and offered its patrons something new, something that they might like a lot. The Wexford Festival Orchestra was contracted to play for all of the Johnstown performances. There was some media criticism however that there were no Irish singers in the cast this year. Agler described it as 'a bad year for the Irish', and explained that those singers that he would like to have included were simply not available for the dates required.[15]

The ShortWorks were held in the Dun Mhuire Hall this year and truly made their mark, culminating in a nomination for Best Opera Production in the Irish Times Theatre Awards for *La tragédie de Carmen*, interpreted by Peter Brooks and directed by Andrew Steggall.[16] The coverage in the press managed to capture this year's unique offering.

> There's ballet, an Italian popstar as a director and an opera that's not actually an opera but is instead a play with music that has been translated by television impressionist Rory Bremner, featuring former *Eastenders* soap star Anita 'Angie' Dobson. The sound you now hear is a combination of opera purists sobbing into their linen handkerchiefs mixed with a stampede of opera novices charging to the Wexford booking office. For this, its 56th outing, Wexford Festival Opera is presenting its most public-friendly programme to date.[17]

Helena Kaupova and
David Greeves in *Rusalka*,
Johnstown Castle, 2007

Agler explained the motivation behind his programme:

> 'Many people have a definition of opera that is quite restrictive. It's really an enormous discipline and I just wanted to show that Wexford could really do anything and everything in terms of opera', he said. 'We are breaking away from the formula of performing three unknown operas that has held for over a generation. We're representing the whole gamut of musical theatre this year … So I do concede that this is anything but a typical Festival.'[18]

This was certainly the year to break with tradition and there was a deserved sense of exhilaration from the Wexford Festival Opera company that they had managed to pull it off. Hennessy summed up the Johnstown experience best, in the programme book foreword, when he said:

> To undertake an endeavour of this scale within eight months of our last Festival could, quite reasonably, have been regarded as over-ambitious. It was certainly a daunting challenge. But the potential to create something really unique in the history of our organization, a truly new occasion for the Arts in Ireland and in the Wexford community is, quite simply, the kind of challenge this organization cannot resist. So, daunting as it may be, it is absolutely the right thing for us to do; to challenge ourselves, to deliver a Festival which we believe will in the future be regarded as a defining moment in our history.[19]

Undoubtedly, a significant amount of hard work had been invested in ensuring that the Johnstown Castle experiment would be a success. Artistically it was seen as just that. Financially, it was not such a celebrated achievement. The entire venture had exceeded expectations in terms of cost, as much as approximately €1 million, and Hennessy and the Board had to deal with this fact, alongside the very real pressures of raising the required revenue to ensure that the new Opera House could be paid for. So, as quickly as the magnificent structure had been erected on the grounds of the old castle, it was dismantled in the same orderly fashion and was committed to the memory of a year like no other for Wexford Festival Opera.

Paul Hennessy, Ted Howlin and John O'Connor on site during the building of the Opera House

Relations in the meantime had become fractured between the Board and the new chief executive, Michael Hunt. Having only joined the company in July 2006, Hunt expressed shock at being told by the chairman that he did not believe that Hunt and the Festival were going to have 'a long-term relationship'.[20] Hunt felt that he had done significant work in building a stronger relationship with the Arts Council during his time at Wexford. He also argued that he had not been told previously that he had to complete a probationary period. He believed that his contract was for seven years, to be reviewed after three years. Hunt secured a temporary injunction, to stop Wexford Festival Board from removing him from the position as chief executive. In the end, the dispute was settled at the High Court and the ensuing statement noted that

> Mr Hunt joined the organization in July 2006 and oversaw the staging of both the 2006 and the recently completed 2007 Festivals. Both these Festivals were outstanding successes for the organization and Michael Hunt's considerable skills contributed greatly to their planning and execution.[21]

Interior of the new Opera House, 2008

In an article that appeared in the *Irish Times*, a plausible explanation was put forward as to why relations had broken down:

> Hunt was in many ways well equipped for the Wexford job. He had experience in venue management at Waterford's Theatre Royal. He had run his own touring opera company, Co-Opera. He had directed opera in Ireland and abroad (including the first Opera Scenes at Wexford in 1982), and he had a secure and imaginative grasp of the issues facing opera in Wexford and in Ireland generally. On the other hand, he was

believed to have encountered difficulties in personnel management, and the negative reaction from the large team of volunteer workers in Wexford is the issue most widely cited as contributing to his downfall at the Festival.[22]

Soon after, David McLoughlin was appointed as interim chief executive. He was the former CEO of Screen Producers Ireland and a film producer in his own right. Chair of the Dublin Film Festival, McLoughlin was given an initial contract of six months. He was joining the organization at a most critical time.

The Board remained focused on the construction of the new Opera House. It was astute enough to realize that this project had to be a proper partnership model, where all parties had a vested interest in a successful outcome. The building project was managed by the OPW and overseen by a Steering Committee that comprised of representatives from the OPW, Wexford Festival Opera and the Department of Arts, Sport and Tourism, with the Committee being chaired by the OPW Commissioner, Clare McGrath. Matt O'Connor was a key member of the Wexford Festival Board at the time, and contributed important insights from his significant experience as an architect and former CEO of the National Building Agency. Due to the fact that all of the boundaries were shared with either businesses or residences, there was a wider impact on the immediate neighbourhood. Scaffolding had to be erected on the surrounding buildings. To pre-empt any issues arising, the design team organized monthly meetings with the local community to quickly identify and seek to address any problems or issues. For the overall success of the project, it was vital to be sensitive to the views of the surrounding community and, although not without its difficulties, this process was managed very well. Don Curtin, Board member and a former town clerk, was tasked with managing relations with the neighbouring households, a role that he executed particularly well. In fact, the Board members were all aware of the enormity of their roles in ensuring that the project would be executed. Billy Sweetman, a partner with PWC, was another key member of the Board at the time, bringing his expertise to bear in assisting in navigating some of the complex issues that arose. Blaise Brosnan, too, brought management expertise and focus to the Board at a time when it was crucially needed. All members agreed to remain on the Board for the duration of the project, so that all Board members could go over the line together and be involved in the momentous occasion that was anticipated.

Furthermore, Hennessy remained in the chair, unopposed during this time.

As the building began to take shape, it was clear early on that it was going to be a truly spectacular venue – the first purpose-built opera house in Ireland. The reinstated terraced building façade on the outside camouflaged the new building perfectly and succeeded in maintaining the element of surprise that was so characteristic of the Theatre Royal, tucked away on a narrow side street. It featured an auditorium for 780 people (an increase of 30 seats on the original projections), a multi-purpose 'black-box' performing space for 175 people and several smaller rehearsal spaces. The main auditorium was fitted with two double-decker orchestra hydraulic pit lifts, to cater for different types of performances. The pit could disappear when not in use and the area was capable of being raised to maximum height to become part of the stage, or mid-height to cater for additional seating. This would increase the capacity of the auditorium to 853 when the orchestra pit was not in use, representing a 40 per cent increase in audience capacity from the original Theatre Royal. Further, the individual seats were 40 per cent bigger than the previous seats and were designed for comfort and with the acoustics very much to the forefront of consideration. Traditional horse-shoe shaped balconies brought the audience closer to the stage and covered the walls on three sides. With all of the additional space, the design was carefully considered so that there was no increase in the distance from the stage to the furthest away seat. A key feature of the new building was the expansive use of walnut and lighting bridges hanging from the ceiling. The effect resembled the inside of a cello and was very impressive. The fly tower externally was clad in copper, hence the distinctive appearance on the Wexford skyline, traditionally bookended by the two church spires. The OPW Architectural Services worked diligently with Keith Williams Architects to achieve the unique effect.

The backstage facilities included dedicated rooms for directors, conductors, designers and singers, an increased number of dressing rooms, chorus rehearsal rooms and prop-making areas. The new layout also included 40 fly bars for scenery changes, ensuring that the opera house would be able to cater for dynamic changes quickly. This was so important at Wexford where the norm was to produce six cycles of three operas. With the improved set-up backstage, the sets and scenery for two operas could be stored overhead in the flys during the performance of the third opera.

One of the fundamental requirements outlined early on in the specifications was the need to ensure the highest acoustic standards for the new building. The

Enrico Marabelli and
Marco Filippo Romano
in *Tutti in maschera*, 2008

support of Arup Acoustics was therefore essential to ensure that the sound was a priority during the design and build phase. The emphasis was on the voice, and enabling the singers to shine, while also balanced with a pure orchestral sound. Arup was certainly a leader in the area of theatre acoustics, having had responsibility for acoustics at the new opera houses in Copenhagen and Oslo, the Wales Millennium Centre, Cardiff, Glyndebourne Opera House and the refurbishment of the Royal Opera House, London. The OPW also acted as Mechanical & Electrical consultants and its biggest challenge here was to provide air conditioning and ventilation that was extremely quiet, so as not to hinder performances. The process undertaken was to use huge motors to deliver vast quantities of air quietly to large plenums under the seating, which in turn delivered large quantities of fresh air into the main auditorium.

Arup Acoustics' senior auditorium designer Jeremy Newton described how the acoustic was carefully considered, particularly in the main auditorium:

> The room is carefully shaped to ensure the right sound reflections to the audience and performers. Where there is need for sound scattering surfaces, these are integrated into the architectural room design. The leather seating has a perforated underside to introduce high frequency sound absorption provided by the audience making the acoustic for rehearsals as similar as possible to that for performance. One of the problems in orchestra pits is that excessive sound build up can contribute to hearing damage to the players. To help reduce this, we incorporated flexible sound absorbing surfaces around the pit. This is particularly important at Wexford, as the pit is designed to accommodate a large overhang underneath the front of the stage.[23]

The decision to clad the auditorium walls in walnut panelling was taken with the acoustic in mind, but the overall effect of the panelling was also beautiful. The exposed lighting bridges overhead completed the impression of a large cello, the wood portraying the body of the instrument and the lighting bridges portraying the strings.

Given the proposed scale and complexities of the new venture, a decision was taken to enhance the organization structure, and it coincided, in May 2008, with the appointment of David McLoughlin as full-time chief executive of both the Festival and the Wexford Opera House. McLoughlin had been fulfilling the role on an interim basis since September 2007.

A discussion that caused much disquiet among Board members and members of the company centred on the naming of the new Opera House. Hennessy, who had been integrally involved in all of the decisions thus far, was adamant that the new Opera House could not be called the New Theatre Royal. Hennessy felt that the term 'Theatre Royal' had connotations of English royalty, and hence should not be used given the investment being made by the Irish government. Further, a difficult conversation had to happen between Hennessy and Tony O'Reilly – the largest private sponsor of the new building – where Hennessy explained that O'Reilly would have naming rights to the main Auditorium only and not to the Opera House itself.

After much discussion and dissension, the Board finally agreed to the name, the 'Wexford Opera House'. 'It will be a total disaster and an insult if Dr Tom Walsh is not honoured' remarked Peter Ebert following confirmation that the Board voted for 'Wexford Opera House' as the name for the building:

> Without him there would have been no Festival. Whoever has an influence should do all they can to rectify the situation. There are plenty of rooms in the theatre that could be dedicated to him ...

said Ebert. He was pleased to note however that the second smaller auditorium would be named after the late Jerome Hynes.[24] It was agreed that the famous bust of Dr Tom Walsh by the late Seamus Furlong would be displayed prominently in the foyer of the opera house.

Throughout the year, the Wexford Festival Opera and its Board were consumed with fundraising. The Arts Council had recently added an extra €200,000 to Wexford's grant, bringing the total funding for 2008 to €1.4 million. Datapac, IT Solutions and Services provider, signed up as the Festival's exclusive IT and telecommunications partner. As the Opera House was beginning to take shape, a local businessman, James O'Connor, offered to organize a fundraiser for the capital project. O'Connor was one of the Festival's most loyal local sponsors. At €1,000 per guest, he managed to convince 25 people to sign up to a dinner at his restaurant, Greenacres. A tour of the opera house before dinner was part of the deal and a local opera singer, Sinéad Campbell, entertained the guests. Matt O'Connor, who was now a Board member, was the tour guide for

Irina Samoylova and Natela Nicoli in *Snegurochka,* 2008

the pre-dinner unveiling of the opera house that was still under construction. The tour walked out onto the balcony and looked down towards the stage into the empty house, where the seats had not yet been fitted. Something did not seem right to Matt O'Connor and Hennessy, who were also observing from the balcony. Once the dinner guests had moved on, O'Connor made his way to the stalls where he proceeded to measure the spaces between the vent holes on the ground that would soon be covered with the seats. To his horror, he realized that the vent holes were in the wrong place. O'Connor and Hennessy re-joined the dinner guests who were contributing so much to the future of the Opera House. They did not divulge that the floor of the building that had been so carefully laid would have to be taken up and re-laid to rectify the error. Hennessy later admitted that it was a conscious decision on the part of those at the helm to relay positive news and updates and not to relay the difficulties (often quite acute) that went along with trying to complete such an expensive and complex project.

These were worrying times for the Board of Wexford Festival Opera. The Arts Council had not agreed to provide the additional funding needed for engaging an Irish orchestra, an initiative that had doubled orchestral costs from €300,000 up to €600,000. Tickets were selling well but every seat needed to be sold to ensure maximum revenue. By September 2008, the financial situation was critical. Hennessy wrote to the Board, urging the members to focus on the situation as a matter of priority and to promote the sale of tickets at every opportunity. He described the circumstances as 'very acute and have to be managed on a day to day basis'.[25] Board members were tasked with redoubling their efforts in a local business fundraising campaign in the hope that the required funds could be found. Wexford still needed to raise €2.5 million of the €7 million it had pledged to raise locally, towards the overall costs of the new building, which now stood at €33 million. 'This is an urgent appeal for funds' Hennessy urged, calling on visitors, local people and the business community to play their part. People were asked to consider endowing seats at a cost of €850 as a way of bridging the funding gap.[26] A beverage manufacturing company – European Refreshments – that included Coca-Cola among its products, was set to establish a research and development facility at Wexford, and agreed to become a sponsor of the Festival. Wexford County Council also made a significant contribution to the development of the Opera House, much to the relief of those working hard to reach their targets. Following this, the County Council continued its support of the Festival each year.

Remarkably, the building project was delivered on budget at €32 million and on schedule. Considering the costs of other recent opera house projects – the new opera house in Copenhagen cost €239 million and the new one in Oslo cost €500 million – Wexford could feel particularly proud of its endeavour. The project timeline had been very tight, and was developed around the requirement to have a building in place for the 2008 Festival. This would mean that Wexford Festival Opera would be without a home for only two seasons. The iconic building was handed over to Wexford Festival Opera on 1 August 2008 and David McLoughlin commended the innovation shown by Keith Williams in its design:

> We continue to be impressed by the vision, ingenuity and creativity which Keith Williams Architects brought to the design and construction of Wexford Opera House.

As Matt O'Connor concluded later:

> all credit must go to our Wexford builders Eugene Cleary and John Doyle – a magnificent and dedicated team driven by local pride.

O'Connor recalled how there was not enough time to carry out a full pre-opening acoustic sound checking in the Opera House, as the deadlines were so tight, 'not to mention we didn't have the funds to pay the orchestra for the tests'.[27]

Amid this financial uncertainty, in early September 2008, Wexford Festival Opera's performers, directors, designers and technical teams arrived to begin rehearsals. Those that had graced the stage of the old Theatre Royal were beyond impressed with the improved conditions and facilities. Meanwhile, Agler was busy pulling together the Festival components, and, given that this would be the first Festival in the new opera house, there would be much attention brought to bear on the standard of productions and on the ambiance of the new space.

For the first time too, the Board had to concern itself not only with an annual opera festival, but an annual programme of activity fitting of the new opera house. Attention would certainly be on Wexford's ability to propel the opera house into full activity as soon as possible. A key consideration for the Board was whether any ancillary activity should have its own artistic identity or whether it should come under the aegis of the Festival. This would depend on a number of factors, not least the financial considerations and the type of productions that the venue would attract. Promoting the new Opera House and protecting the Festival brand were foremost in the minds of the Board members and to this end, Thomas de Mallet Burgess was invited to become creative director to support the Board in developing policies around the use of the facility and to fill a programming role. De Mallet Burgess was Director of TEAM Educational Theatre Company, a theatre in education company that worked with primary and post-primary schools. He had also directed *La vestale* at Wexford in 2004.

> The activity in the new theatre is ridiculous. Snaggers, acousticians, stage crews, and staff all in each other's way. There will be an 'Open Day' next Sunday – 1,200 have signed up and there is a waiting list of several hundred more. Not bad for a small Irish town,

wrote Agler to Sue Graham-Dixon, Wexford's UK press agent, in early September 2008.[28] It was true that there was significant interest in the new building from local people. The Opera House organized tours of the building every Saturday at 1p.m. for the first six months. Within the first four weeks alone, 20,000 local people had taken part in a guided tour.

In advance of the Festival opening, McLoughlin approached Clare Deignan of RTÉ about the possibility of organizing a launch event in Wexford. McLoughlin managed to secure a great coup in getting the agreement of RTÉ to broadcast the popular light entertainment show, *The Late Late Show*, from the Wexford Opera House. Taking place on 5 September, this was only the fourth time in 48 years that the show was broadcast outside of the RTÉ studio in Dublin. Although it was very much an RTÉ-run event, including the presence of the RTÉ Concert Orchestra, there was plenty of local participation, with the Wexford sports teams (football and camogie) invited to take part in the celebration. Among the guests to perform live was the mezzo-soprano Katherine Jenkins, who was the first opera singer to perform from the new Wexford Opera House. The Opera House was formally opened by the Taoiseach, Brian Cowen. In many ways, the new Opera House was a perfect example of what was possible during the Celtic Tiger era – the ability to create something unique and world class with the support of state funding, something of which the whole country could be proud. Cowen of course knew at this stage that a financial crisis was looming. He spoke to the host of the show, Pat Kenny, about the significance of this publicly funded asset for the country as a whole. It would soon become clear that Ireland faced an uncertain future.

The Festival itself was launched a number of weeks later, on 16 October, by Martin Cullen, Minister for Arts, Sport and Tourism, to an eager crowd on Wexford's quay front. The first opera to be performed in the new Wexford Opera House was *Snegurochka* by Rimsky-Korsakov. The other operas chosen

John Bellemer and Caroline Worra in *The Mines of Sulphur*, 2008

by Agler for this historic year were Bennett's *The Mines of Sulphur* and Pedrotti's *Tutti in maschera* and the Festival ran for 18 full days.

'With the opening of the new Wexford Opera House, something both wonderful and a little strange has happened', Fintan O'Toole wrote in his *Irish Times* article:

> The wonderful bit is easily stated: Wexford now has what is unquestionably the finest performance space in Ireland. The new theatre is not just beautiful, it is also technically superb, with a stage

that can be used in three different configurations, top-class lighting and stage machinery, an orchestra pit that actually looks big enough for the job, and above all, an acoustic that is almost eerily good. The strange bit is less straightforward: it is far from clear what can or should be done with this stunning facility when it is not being used by the Festival. That is not, it should be emphasized, a complaint. No place in Ireland deserves a building as good as this one more than Wexford does. Even for those of us who can't entirely shrug off our scepticism about opera, the Wexford Festival is a remarkable phenomenon. To create a world-class opera festival in a medium-sized Irish town in the 1950s and to sustain it for 57 years on the basis of the community's voluntary commitment is no mean feat. To do that while deliberately eschewing the standards of the operatic repertoire and specializing in neglected and forgotten works is a death-defying stunt. For that, and for the vision of the late Jerome Hynes who saw both the need and the opportunity for a radical redevelopment of the old Theatre Royal, Wexford should be spared even the tiniest whiff of begrudgery.

It is also true that the new opera house is something in which everyone in the country should take some pride. Even if you hate opera and have no intention of visiting Wexford, the project stands as a rebuke to all the stupid negativity about the capacities of the public sector. In an era (now rapidly fading) when we were told that only the profit motive could create efficiency, it is worth noting that this public project was delivered, not just to a high standard of excellence, but on time, on budget, and in spite of formidable technical challenges.[29]

Only time would tell whether or not Wexford had over-extended itself with regard to such an ambitious project – certainly, at times, it appeared that the financial burden of delivering the new opera house would be insurmountable. The challenge was now to make it work. With a critical international financial situation unfolding, this challenge was greater than ever.

CHAPTER 12

JUST ONE OF THOSE CRAZY THINGS

2009–12

Just ten days after the *Late Late Show* event at Wexford Opera House, the international media reported that Lehman Brothers, the global financial services firm, had filed for bankruptcy. There was an immediate and chilling inevitability that economies around the world were about to be hit by recession. Within days of the Festival then, the Irish government, a Fianna Fáil coalition, officially conceded that Ireland was in the midst of a recession. Ireland was, in fact, the first country in the Eurozone to enter recession. The Wexford Festival Board and its executive looked on in horror as the entire landscape changed dramatically around them. The impact of the economic crash on this new opera house would be significant, and it would take a mammoth effort to keep the doors open and survive this latest and most acute crisis. As Michael Dervan pointed out,

The Wexford Festival is one of those crazy things that should never have happened. No, I'm not suggesting a comparison with the current financial crisis. Think instead of something along the lines of man learning to fly, or the invention of submarines … It's unfortunate that the Arts Council's long-promised quantum leap in the funding of opera has yet to materialize. And doubly unfortunate that the Festival has taken possession of its new house at a time of unprecedented international financial turmoil and the certainty of severe cutbacks in public funding of the arts. If necessity is the mother of invention, Wexford is at the point in its history where inventiveness is going to be crucial to survival. The complexity of the current challenges will call on Wexford's craziness to an extent never seen before.[1]

Luckily, the 2008 Festival did not suffer as a result of the impending economic downturn. In fact, there was a feeling of jubilation during the Festival. There were too many achievements to celebrate and the Board and staff of Wexford Festival Opera had waited a long time for this moment. They did feel that luck had been on their side in getting the new opera house completed on time, as any delays in the building of the state-of-the-art facility would have been detrimental to its very completion.

The critics were unanimous in their praise of the Festival this year and the new Opera House was celebrated by all who visited Wexford. According to Andrew Clark in the *Financial Times*: 'With the new opera house stealing much of the limelight, the 58th Festival may go down as the most successful of all'.[2] The *Sunday Business Post* was also full of praise for what Wexford had achieved:

Wexford Festival Opera faced an enormous task in opening its new premises and staging a festival simultaneously. That it was an outstanding and memorable success is testament to the vision of its founders, the initiative of its management, and the spirit and unstinting support of its community. Bravo, Wexford, a triumph in more than one way.[3]

There was an enormous sense of accomplishment that was felt not only by those in Wexford who had worked so hard to realize this dream, but was also recognized by journalists and visitors alike. 'At a stroke, the Festival can be what

Barbara Quintiliani
and Marco Caria in
Maria Padilla, 2009

it's always tried to be: world class', concluded one journalist, who had made the pilgrimage to Wexford.[4] There was a feeling this year that the entire arts community, at home and abroad, was proud of what Wexford had managed to achieve.

The Festival, and in particular the Opera House, picked up a number of awards following its opening. Wexford was included in third place on the Top Ten Destinations for Opera Lovers, which was published by the prominent Frommer's organization. The Opera House also won an Irish Times Theatre Award for special achievement, an Opus Architecture and Construction Award, a Royal Institute of Architects in Ireland (RIAI) Best Cultural Building

Laura Vlasak Nolan in *The Ghosts of Versailles*, 2009

Award, and a coveted award from the Royal Institute of British Architects for architectural excellence. On a more sobering note however, there was still substantial borrowing arising from the construction of the new building and the work of the Foundation continued, under the stewardship of Liam Healy, to try and bridge the funding gap.[5]

This debt carried over into 2009 much to the despair of those working so hard to develop a successful programme for the coming Festival. Moreover, there was little appetite for raising money because all individuals and businesses were hit to some degree by the recession. The timing did not seem right to ask people to consider funding the Wexford Festival. The Finance Committee, led by Pat Caulfield, former Managing Director of Nutricia, had the difficult task of navigating through this period of austerity. Agler felt the full impact of this burden when he was asked to put a plan together that was deliverable within the new and more stringent context. He produced a plan for the Board in February, outlining how the Festival needed to be reduced from eighteen days to twelve once again, with four cycles of three operas. ShortWorks and concerts were to be cancelled, along with the Dr Tom Walsh lecture series. Agler suggested reintroducing the Late Night Cabaret, which had been popular at Wexford in previous years. Wexford committed to an impressive co-production with the Opera Theatre of St Louis, which would have been impossible to stage if Wexford had to fund the production completely.

Although not all Board members were enthusiastic, Hennessy was supportive of the co-production model, realizing that it was going to be necessary for Wexford to explore these opportunities in the future. Agler had conducted at the Opera Theatre of Saint Louis on a number of occasions and was also impressed with its apprentice programme in theatre arts. He suggested to the Board of Wexford Festival Opera that a similar model could be very successful at Wexford. He subsequently researched similar programmes at Santa Fe and at the Banff Arts Centre, where he had been Music Director, and felt that the programmes offered fantastic opportunities for young people to get experience and a possible route into the industry.[6] The Board agreed in principle with the idea, however the implementation of the programme would be a difficult task with all of the competing priorities and financial strain that Wexford Festival Opera now faced.

Agler remained concerned that the cost of the Wexford Festival Orchestra was such that it put significant pressure on the artistic budget. He compared the 2005 orchestral costs of €217,000 to the sum quoted for 2009 which was €615,000. It was extremely difficult to absorb this increase, and Agler was quick to point out that the business model for delivering quality opera productions that had worked for the more intimate Theatre Royal would be insufficient for the new theatre.[7]

Wexford Festival Opera was not alone in grappling with complex and sustained financial difficulties. The impact of the recession had, without doubt, a profound impact on the entire cultural landscape in Ireland. The Arts Council was forced to rationalize its funding model to ensure viability into the future. Following a plan developed by Randall Shannon, opera advisor to the Arts

Council, it was proposed that from 2011 onwards, all opera in Ireland would be produced by a new single company. This idea had been mooted previously, but now there was a sense of greater urgency to move ahead with the plan. This was potentially a very damaging proposition for Wexford. In the summer of 2009, the Wexford Festival Opera Board penned a response to the draft plan and outlined critically why the plan, in its current form, would have a detrimental effect on Wexford Festival Opera. The main concerns centred on Wexford's ability to maintain its excellent reputation within a new model and it felt that there would be an acute difficulty in retaining sponsors, friends and funders if Wexford was subsumed into a new organization. The concept of being an International Opera Festival on the one hand, and a community-based Festival on the other, was one that Wexford was comfortable with when in charge of its own affairs. This was best shown through the willingness of volunteers to participate in such numbers, and with such professional standards at Wexford. The two components were complementary to one another. Now, however, this structure was in jeopardy, as the volunteer support network and the local community organization concept would surely suffer as a result of any move towards a national entity. There was also the very immediate problem that the ability of Wexford Festival Opera to fundraise for its current season was compromised by the publicity surrounding the Arts Council's intentions. Wexford Festival Opera's future seemed uncertain once again.

Wexford's counter-proposal to the Arts Council included plans for presenting a year-round programme of events, with a separate Dublin production taking place after the October season in Wexford. Following this, two main opera productions would be produced and rehearsed in Wexford in the spring. Touring productions would also form part of the strategy for Wexford in the new proposed model.[8] It was to be an anxious wait for the Board at Wexford Festival Opera to see the conclusions of the Arts Council review.

At the same time, significant governance restructuring was afoot and it was decided that Wexford Opera House would be governed by a separate Board to Wexford Festival Opera. The intention was to make both organizations operationally independent, which made sense, as the Opera House would need to set out its own strategic framework for sustainability and development. The Arts Council did not provide funding for the Opera House – its funding relationship was solely with Wexford Festival Opera. This was Hennessy's last year as chairman of the Board. He had had an arduous and ultimately

Kishani Jayasinghe
and Paula Murrihy in
Une éducation manquée, 2009

Wayne Tigges, David Trudgen, Bradley Smoak, Leslie Davis, Kiera Duffy, Abigail Nims, Owen Gilhooly, Michael Kepler Meo, Frank Kelley in *The Golden Ticket*, 2010

rewarding tenure as chair, combining his business acumen and genuine love of the Festival to best effect. Following the death of Jerome Hynes, Hennessy was the driving force behind the vision for the Opera House. He worked diligently to see that vision become a reality, and brought many others along with him on that journey towards a truly outstanding outcome.

The Ghosts of Versailles by John Corigliano, a co-production with Opera Theatre of St Louis, US, was one of the operas presented in 2009. The composer travelled to Wexford for the production and reported that he had a wonderful time there. Agler had encouraged the Board to cultivate a genuine relationship with the company in St Louis as he felt that there was much to learn from its Board, volunteers and staff there. The reviews were excellent for this co-production at Wexford, 'Even those who did not like the opera, didn't think it was an opera, don't approve of American works (or opera in English) in Wexford admitted that work was splendidly produced', remarked Agler to the Board after the Festival had ended.⁹ The technical requirements of the production were very difficult and Agler was pleased that Wexford had managed to pull it off successfully and with precision. Describing a feeling of 'quiet pride', Agler praised the performances of Owen Gilhooly and Paula Murrihy, along with five Irish dancers who were an integral part of the cast. He reminded the Board however that Wexford could simply not afford to put on a production of this magnitude if all the costs had to be borne by Wexford alone.

The second opera, Donizetti's *Maria Padilla*, was also extremely well received, and was, as Agler described, 'a "real" Wexford opera – an excellent, unjustly neglected work'. Barbara Quintiliani, the American soprano, was singled out for praise and she received a rapturous applause, coupled with the customary banging on the old Theatre Royal floorboards, following her last aria. The first of the double bill operas, *Une éducation manquée* by Chabrier, drew less attention than *La cambiale di matrimonio* by Rossini, which did not receive the positive acclaim from critics that was hoped for. Agler was an advocate of the pre-performance talks that had proved popular in Wexford and he was keen to ensure that they remained part of the offering this year. Roberto Recchia gave the talks for the double bill, which he directed, and for *Maria Padilla*. Michael Shell, who played the part of Wilhelm and was assistant director of *The Ghosts of Versailles*, gave the pre-performance talk about this opera. The European Broadcasting Union (EBU) began broadcasting from Wexford this year, allowing the performances to be heard throughout the EU as well as in Australia and Canada.

Despite positive reviews following another successful season, Agler voiced some general disappointment with the standard of operas this year, citing compromises that had to be made over late changes to operas and the physical productions. He referred to a conversation with the journalist Andrew Clark from the *Financial Times* after the Festival, where Clark commented that 'much was forgiven of Wexford when it had to deal with the difficulties of the Theatre Royal. Those days are over'.[10] The spectacular new Opera House had served not only to open up possibilities for productions not possible in the past, but it also increased the expectations of the press and visitors alike. It was incumbent on Wexford to reach these standards. Notwithstanding this, an unusually high number of theatre directors visited Wexford during the 2009 season. One director reported being particularly impressed by the professionalism shown by the voluntary staff and indicated that it would simply not be possible to get the same high standard of volunteerism in Italy. Agler also signalled to the Board that some of the visitors that had attended this year had voiced their disapproval about the concept of an Irish National Opera Company that might include Wexford. This unresolved matter continued to be a worry for Wexford.

At last, the clarity that Wexford Festival Opera had been waiting for arrived, with an announcement by Minister Martin Cullen, just days before he resigned from political life. Irish National Opera (INO) was to be established from a merger of Opera Ireland (OI) and Opera Theatre Company (OTC), both of which were heavily reliant on state funding. Wexford Festival Opera, its Board, staff and patrons, were in equal measure delighted that this National Opera Company had not forced a merger of the three opera companies, dragging Wexford Festival Opera into the mix. There was still a level of scepticism nationally as to why the merger was required, with those in some quarters suspicious that it was no more than a cost-saving measure. While Opera Ireland had presented 'grand opera' during bi-annual seasons at the Gaiety Theatre in Dublin, Opera Theatre Company was a national touring company, focusing on works outside of the well-known repertoire. The aims and objectives of both were separate up to this point, as were their audience bases. Only time would tell how and if the merger would benefit opera in Ireland and whether the funding would stabilize and even increase over time.[11]

Of course, Wexford's new iconic building continued to dominate discussions of patrons and visitors:

> It is my determined conviction that the future of the Festival has absolutely nothing to do with the new theatre. It has everything to do with renewing the ingredients, which brought it such national and international renown,

declared Agler, hitting on a theme that was to continue to plague Wexford Festival Opera over the coming years.[12]

But it **was** all about the building, not least because the €7 million had not yet been raised in full and there was no clear picture as to how Wexford Festival Board could pay off its debt while keeping the Festival afloat at the height of a recession. The national picture looked bleak for the arts, with the Minister for Arts, Sport and Tourism, Mary Hanafin, admitting in April that she was 'not confident at all' about retaining the current levels of funding for the arts. 'We have to take €2 billion out of the economy in current expenditure next year so it's going to have to come from somewhere', she explained. 'It's a question now of trying to balance it out as far as possible and making sure no one area suffers', Hanafin admitted. It was an important endorsement of the Festival when Hanafin went on to say that she believed that Wexford Festival Opera and its new Opera House was 'worth every penny' invested by the government.[13]

A number of fundraising initiatives were rolled out in 2010, in an attempt to keep focus on the task of staying afloat. The work of the Wexford Festival Foundation was coming to a natural end and it was seen as important to develop new initiatives to capture people's attention in different ways. A President's Circle campaign was launched, along with the idea of a Legacy Society, with the respective goals of raising funds for current initiatives and securing the future of the Festival.[14] Through local press releases, the public was made aware that Wexford Opera House did not receive any state support for ongoing operating costs or overheads. Apart from a modest local authority grant, the venue relied on box office income alone to sustain its business.

Meanwhile, the Wexford Opera House continued to pick up many awards. It won the 2010 Civic Trust Award and the 2010 LAMA Award. In the same year, it picked up an international architecture award for Excellence in Design from the American Institute of Architects. This represented the seventh architectural award made to the venue since its opening in 2008 and was one of only six given out by the American Institute of Architects in 2010. The Institute

Kiera Duffy, Wayne Tigges, Abigail Nims,
David Trudgen, Bradley Smoak, Miriam Murphy,
Noah Stewart, Michael Kepler Meo, Frank Kelley,
Leslie Davis in *The Golden Ticket*, 2010

was highly complementary about the skill in which such a large building was tastefully woven into the fabric of the town, noting that

> its large scale has been successfully orchestrated through careful arrangement of its forms, resulting in a rich townscape composition alongside Wexford's two Puginian church spires.[15]

Along with the building awards, Agler and the Board were particularly pleased to receive the 'Best Opera' award at the Irish Theatre Awards in March of this year for Agler's 2009 production of *The Ghosts of Versailles*.

In May 2009, former chairman of Wexford Festival Board, John O'Connor, died at the age of fifty-seven. He had served on the Board for fifteen years and was chairman from 1992 to 1997. It was widely accepted by all of his colleagues that he had made an immense contribution to Wexford Festival Opera during the time he was involved. He was known for his ability to analyse and simplify complex issues and was instrumental in pushing for the acquisition of the adjoining properties, which ultimately enabled the building of the new Opera House.[16]

The operas chosen for 2010 were *Virginia* by Mercadante, *Hubička* by Smetana and the European premiere of *The Golden Ticket* by composer Peter Ash with a libretto by Donald Sturrock. Ash and Sturrock were in Wexford for the première, along with Felicity Dahl, widow of Roald Dahl, which added to the excitement of the event. *Virginia* was broadcast live to 24 countries around the world, and it was reported that about 1 million people tuned in to hear the opera. Six students from the local girls secondary school took part in the production. It was to be the second time that *Hubička* was performed at Wexford, having been first heard on the Theatre Royal stage in 1984, sung in English. This year, it would be performed in Czech, with the Czech Chorus. However, Agler defended his decision to stage the opera once again at Wexford, stating that the opera was still relatively unknown and that he had consulted with the former artistic directors at Wexford and they concurred with his interpretation of the policy.[17] It was also a co-production with Opera Theatre of Saint Louis, US. It was a conscious decision to pursue co-productions at this point in an attempt to survive the recession. It was the first time that all former living artistic directors were present at the Festival together. It was Brian Dickie's first time to visit the Festival in quite some time, and Agler was

Ivan Magri, Angela Meade, Hugh Russell and Festival Chorus in *Virginia*, 2010

particularly delighted that he chose to return. 'As you know Wexford has a crucial importance to me', Dickie wrote to Agler following his return home:

> It was the first thing I did on my own and was a fantastic opportunity. I learned a huge amount and made lifelong friends. So to feel the warmth of the welcome and to be there and be reminded of my good fortune to have it as part of my life – a big thank you to you. Wexford is a miracle …[18]

A number of Irish singers joined the cast this year, including Owen Gilhooly (as Lord Salt in *The Golden Ticket*), Gavin Ring, who sang in the chorus and performed Marcello in *La bohème*, Miriam Murphy, who sang the parts of Mrs Gloop and Grandma Georgina, and Marcella Walsh who sang the part of Tullia in *Virginia*. Frank Kelley, who had performed at Wexford many years previously, sang the part of Grandpa Joe in *The Golden Ticket*. The Festival had hoped to engage with a larger international audience this year and *The Golden Ticket* was certainly an attempt to extend the reach of the Festival beyond its usual boundaries.

Wexford Festival Opera also took the brave decision to extend its schedule this year to 15 days, from 16 to 30 October. It was delighted to report that sales of tickets had surpassed the sales of 2009. Breaking with tradition, the Festival opened on a Saturday and was officially opened by the Minister for Tourism, Culture and Sport,[19] Mary Hanafin. Following in his father Seán's footsteps, Peter Scallan became chairman of the Festival in 2010. His father had held the position from 1971 to 1976. Having spent many years as an executive and non-executive director with Celtic Linen, Scallan formed his own company in 2008. His involvement with Wexford Festival Opera however, both as a volunteer and a trustee, stretched back to 1993.

In 2011, Colm Tóibín reflected:

> If you did a proper sociological study of the committees that have run the Wexford Opera Festival and the volunteers who work for it, you would find a cross-section of the town who believe in good music, in serious singing, in putting on the best show possible, and who are ready to work for that … Just as the old Theatre Royal was an unlikely jewel in the narrow street of a port town, so too the new opera house, whose creation took dedicated work and serious planning, with its modest façade and its perfect acoustics, is a monument to a civic spirit, a sort of modest sophistication, which is a fundamental part of Wexford …[20]

The year 2011 was the 60th anniversary of the Wexford Festival and the 100th anniversary of the birth of Dr Tom Walsh. It had been an incredible journey throughout those 60 years. The year got off to a very good start with the announcement that Mercadante's *Virginia* – the 2010 production – won the award for 'Best Opera' at the Irish Times Theatre Awards.

There was much talk in 2011 about the fact that the government and the

Arts Council were perceived to have failed opera in Ireland, marked by the lack of progress in the establishing of Irish National Opera. Although the proposed merger of Opera Ireland and Opera Theatre Company had been announced in late 2010, the new Minister for the Tourism, Culture and Sport, Jimmy Deenihan, decided to drop the plan for a merger altogether. It became clear that the Minister's decision was arrived at following a report that was commissioned to cost the set-up of the new entity. Although relieved that it would continue as a stand-alone entity, Wexford had more than a passing interest in the outcome of the deliberations. A firm of international consultants, Proscenium, a Viennese company headed by former opera singer Rudolf Berger, concluded that the project would need to be funded to the amount of €12 million for the first three years, and €4.5 million per year after that. It reported emphatically that the project needed to be funded properly in order to give it any chance of success, or not at all. If the commitment to the medium- and long-term vision could not be made, it would be better to leave in place what already existed – Opera Ireland and Opera Theatre Company.[21] This was enough for the government to draw a line under the protracted saga and it decided not to proceed.

But it wasn't as simple as agreeing to reinstate the status quo. The former Minister, Martin Cullen, had already invited Ray Bates, former head of the National Lottery, to chair an interim board of the proposed Irish National Opera in March 2010. Opera Ireland, which was carrying significant debt at this point, had agreed to wind down its operations to make way for the new entity. It would have to come to an arrangement with the government regarding its outstanding debt if it was to have any chance of re-emerging as a functioning opera company; however, the government was adamant that it was not responsible for any outstanding debt. Opera Ireland had disbanded, its staff and management were laid off, in what the *Sunday Business Post* described as 'Opera Ireland's final tragic act'.[22] The new Convention Centre in Dublin had been waiting with interest on the announcement of a potential Irish National Opera company too, as it had been recommended in the consultant report as a potential permanent home for the proposed company. Although not a publicly owned building, the government had secured a long-term contract for the Convention Centre from Treasury Holdings.

On the other hand, Opera Theatre Company was not so badly impacted by the news that the project was abandoned. It was still in a position to see out its season, up until the following March. Virginia Kerr, who had represented the

Jack Power and Stephanie Kinsella in *A Village Romeo and Juliet*, 2012

company on the interim Irish National Opera Board, said that the Board was highly frustrated with how things had turned out, but that they could not find a way forward with the proposal. 'We just faced an insurmountable wall: it was as simple as that', she said.[23]

And so, after much planning and a tense wait, it was clear that the planned strategy of the government taking over responsibility for opera in Ireland had not paid off. It had failed to find a solution and the responsibility was passed back to the Arts Council. Pat Moylan, chairman of the Arts Council, said it would prepare an assessment for the government of the issues around the

John Bellemer and Jessica Muirhead in *A Village Romeo and Juliet*, 2012

financing of opera up to 2013. 'Opera has been an area of concern for the Council for many years and we intend to consider a broad range of perspectives in developing a comprehensive assessment', she said.[24]

Although Wexford was not caught up in the drama of the national opera discussions, it had more than its own share of issues to deal with locally. The Wexford Festival Board revealed that the Wexford Opera House, as a standalone entity from the Festival, had been losing money since it opened in September 2008. This meant that the Opera House was forced to put a plan in place to charge rental rates to community and arts groups for hiring the building, with a view to saving about €225,000 per year. The Opera House itself was not receiving any funding from the Arts Council so it was important to build up the business of hiring out the venue as much as possible across the entire year.[25]

Meanwhile, Wexford Festival Opera received its grant of €1.73 million from the Arts Council, this time for fifteen months of activity, as opposed to the usual annual grant.[26]

Agler had long hoped for a chance to develop a chorus for Wexford, and the opportunity presented itself in 2011 to make this happen. The Prague Chamber Choir, a professional choir that was cast and managed independently of the Festival, had performed at the Festival since 1995.[27] Although the standard of this chorus had been exceptionally high starting out, it was becoming increasingly difficult to encourage the very best singers to come to Wexford for the fee offered. Many had stopped coming altogether and this had started to impact on the overall quality of the chorus. It came down to a decision to either find additional funds to pay the chorus, or to look for an alternative solution. Agler sought the help of Elenor Bowers-Jolley in London to assemble a chorus. Bowers-Jolley gathered an impressive array of singers from across the world – thirty-six in total – including Irish, English, Canadian and Australian singers. It was a truly international chorus, with Irish singers making up about one quarter of the total number. Bowers-Jolley became the chorus manager of the Wexford Festival Chorus and Gavin Carr, who had worked with Wexford Festival Opera for a number of years, became the chorus master. The members of the chorus also sang small roles in the operas and took part in the Opera Scenes. The establishment of the new 'English (speaking) choir', as it was known locally, was heralded as a positive departure for Wexford.

The Festival ran for sixteen days and was officially opened by Taoiseach Enda Kenny from the quay front. The mainstage productions were *La cour de Célimène* by Thomas, *Maria* by Statkowski and *Gianni di Parigi* by Donizetti. *Maria* was a co-production with Kraków Opera, Poland. Claudia Boyle sang in the title role of *La cour de Célimène* and was a popular choice with patrons. A special ceremony was organized to honour Dr Tom Walsh and a plaque in honour of the Festival's founder was unveiled by patron of the Festival and President of Ireland, Mary McAleese, in what was to be one of her last public engagements before her time as President came to an end.

To coincide with 'European Year of the Volunteer' and Wexford Festival's 60th anniversary, Wexford decided to launch its own Volunteer Award programme. It was sponsored in its first year by Zurich Insurance Group, the global insurance company that had a large operation in Wexford town. Zurich had entered into a three-year production sponsorship deal with the Festival and the sponsorship of the volunteer programme was a welcome addition. The Volunteer programme in Wexford was the envy of many arts organizations, and it was no exaggeration to say that the Festival would not have been able to continue for sixty years without the support of so many dedicated volunteers. It was agreed that the award would be made on an annual basis to a volunteer who displayed outstanding leadership and enhanced the development, patron service and longevity of Wexford Festival Opera.[28] As one reporter who had attended the awards ceremony noted:

> I had no idea how embedded in the culture of the Festival they were until I went there. There was no discernible distinction between professional staff and voluntary staff – they were all informed, enthusiastic and possessed a rare sense of pride in and belonging to the Festival. This is real, long-term community development and who would have thought that Opera could help to achieve this – not its traditional moniker. Perhaps it just goes to show that the arts are inherently open activities – that work best when people from across our communities participate in them, nurture them and make them a part of their everyday life.[29]

Right from the beginning, with Walsh's impossible dream, the tireless work of local people had been key to the success of Wexford Festival Opera. Nicky Cleary, who died in this year, was one such person. He had worked assiduously for fifty-eight years, across many functions, to support the Festival. He served as a Festival volunteer, as well as a Council member, trustee, and as the Theatre Royal Stage Director and was instrumental in training and mentoring generations of stagehands and technicians. He was a quintessential volunteer and had made a significant contribution to the Festival over a long period of time.[30]

Again, Wexford showed signs of remarkable resilience in battling its way through the recession. Responding to how Wexford was surviving despite the economic crisis that still loomed large, Agler commented: 'Our budget has always been small. We are of necessity crisis-trained masters of adaptability'.[31]

The decision to revert to a twelve-day Festival in 2012 was taken before the 2011 Festival had concluded and was taken as a direct consequence of the difficult economic situation. It was not a popular decision locally, as businesses in the town felt that they should have been consulted before the final decision was made. Furthermore, they felt that an analysis should have been carried out on the 2011 season to gauge the success of the fifteen-day Festival, before agreeing to cut it to twelve days. Peter Scallan, chairman, explained that although Wexford Festival Board had made significant strides in addressing its debt, there was still a way to go. He also noted that on days during the Festival when there was no opera, it was still costing approximately €30,000 a day, meaning that they had spent almost €100,000 in 2011 on 'dark' nights alone. This was simply not sustainable.[32]

Scallan concluded his three-year term as chair and made way for Ger Lawlor. Lawlor had been involved with the Festival for many years and was appointed to the Wexford Festival Council in 1984. He was a professional photographer, as well as organist and choirmaster at Wexford's Church of the Assumption. Passionate about music and opera, Lawlor received his mentoring in opera from Dr Tom Walsh and Seamus O'Dwyer (from the original Wexford Opera Study Circle) and held a number of voluntary artistic and administrative roles with the Festival over many years, including as chairman of the Artistic Advisory Committee and as a member of the working group that liaised with the design team of Wexford Opera House.

Fundraising was still the main topic of discussion at all of the Board meetings, and all those involved realized that more needed to be done to extend the opportunities for bringing in money. Wexford still had its loyal supporters, and these included Patricia Mellon, who had attended the Festival with her husband, John, for many years. Patricia made a monthly pledge towards the sustainability of the Festival, a commitment that she has carried on since. One decisive action that was taken was the establishment of a National Development Council. Its role was to provide a focus for development funding for the Festival and to take a leadership role in encouraging others to support the Festival financially. Terry Neill accepted the position of chairman of the Development Council. A graduate of Trinity College Dublin, Neill held an MBA from London Business School, where he was also a governor for thirteen years. In his thirty-year career with Accenture/Andersen Consulting he was based in Dublin, Chicago and London. He was chairman of Andersen Worldwide and Accenture, and was a director of Bank of Ireland Group and CRH plc and UBM plc. Neill, along with his wife Marjorie, had attended opera in Wexford for many years and would become significant donors of Wexford Festival Opera.[33]

There was also a renewed focus on the overseas market. The American Friends of Wexford Opera initiative was launched in September 2012, as Wexford believed it also needed to concentrate its efforts in the United States. The launch was hosted by Loretta Brennan Glucksman, chair of the American Ireland Fund, who invited over 60 guests to her home in New York, where she outlined to them the unique success of Wexford Festival Opera as a festival of international significance. The initiative was intended to strengthen the Festival's media profile and its donor and audience base in North America. The event featured an intimate recital by Wexford company member Luigi Boccia, an Italian-American tenor, and was attended by prominent individuals from New York, who, it was hoped, might venture to Wexford to explore it for themselves.[34]

Behind the scenes, Wexford was working hard to put together proposals to bring opera outside of Wexford. It was a goal of the Board to identify and test possibilities, and they were committed to seeking out options in this regard. But its inability to make any inroads outside of Wexford came back to one thing – there was simply too much to do to ensure that the Wexford Festival was the best it could be, with a small number of dedicated people working towards this goal on an annual basis. This continued to be a source of frustration for the Board, the chief executive and the artistic director; however, they were all agreed that it was on the quality of the annual Wexford Festival that their success or failure would be ultimately judged. Wexford Festival Opera watched with interest then as Wide Open Opera was formed in 2012 by Fergus Sheil and Gavin O'Sullivan, receiving what was a record first-time grant from the Arts Council of just over €600,000 in 2012.

Back in Wexford, Agler was busy trying to piece together the Festival for 2012. In a report to the Board early that year, he outlined the very real possibility that White's Hotel might not be available as a venue for the ShortWorks for this year's Festival. This news generated mixed feelings. The Festival had relied on White's Hotel as a venue since its inception. However, some believed White's to be wholly unsuitable for ShortWorks and favoured exploring other options. Other venue options in the town were limited however to the Dun Mhuire Hall, which had not proven popular with the Festival's patrons for ShortWorks, and the Jerome Hynes Theatre, limited in terms of space. Agler suggested that the executive would explore the possibility of hiring a temporary structure

– he suggested a Spiegeltent – which were beginning to become popular as venues around the world. This option, he deduced, could be used as a late-night performance venue and could also be used for post-performance gatherings, akin to a 'Festival Club'.[35] A document was prepared to outline the rationale for renting a temporary structure and a comparison of costs was drawn up between the proposed Spiegeltent and the Jerome Hynes Theatre. By a very small margin, it was deemed that the Jerome Hynes Theatre would suffice for the type of events proposed for the 2012 Festival.[36] Interestingly, the Spiegeltent did come to Wexford this year, although not at the behest of Wexford Festival Opera, but as a private venture operating within the Fringe Festival.

The 2012 Festival took place over twelve days straight through, beginning on Wednesday 24 October. The operas performed were *L'arlesiana* by Francesco Cilea, *Le roi malgré lui* by Chabrier and *A Village Romeo and Juliet* by Frederick Delius. A generous donation was received from Freddie and Michael Linnett towards production costs this year, which helped significantly in what was a difficult financial year. Elavon also came on board as production sponsors in this year. *Le roi malgré lui* was a co-production with Bard Festival, New York. Agler was forced to change his plans this year due to being unable to obtain a manuscript for *Francesca da Rimini*, a Saverio Mercadante opera that he had planned to produce. The opera, originally written in 1831, was never performed in the opera house for which it was written, which burned to the ground before the opera was produced. A handwritten manuscript of the opera did exist but had never been printed. Agler tried but failed to get a copy printed in time, hence the rare opera had to be shelved and *L'arlesiana* was produced in its place.[37] The production of *L'arlesiana* was subsequently sold to Jesi, Italy. The production of *A Village Romeo and Juliet* marked the 150th anniversary of the birth of the British composer Delius, and offered an opportunity to two Wexford teenagers to make their debut on the Wexford stage as the childhood versions of the main characters.[38] Agler had purposely sought out local young people to participate in the production, carrying out open auditions that involved singing and acting. 'The roles for this opera are very demanding for such a young age but having heard many young singers in local choirs, I felt that we should at least begin our search here', Agler said. 'We discovered that we could have cast the roles three times over, such was the quality of the talent', he added.

The ensuing reviews were positive. Agler had worked hard to guarantee high quality productions, and the new Opera House had certainly added to the opportunities for really special performances. Agler and the Festival Board remained very sensitive to the positioning of the Opera Festival in its local community and the desire for a quality all-round Festival experience and atmosphere for its patrons. It seemed that efforts in this regard were paying off. 'And then there's the Festival's secret weapon – its people', David Mellor reported, as the 2012 Festival came to a close.

> They really want you to have a good time and nothing is too much trouble. If there's a more warm-hearted, less stuffy place to enjoy opera, I have yet to find it,[39]

The lack of Irish singers in the cast continued to be a source of criticism in media circles. 'Agler's achievement represents a particularly dogged commitment', commented journalist Michael Dervan:

> The first 55 years of the Festival saw seven operas in English, three by Irishmen, three by Englishmen, one by an American. The last eight years, with Agler in charge, have brought five operas in English, four of them by Americans, and, in the piano-accompanied productions that the Festival bills as ShortWorks, a further six, all but one by Americans. If only Agler had the same grá [love] for Irish singers that he does for English-language opera – Irish voices are once again notable in this year's Festival by their absence.[40]

Wexford had defended its position many times before, and David McLoughlin, chief executive, defended the company once more in a letter to the Arts Council on the matter.

> Throughout David Agler's current tenure as Wexford's artistic director, several established Irish singers have been invited to sing with us … They declined for much the same reason singers do everywhere – they are engaged, don't want to take the time to learn a role they will probably never sing again (as is the case with the rare Wexford operas), or the fee is not adequate (an ongoing Wexford issue). The claim that Wexford is not interested in Irish singers is untrue …[41]

CHAPTER 13

THE PURPOSE OF OPERA IS TO CHANGE THE WORLD

2013–16

Wexford Festival Opera succeeded in its bid to host the Opera Europa Conference in Wexford in 2013. This was a significant coup and ensured that an impressive line-up of opera personnel made their way to Wexford this year. It was the first time that the Conference was held in Ireland and the team at Wexford understood the importance of showcasing Wexford Opera House and the Festival experience to those that visited the town for the event.[1] Colm Tóibín was invited to give a speech at the closing of the Conference that was held during the Festival of 2013, and his words resonated with many who had given so much of their time, their expertise and their support to ensuring that Wexford Festival Opera would live on.

'It seems to me that the purpose of opera is to change the world', Tóibín declared to a captive audience who had travelled from all over Europe to Wexford for the occasion.

In 1971, when I was sixteen, the only live music I had heard was in a church ... I was a boarder in St Peter's College in Wexford. It was agreed in that autumn that anyone who came to the music room four afternoons in a row and listened to recordings of opera could attend the dress rehearsal of *The Pearl Fishers* which was being performed at the Wexford Festival Opera. The tickets were very cheap. I went there, just so I could get out of the confines of the school for a night, but slowly in that week, the music took me over, the idea of aria, duet, motif and pattern began to fascinate me. It was something I had never thought about before.

The performance itself came as an enormous and liberating shock, it introduced me to the idea of soaring beauty. The intimacy of the space, the fact that the Theatre Royal was filled with opera lovers from Wexford town itself who had bought cheap seats for the dress rehearsals, or friends of the volunteers who got tickets for this each year as a special gift in the same way as sports lovers might get tickets for a final, all this made a difference. I have a vivid memory of the awed silence in the audience, and then of the women's chorus, of the yellow lighting, and then of astonishing voices of the soloists, and then the story itself in all its drama, hitting the enclosed places within the nervous system of us all with its exquisite patterns of sound.

I remember back in school that night being excited and unsettled by the idea that there was a world beyond my world, a world where people would travel distances to have a close brush with beauty ...

Thus began my adventures in opera. It simply entered my spirit and it lingered there and it became powerful. It offered me a relationship to soaring beauty, to the idea that there was a world beyond the visible world, or the material world, or the everyday world, which was filled with mystery. It offered a drama of human striving at its most developed and serious, it suggested mystery, as human relations are filled with mystery, as light is filled with mystery, as sound is filled with mystery. It paved the way for a life lived more sonorously, a life open to possibility and otherness and strangeness.

What I am saying is that it taught me how to live.

Maybe that is why we work in the way we do, why we raise money and put opera programmes together, why we go out and find sponsors,

Lucia Cirillo, Helena Dix and chorus in *Cristina, regina di Svezia*, 2013

why we train singers and musicians and front-of-house staff so that we can, in ways which are hard to pin down but all the more powerful for that, teach others and indeed ourselves, how to live, how to pay attention to the world in all its fleeting beauty'.[2]

Tóibín had managed to articulate beautifully what Wexford Festival's stalwarts had known intrinsically – that for all those who had become part of it, the impact of opera at Wexford was incredibly powerful.

Sadly, one of the real characters of Wexford Festival Opera died this year with the passing of Jim Golden, following a short illness. Golden epitomized what it was to be a selfless volunteer, who gave all of his expertise and time to a cause in which he believed passionately. He was a much-loved character of the Festival, his gruff manner and his intense loyalty seemingly endearing him all the more to his friends at Wexford Festival Opera. It was of great pride to him that he had been selected to take on the role of chairman of the Board and he was particularly aware of the need for the chairman to build solid relationships with the artistic directors, who were ultimately the figureheads of the organization. As Brian Dickie articulated upon hearing of Golden's death:

> Oh dear Jim – they said I should not make you a saint. But you are – the most selfless dedicated 'volunteer' I have encountered in my long career in our beloved opera business. From those early days in the 1960s when you put in sub-human hours in charge of the Box Office, right through your 'career' with the Festival as you rose meteorically to the top job, you set an example of leadership. Your love and humour affected all whom you touched. You were a shining light in what must have taken in many dark and difficult moments. God bless you St Jim – RIP in the sure knowledge that you made a difference.[3]

Agler had become a particularly close friend to Golden and often turned to him for advice on how to navigate some of the political situations that would present themselves at Wexford. Elaine Padmore before him, had maintained her friendship with Golden too and they were in contact regularly. Agler had a particular empathy for what had gone before him, and what would come after. Reflecting on what he had achieved with and for Wexford, it was fair to say that Agler had transformed many elements of the Festival, quietly and without circus. This would be Agler's ninth season at Wexford, and in that time, he had been part of the opening of the new Opera House, he was instrumental in the formation of the Festival's own orchestra and chorus and he had transformed the Opera Scenes into 'mini opera' format, along with giving further weight to the importance of the orchestral concerts and recitals as part of the overall offering. He always gave careful consideration to the Dr Tom Walsh lecture, believing that the link with the past was integral to what Wexford was about and he was keen to hear the stories of Wexford Festival Opera throughout its history. He managed to build strong relationships with former artistic directors. Agler used Elaine Padmore and Brian Dickie, in particular, as sounding boards for some of his ideas for Wexford and they were more than happy to oblige. As

Padmore commented to Agler at the beginning of his tenure;

> If there's anything at all I can do to help you, or if you want to sound me out on anything, just ask. I still have Wexford engraved on my heart! Above all, enjoy it![4]

In September of 2013, the inaugural American Friends of Wexford Festival Opera New York Gala Dinner took place at the Mandarin Oriental overlooking Central Park. This was an important event in building and enhancing a profile for Wexford Festival Opera in the United States, and was an attempt to expand the Festival's donor base to enable Wexford to continue its mission. The honoree at the gala was Dr T. Pearse Lyons, an Irish biochemist and President and founder of Alltech, who received the Wexford Opera Patron of the Arts Award from Loretta Brennan Glucksman.[5] The award marked his significant contribution to and support of the performing arts, particularly through the development of emerging operatic talent, demonstrated through the Alltech Vocal Scholarship Program at the University of Kentucky Opera Theatre. Angela Meade, Wexford alumna, was the special guest performer on the night, along with several young singers from the University of Kentucky Opera Theatre. Meade had made her European debut at Wexford in 2010 in *Virginia*.

Errol Girdlestone, the British conductor and composer, took over the role of chorus master at Wexford.[6] Agler chose a double bill as part of the 2013 season – *Thérèse* by Massenet and *La Navarraise*, also by Massenet. Rota's *Il cappello di paglia di Firenze* was also chosen. But the stand-out production of this season was *Cristina, regina di Svezia* by Jacopo Foroni, which went on to win Best Re-discovered Work at the International Opera Awards. The young Australian soprano, Helena Dix, was nominated in the Best Young Singer category, for her title role in the same opera.

During the Festival, Wexford announced a new partnership with the Lir Theatre in Dublin, the National Academy of Dramatic Art at Trinity College Dublin and with the Institute of Art, Design and Technology (IADT) in Dun Laoghaire, Dublin. This would result in opportunities for interns to work at Wexford and gain valuable mentoring experiences and an introduction to work in a purpose-built professional opera house.[7] Ecclesiastical Insurance and Financial Services took over as sponsors of the Volunteer of the Year award this year and also signed up to become production sponsors of the Festival. There

Na'ama Goldman as Salomé
and Emma Watkinson as
Hérodias's page in *Salomé*, 2014

was more good news for Wexford Festival Opera in 2013 with the announcement that there would be a small increase to its Arts Council grant. This rounded off seven consecutive years of funding by the Arts Council without any cut in funding, which the Arts Council affirmed was a testament to its commitment to support Wexford Festival Opera.[8]

Agler was very clear about the fact that Wexford could never be what some wanted it to be – a National Opera company, satisfying the needs of all. 'The Opera House is the reward for Wexford' he said,

> which for six decades stubbornly and prudently persisted in creating something unique. It draws people from all over the world. With the demise of Opera Ireland, the Festival is really the only true operatic establishment in the country, but it cannot become the national company. I sense the frustration of the Irish audiences who really love opera and come to Wexford to hear rarities, yet have no opportunity of hearing a *Don Carlos* or whatever at home. It's not good for Wexford that there is no major company in Dublin. We are under pressure to take up the aspirations and political needs of everyone – but Wexford cannot do that.[9]

There was change afoot in Dublin, however. Rosemary Collier was announced as the new chief executive of Opera Theatre Company and Fergus Sheil, founder and artistic director of Wide Open Opera, took on the role of artistic director of the same company.[10]

Agler was proud of the fact that he had managed to create stability for the orchestra and chorus at Wexford, while addressing the age-old criticism that there were not enough Irish musicians engaged during the Festival. By 2013, nearly 90 per cent of the orchestral players were coming from the Irish freelance community. Joe Csibi took over as the Orchestra Manager and Fionnuala Hunt, the accomplished violinist, remained a popular choice as leader of the orchestra. Yet Agler never felt that Wexford got the credit it deserved for its achievements in this regard. 'Behind the scenes, it's never been more Irish', he argued,

> and it's the right thing to do. But we have to balance it with the ambition – going right back to Tom Walsh – for an international festival, where people come to hear international singers.[11]

Alexander Sprague, Chad Johnson, Quentin Hayes, Matthew Worth, Ian Beadle and Festival Chorus in *Silent Night*, 2014

Agler was certainly making his mark in Wexford. Although he was quick to point out that it was not the job that he had signed up for, he described it as 'the greatest job I've ever had'. With the death of Jerome Hynes, an organic restructuring meant that from the outset, Agler had to take on a more administrative role to ensure that certain elements were completed to standard and on time. He had less time to dedicate to conducting, but he accepted that it was for the greater good:

> I've done so much fantastic music with so many wonderful people, and I like what I'm doing now…I like putting young people together,

and I love the mentoring process because I was so well mentored myself. I have a sort of spiritual view of what being an artistic director here entails. Wexford has a clear mission and a good bit of magic ...[12]

There was another significant change to the leadership at Wexford Festival Opera in 2014. Sir Anthony O'Reilly, who had been President of the Festival since 1993, stepped aside to make way for Sir David Davies, a banker and international businessman who had been attending the Festival for many years. Davies was awarded the Knights Bachelor in the 1999 New Year's Honours list in Britain for his contribution as chairman of the Advisory Committee on Business and the Environment. Davies had also acted as a director and trustee of a number of arts organizations, notably Glyndebourne Festival Opera, Royal Opera House Trust, Grange Park Opera, the Irish Heritage Trust and chairman of Wexford Festival Trust (UK). His home in Ireland was in Abbeyleix, Co. Laois, which he had spent many years carefully restoring to become one of the finest stately homes in the country.[13]

Wexford Festival Opera was indebted to O'Reilly, its outgoing President, for many things, not least his contribution to ensuring that the Opera House was more than just a pipe dream. His significant contribution was not only a financial one, but his powers of persuasion and his credibility as a businessman ensured that Wexford Festival Opera was able to get a seat at the table with the Taoiseach for the all-important conversation about government support for the Opera House venture in Wexford. Without his hands-on support, it was widely accepted that the project would have struggled to gain traction.

Given Agler's sensitivity to the criticism about lack of opportunities for Irish artists at Wexford, he was keen to explore any possibility that might demonstrate Wexford's contribution to the musical landscape in Ireland, without undermining the mission of Wexford Festival Opera itself. In 2014, he had a series of meetings with the organizers of the Veronica Dunne Singing Competition to explore any potential opportunities for collaboration. The competition had been established in 1995 by the well-known Dr Veronica Dunne and occurred every three years. It was sponsored by the Friends of the Vocal Arts, a not-for-profit charitable organization, and its mission was to find and foster vocal talent and help to build international careers. The Committee was chaired by Diarmuid Hegarty, President of Griffith College, Dublin, and Veronica Dunne herself was its artistic director. The competition had become a member of the Federation of World Competitions. As it happened, members of the Committee were very interested in discussing a potential collaboration with Wexford. Strategically, it seemed to make sense from Wexford's perspective as it was an opportunity to enhance its reputation in nurturing Irish talent. Agler had originally hoped to begin his own vocal competition in Wexford and believed that Wexford Festival Opera would be the obvious home for any such competition. However, he didn't think that it would make sense to compete with the already established Veronica Dunne competition which had built up an impressive reputation. He hoped that any association with this competition would open up new audiences, from Dublin in the main, for Wexford Festival Opera and would demonstrate Wexford's commitment to the Irish music scene and in particular Irish singers.

In the lead up to this year's Festival, the American Friends of Wexford Opera hosted the New York gala dinner at the Pierre Hotel in New York. The American Ireland Fund, which had supported Wexford Festival Opera for many years, joined in hosting the event. Guests were welcomed by Loretta Brennan Glucksman, Honorary Patron of American Friends of Wexford Opera and chairman emeritus of the American Ireland Fund, along with Shane Naughton, Board Director of the American Ireland Fund. Those invited enjoyed a performance by Wexford Opera Alumnus Award recipient Bryan Hymel, who had made his European debut at Wexford in *Rusalka* in 2007. He was the leading tenor the following year in *Snegurochka*, the opera which opened the new Opera House in 2008. Hymel was joined in New York by the French-Canadian soprano Marie-Ève Munger. Brennan Glucksman made a presentation to newly appointed Consul General of Ireland Barbara Jones, who attended the evening as guest of honour, marking her first official engagement in her new post. Originally from Enniscorthy, Wexford, she spoke of how proud she was of her native county which was now forging a 'new bridge of voices' with America.

The three operas chosen for the 2014 season were Mariotte's *Salomé, Don Bucefalo* by Cagnoni and Pulitzer prize-winning American opera *Silent Night* by composer Kevin Puts. Proceeds from the American Friends of Wexford Opera gala dinner directly benefitted this production.

Silent Night proved to be a bigger success than anticipated, although the British press was not as enthusiastic as the audiences had been. As Agler noted in an email to Brian Dickie after the Festival, 'most nights there was

Annunziata Vestri in *Guglielmo Ratcliff*, 2015

nearly a minute of silence at the end of the performance'.[14] Both Puts and the librettist, Mark Campbell, came to Wexford to attend a performance of the opera and to give the Dr Tom Walsh lecture. In selecting *Silent Night*, Agler had made a clever choice. He believed that the Festival was justified in making an important contribution to the centenary commemorations of the Great War, a war in which nearly one thousand Wexford men had lost their lives, forty in a single day on 19 October 1914. A century later, to the week, Wexford had the opportunity to stage the European premiere of *Silent Night*.[15]

It was a very moving production, and it stirred the emotions of the audiences each night. *Silent Night* went on to win two awards – the *Irish Times* Best Opera Production and the inaugural An Post Irish Stamps Audience Choice Prize. The Audience Choice category contained seventeen nominations, predominantly theatre nominations with just two operas among the list. Agler and the Wexford company were particularly encouraged to have managed to win in this category. The production of *Silent Night* was subsequently rented to Atlanta Opera, Glimmerglass Festival, Washington (DC) National Opera and Austin Opera – all in the United States.

The Orchestra Education workshops for primary schools were developed this year, and Joe Csibi, Orchestra Director, put together a programme that included a trumpet player, a percussionist and a violinist to deliver these workshops to schools in the town. It proved to be a very popular initiative, with positive feedback received from a number of school principals in this regard.[16]

For some time now, executives and the Board at Wexford had discussed the fact that the Wexford Opera House was the only purpose-built opera house in Ireland and was worthy of state recognition and financial support. The state had invested heavily in the building and there had been no further dialogue about how ongoing financial support might be provided. It was clear that the building needed to be able to absorb its operating costs by ensuring that more events took place there across the year. In relation to state recognition of the status of the building, an interesting possibility presented itself in 2014. The Minister for Arts, Heritage and the Gaeltacht, Heather Humphreys, was invited to open the Festival and it was mooted that she could confer the title of 'National Opera House' on the building at the same time. David McLoughlin had had a number of meetings prior to this with Niall O'Donnchu in the Department of Arts, Heritage and the Gaeltacht[17] and with Humphreys and her predecessor, Jimmy Deenihan, who were amenable to the proposition.[18] The advantages to achieving national status were threefold. The upgraded status would benefit the marketing and promotion of the Opera House as the only purpose-built opera house in the country and it was hoped that this would attract other events to the venue throughout the year. Added to this, national status for the Opera House would mean that Ireland was no longer the only country in the EU to be without a national opera house. Third, and most crucially, this change in status would mean that Wexford could bid for funding from the government for capital investment for the opera house. There had been no prior agreement with the government for ongoing financial support once the opera house was up and running, hence this option was a critical one.

Minister Heather Humphreys did, in fact, make the historic announcement at the official opening of the 63rd Wexford Festival Opera. In front of an estimated 18,000 people who lined the quay front of Wexford, she confirmed that the iconic building would be renamed 'the National Opera House'. She confirmed her support for this decision, by saying that

> The Wexford Opera House is Ireland's only acoustically purpose-built Opera House, and it has been a major addition to our cultural infrastructure since the state-of-the-art building was opened in 2008. The Irish people, through funding from my Department, have invested in this Opera House, and I think it is fitting that it is renamed the National Opera House.

This was a significant achievement for McLoughlin and Ger Lawlor as chairman in particular. McLoughlin added that

> the official recognition of Wexford as Ireland's National Opera House will help secure a legacy in opera in Ireland for generations to come, but perhaps more importantly deservedly recognizes the State's previous significant investment in the creation of what has been internationally acclaimed as 'the best small opera house in the world'.

In a memo to staff following the announcement, McLoughlin explained that the Wexford Opera House would not become a national cultural institution, in that the Minister was not seeking to appoint members to the Board of the Opera House. McLoughlin had negotiated these terms in advance with the Department and it was agreed by both parties that Wexford Festival would retain its autonomy.

Early 2015 was taken up with plans to collaborate with the Veronica Dunne Singing Competition. Hennessy and Agler were the driving forces behind this ambition, as they believed that Wexford Festival Opera would benefit from an association with the prestigious competition. A Memorandum of Understanding was drafted and agreed by both parties in the hope that a partnership would yield benefits. The announcement was made in July 2015 of the intention to

Daniela Pini in *Herculanum*, 2016

collaborate, with Wexford Festival Opera hosting one of the auditions. The Wexford Festival Opera Orchestra would be the orchestra for the final of the competition in the National Concert Hall, Dublin, and the winner would be invited to perform at the Festival in 2016. Agler, who had been on the jury for the 2010 competition, welcomed the announcement, stating that:

> I warmly welcome this alliance between two iconic Irish institutions, both dedicated to discovering the next generation of promising singers. I know that Dr Dunne and I take great pride in the contributions that her Competition and the Festival make in helping to launch the careers of so many gifted artists. And to have the splendid Wexford Festival Orchestra become the Orchestra of the Competition is a great satisfaction, as well. The combination of the unique strengths of both our organizations will ensure the viability and success of the Competition for many years to come.

However, despite the efforts of both parties, the collaboration never fully mobilized. Having collaborated for the 2016 competition both parties agreed

Carolyn Sproule in *Vanessa*, 2016

not to pursue the alliance any further for future competitions. The Wexford Festival Orchestra played for the scheduled singing competition, following which the organizations parted ways.

The 64th Wexford Festival Opera season opened on 21 October 2015 with *Koanga* by Frederick Delius, followed by *Guglielmo Ratcliff* by Pietro Mascagni and *Le pré aux clercs* by Ferdinand Hérold. *Koanga* was generously sponsored by the Delius Trust. *Le pré aux clercs* was a co-production with Opéra Comique, Paris, France. The three daytime ShortWorks operas were: *The Portrait of Manon* by Jules Massenet, *Tosca* by Giacomo Puccini and *Hansel and Gretel* by Engelbert Humperdinck. As part of the Festival's effort to reach out to the local community,

Claire Rutter, Michael Brandenburg, Carolyn Sproule and Festival Chorus in *Vanessa*, 2016

school children were invited to appear in the Children's Chorus of the opera *Hansel and Gretel,* which formed a key part of this year's programme. In all, the Festival included fifty-two events over twelve days, with offerings of concerts, lunchtime recitals, lectures and talks. The *Spectator* singled out *Koanga* for praise:

> Fatally flawed but with some heroic musical moments, *Koanga* is exactly the kind of show only Wexford could – or would – dare stage. A world-class opera festival specializing in obscure rarities based in a tiny coastal town – Wexford is the ultimate Irish joke. The punchline? It's bloody brilliant.[19]

Ted Howlin was honoured this year in the Ecclesiastical Volunteer award programme for his dedication to Wexford as a volunteer over thirty years. Wexford Festival Opera lost two significant contributors this year, first with the death of Mairéad Furlong, who had joined the Wexford Festival Council, as it was known at the time, in 1968 and retired from the Board of Directors in 2003, remaining on as a trustee. A former member of the Arts Council, Furlong had made a significant contribution to the Wexford Festival in particular, spanning over 50 years. The Festival in 2015 was dedicated to the memory of Liam Healy, who also died this year. Healy was the chairman of the Wexford Festival Foundation from 2004 to 2011 and he was lauded throughout his involvement for his immense leadership abilities in undertaking the very difficult task of finding the funding to turn the idea of a new building into a reality. He was relentless in his approach, professional and selfless in his desire to ensure success. His involvement was critical at a time when the Festival so badly needed the skills that he had to offer.[20]

In the immediate lead up to the Festival, there was much talk among Board members about the tradition of wearing formal attire to the operas and to Festival evening events. Some of the patrons loved the tradition, citing it as one of the unique and important parts of the entire experience. Others did not care for it at all, hence there was often discussion as to how to retain the tradition without frustrating patrons. Hennessy recalled being told by a former chairman of the Festival that any events taking place after 6p.m. required black tie attire; formal wear would not be required for a Festival event that concluded before 6p.m.; where an event began before 6p.m., but ended after 6p.m., the dress code was optional. This had been the unwritten rule since the beginning of the Festival in 1951 and the Board was keen to see it continue. 'I think the issue is making sure we don't reach that "tipping point",' Hennessy wrote to McLoughlin,

> but I don't believe we can go the compulsory route. I think our message that 'we dress to celebrate not to intimidate' is spot on. I can only suggest that we promote this concept a bit more rigorously. The current decline is best rectified by stealth rather than by a 'big bang' approach.[21]

The operas chosen for the 2016 season were *Herculanum* by Félicien David, *Vanessa* by Barber and *Maria de Rudenz* by Donizetti. A co-production with

Minnesota Opera and described as the 'most resounding fiasco of Donizetti's career' at its première in 1838, the opera attracted some favourable reviews following its Wexford production. The chorus was singled out for praise, as was its chorus master, Errol Girdlestone, for the dramatic portrayal of the story, topped off by the flamboyant costumes and intense makeup. Brian Kellow, editor at *Opera News*, favoured *Vanessa*, admitting that it 'isn't really a masterpiece, but Wexford's production almost made it seem like one'.[22] Kellow was an avid supporter of Wexford Festival Opera, often writing about his sense of anticipation leading up to the Festival season at Wexford:

> In this age of global economics, travellers may have more difficulty than ever seeking out a place that is like no other. For me, one of those places is Wexford … home to Wexford Festival Opera, one of Europe's most distinctive musical institutions …[23]

CHAPTER 14

A PLACE LIKE NO OTHER

2017–20

In early 2017, the Arts Council announced a series of initiatives and grants under its new opera strategy, including an open call for main-scale Irish opera provision for Dublin and other cities, as well as support for opera artists. Its strategy outlined a plan to provide for the production of Irish-produced main-scale opera in Dublin, with options for touring to other cities. The announcement of the open funding call came in the wake of a review of opera policy and provision in Ireland, which had taken place the previous year and the objective, according to the Arts Council, was to ensure a more balanced and sustainable approach to national opera provision. Following the application assessment process, the Arts Council would put in place a multi-annual funding agreement with the successful company, with performances expected to begin in 2018. Wexford was still funded on an annual basis by the Arts Council. Wexford Festival Opera had to now consider how it would approach this opportunity.

Agler and the Board had been contemplating moving ahead with plans to produce a Spring season. Agler wrote to Joe Csibi, Orchestra Manager, to gauge the support of the Festival orchestra for such a venture. Csibi's response was overwhelmingly positive and for the first time, there seemed to be a real hope of extending into the spring.[1] The announcement of the Arts Council grant then presented both a challenge and an opportunity for Wexford. The successful application would effectively culminate in the establishment of the Irish National Opera model, a model that had long been mooted but had come to nothing. For Wexford, it was an opportunity to get funding for some of the plans that they had long hoped to see come to fruition, namely the opportunity to bring the Wexford Festival Opera offering outside of its home at the National Opera House. At the same time, it presented a challenge, in that it was now a competitive process and Wexford would have to bid for the right to extend its offering.

Wexford Festival Opera decided to put together a comprehensive proposal for the provision of main-scale opera for the period 2018–20. This proposal outlined a new programme focusing on works not produced in Ireland for many years, performed over three nights in the Bord Gáis Energy Theatre in Dublin, and selected operas to be performed in Wexford and Cork. It outlined the Irish National Opera concept as a subsidiary of Wexford Festival Trust, in the same way as the National Opera House was a subsidiary company of Wexford Festival Trust.[2]

It was an anxious wait to see how Wexford had fared in the funding competition as the result would have a significant impact on Wexford's strategy for development. Before long, Wexford received a letter from the Arts Council indicating that it had not been successful with its bid. Instead, a multi-annual award had been made to Fergus Sheil for his proposal to deliver opera in the capital, with touring opportunities to other major cities and towns. After many years of false starts, Irish National Opera was now a reality – with Sheil as its artistic director. Following various attempts by the government to establish Irish National Opera previously, this new company was a merger of Opera Theatre Company, and Wide Open Opera, Sheil's project-based company which was founded in 2012. Although Wexford's proposal had not been successful, the Board and executive at Wexford nonetheless hoped that the assessment panel was left in no doubt as to Wexford's ambitious plans to bring more of Wexford's renowned productions to new audiences throughout the year and throughout the country.

Meanwhile, there was a great deal of excitement building around the fact that Fiona Shaw had been chosen to direct Cherubini's *Medea* as part of the 2017 mainstage programme. Shaw was a well-known Irish actress and director

Filippo Fontana and Matteo D'Apolito in *Margherita*, 2017

and had played the part of Medea many years previously in the play at the Abbey Theatre in Dublin. This sense of anticipation translated into early ticket sales, much to the delight of the Wexford Festival Board and company alike. Not for the first time, Visa, the multinational financial services corporation, signed up as a production sponsor. Shaw was generous with her time leading up to the Festival, and had participated in organized fundraising and marketing events, including a talk in the Merrion Hotel in Dublin.

Again, Joe Csibi worked closely with Agler to agree a programme of music as part of the Orchestra Education programme for local schools. This programme took place during the Festival and was facilitated by members of the orchestra.

Charles Rice and Anne Sophie Duprels in *Risurrezione*, 2017

It had become a very popular addition to the local engagement events taking place in the town in October.

However, when Festival time came round, the excitement gave way to anxiety over whether the Festival would be deemed a success. Not least of the worries centred on the fact that Wexford was hit by an immense storm in the week leading up to, and the first days of the Festival. It was not possible to run the dress rehearsal for *Medea* due to the conditions and loss of electricity – a situation that naturally caused great angst to Agler and his team. It was certainly a tense build up. 'The storm caused chaos for us', Agler wrote to his now confidantes, Brian Dickie and Elaine Padmore:

> Lost the *Medea* dress (rehearsal), ran *Margherita* last night without any stage lighting, Wi-Fi down so tills and other systems not reliable, neighbourhoods surrounding town still without water and electricity. Fiona Shaw has cancelled her Tom Walsh Lecture. We are, in very nearly every respect, not ready.[3]

Along with *Medea*, the other operas chosen for the 2017 Festival were *Margherita* by Jacopo Foroni and *Risurrezione* by Franco Alfano. *Margherita* was a co-production with Oldenburg Opera, Germany. Under the ShortWorks programme, the Festival presented the world premiere of *Dubliners* by Andrew Synnott, two operas based on *Dubliners* by James Joyce. The production of *Medea* polarized opinion and attracted very mixed reviews. Emer O'Kelly, however, praised Shaw's bravery in stepping outside of convention:

> Whether audiences hoped for pretty 18th-century costumes (Cherubini's era) or flowing classical robes (Greek legendary garb), I'm not sure. But a lot of them sure as hell didn't like what they saw. I thought it was extraordinarily touching and vulnerable, and superbly sung, conducted and acted.[4]

The Taoiseach, Leo Varadkar, was the guest of honour on the closing night. Actress Joanna Lumley also came to town this year for the Festival, to support her husband, Stephen Barlow, who was conducting *Medea*. She appeared on the podium for the fireworks display, much to the excitement of the thousands of local people who were gathered on the quay to experience the opening night display.

Those that were working so hard to maintain the high standard of Wexford Festival Opera were overjoyed to learn that the Festival won the Best Festival Award in the International Opera Awards for 2017. It was particularly thrilling for Agler who had maintained his focus and resolve and had delivered successful programmes year after year. It was also deserved recognition for Wexford's volunteers who played such a vital part in creating the overall atmosphere during the Festival, and was an acknowledgment that the town itself, including its businesses and local council, also played an important part in ensuring the success of the overall venture.

> On Sunday evening last at the Coliseum Opera House in London, the opera world's leading lights attended the announcement of the International Opera Awards. In the category for Best Opera Festival, there were six nominations for festivals as far apart as France and the US. Wexford Opera Festival walked away with the award. It seems trivial to use the word 'congratulations' because Wexford Opera Festival deserves much more than that. I am in awe, and so very proud of what they are achieving in Wexford,

Yasko Sato and Festival Chorus in *Il bravo*, 2018

Ursula Hough-Gormley wrote in the *Irish Times* upon hearing of Wexford's tremendous success at the awards ceremony.

Another former chairperson, Barbara Wallace, died in July 2017. She had been chairperson of Wexford Festival Opera for five years and had been instrumental in fundraising, particularly in the fateful year of 1987, when the Arts Council withdrew its financial support. Her leadership and drive ensured that the money was found and the Festival was staged. Wallace had relaunched the Friends of the Festival programme, which had not been performing to the level required as a revenue generating programme. She restructured it to make it more appealing to patrons, introducing advance booking, which proved very popular and which yielded much higher membership to the scheme. Wallace was also credited with encouraging Tony O'Reilly to take more than a passing interest in the Festival, leading to the Ireland Funds support in 1987 and the long-lasting relationship between O'Reilly and the Festival.[5]

With another successful Festival behind them, Wexford Festival Opera set about preparations for 2018. This would be a critical year for the Festival, not least because it would be Agler's penultimate Festival as artistic director. His contract had been extended a number of times up to this point. The search began in earnest for his replacement. It was an international search and there was much interest in the position. Agler was keen to stress the importance of a professional approach to recruiting his successor, 'something that reflects our standing in the international opera community', he added.[6] Elaine Padmore was also consulted to ensure that the job description was an accurate reflection of the role being advertised.

At the opening ceremony of this year's Festival, the Minister for Culture, Heritage and the Gaeltacht, Josepha Madigan, told the crowd gathered that her department had decided to make a significant investment in the National Opera House. 'I am conscious that we are celebrating this year the tenth anniversary of the opening of this magnificent Opera House,' she told the community on the quay front;

> I am delighted to announce that my Department will be investing €1 million in necessary updating and refurbishment works over the next three years to protect the State's significant investment in this building and to ensure that the National Opera House continues to operate at the highest quality levels for many years to come. In opera, Wexford is a global leader. In the arts, Wexford is a national example. This Government is deeply appreciative of this and is strongly supportive of the arts and Ireland's arts community.[7]

McLoughlin and Hennessy[8] in particular were delighted and relieved with the news, as they had been involved in protracted discussions with the government over a number of years about the National Opera House's need for some level of public subsidy to ensure that the highest standards could be maintained.

For Agler's penultimate season, he chose a double bill, *L'oracolo* by Franco Leoni and *Mala vita*, by Umberto Giordano. Both operas included a local children's chorus. *Dinner at Eight* by William Bolcom was also chosen – a European premiere and a co-production with Minnesota Opera. *Il bravo* by Mercadante was the third opera performed in 2018. Loughlin Quinn, businessman and philanthropist, and his wife Brenda, donated generously to the newly established production consortium for *Il bravo* and also hosted a fundraising lunch on behalf of Wexford Festival Opera. Brenda had recently joined the National Development Council. The Festival ran from 19 October to 4 November. RTÉ Lyric FM was particularly delighted with its collaboration with Wexford Festival Opera this year, enabling Wexford's opera offering to be delivered to communities and homes across the globe.[9] Anne Reck, a volunteer in the wardrobe department for forty years, was called to the stage by Agler before the curtain was lifted on the final night, and her dedicated years of service was acknowledged with a heartfelt round of applause from the audience.

The reviews of the operas were very positive and it was deemed to be another very successful Festival. But it was not a good year in general for Wexford. In fact, in the weeks surrounding the Festival, there was a lot of tension and angst about how the season had played out. Ticket sales were down in 2018. It transpired however that ticket sales for many cultural events and Festivals in Ireland had suffered in the same year. A decision was taken quickly to contract the Festival to 12 days for 2019 to offset some of this loss. This was particularly disappointing for Agler, as 2019 would be his last year with Wexford. The ticket sales were not the only issue affecting the budget. In fact, there was a series of occurrences that came together to put significant pressure on the finances. Along with the lower-than-average ticket sales, the income raised from donors and sponsors was also lower than had been projected. Coupled with this, the artistic budget was stretched this year as a result of higher-than-average production costs associated with the very ambitious programme that was presented.

Just four weeks after the close of the 2018 Festival, Wexford was hit with one of its most significant challenges that would threaten its very existence. Wexford received the devastating news that the Arts Council had decided to postpone making a decision on Wexford's funding, without a guarantee of any funding at all for Wexford for the coming year. Wexford was plunged into crisis, and paralysed in its planning for 2019. All attention turned to engaging with the Arts Council to understand the root cause of this delay in the funding decision. The Arts Council looked for clarification on the Festival's financial situation following the 2018 season and assurances as to the financial stability

Goderdzi Janelidze and Olafur Sigurdarson in *Don Quichotte*, 2019

of the company. To this end, an audit of Wexford's financial affairs was sought to provide all necessary assurances for the Arts Council. It was widely accepted that the Festival could not survive without its funding from its principal sponsor. Nevertheless, Wexford Festival Opera had planned to announce its repertory for 2019 along with the actual Festival dates the same week and there would be longer term consequences to their ability to stage the Festival if delays occurred at this time.

So Wexford Festival Opera went ahead and announced its plans, while working on the ground with the auditor, in the hope of being able to prove to the Arts Council that it was a financially stable organization, with appropriate

Festival cast and chorus
in *Adina*, 2019

management structures to support such a cultural institution.[10] It was a baptism of fire for the incoming chairwoman, Dr Mary Kelly, who took over the role from Ger Lawlor in the middle of this crisis. Lawlor's term had come to an end, following six years at the helm. Kelly had been on the Board of Wexford Festival Trust since 2017 and had served as Director General of the Environmental Protection Agency (EPA), which was an important sponsor of Wexford Festival Opera. She was also the chairperson of An Bord Pleanála (Planning Board) for seven years.

By the beginning of 2019, the Festival was in disarray. There was so much preparation to be done for the season ahead, and the level of financial uncertainty that Wexford Festival Opera was operating within was extremely challenging. Agler was in a particularly difficult position, as he grappled with trying to lay out a plan within an ever-contracting artistic budget. He wrote to his confidante, Elaine Padmore, describing the current situation as 'utterly grim'.[11] Having announced the repertory for the coming season, Alger realized that the programme would be too expensive to stage, and concluded that he would have to revisit his selection. He met with some opposition to naming a new programme however. For fourteen years, he had been at the helm at Wexford and the fact that his last year would be marred with the level of restriction being placed on his artistic output was particularly disappointing for him, as he outlined in his letter to the chair of the Board.

> For the 14 Festival seasons I have planned for Wexford I have never been asked to justify the operas I produced and, indeed, I do not believe I am contractually obliged to do so … I have presented 42 main-stage productions containing 47 different operas, many winning Irish and international awards. After a month of work and consultation I conclude that I am not able to produce a season of the artistic quality and musical standards which the public have come to expect of Wexford. Therefore, I am submitting my resignation as Artistic Director of The Wexford Festival.[12]

It was clear to all that there was a lot at stake here. Finally, the news that had been keenly awaited arrived. In March, the Arts Council confirmed its grant for the 2019 Festival.[13] Tensions abated and Agler was persuaded to see out the 2019 Festival, with additional responsibility being passed over to the artistic director designate. This role had been won by Rosetta Cucchi. Cucchi knew Wexford well, having first worked at Wexford as a répétiteur with Luigi Ferrari in 1995. She went on to direct in the Opera Scenes in 2003 and from there, she made her mainstage directorial debut with Braunfels' *Prinzessin Brambilla* in 2004.When Agler arrived on the scene in 2005, Cucchi worked as his associate for his entire tenure. She was full of ambition for Wexford and worked well with Agler over many years to realize his vision for the Festival. Soon, it would be her turn to put her stamp on the artistic endeavours at Wexford.

Once the Arts Council grant was secured, preparations got started in earnest for the season ahead. The executive worked hard to realize any potential development income that could be generated to ensure that the Festival being produced in the Autumn would be of a standard befitting Wexford Festival Opera. Agler concentrated on the operas, working closely with Cucchi to ensure a steady transition once the Festival was over.

After a very unsteady start to preparations, the Festival overall turned out to be a popular one with the patrons although the reviews were mixed. *Don Quichotte* by Massenet opened the Festival and received broadly positive reviews. *Dorilla in Tempe* by Antonio Vivaldi was the first Baroque opera to be performed at Wexford in over thirty years, but proved to be a less popular choice with audiences. The opera was sponsored by Danone, who had become an important and regular production sponsor over the past decade. Danone had also contributed to the Foundation to support the building of the National Opera House. The Festival staged the world-premiere of Andrew Synnott's *La cucina*, as a complement to Rossini's *Adina*, a co-production with the Rossini Opera Festival. *Adina* and *La cucina* were directed by Cucchi. The Taoiseach, Leo Varadkar, made his way to Wexford once again to see a performance of the double-bill. Along with Synnott's opera, the work of another Irish composer featured on the main stage in 2019. A concert version of *The Veiled Prophet* by Charles Villiers Stanford was presented in association with Heritage Music Productions, led by international pianist Una Hunt and supported by a grant from the Arts Council. It was fitting that Eleanor White received the Ecclesiastical Volunteer of the Year award for five decades of volunteering with Wexford Festival Opera, across a number of different areas.

And so, 2019 was Agler's last Festival as artistic director with Wexford. He had served the Festival for fifteen years, longer than any other artistic director before him apart from Tom Walsh, who also served for fifteen years.[14] Looking

Luca Nucera
and Emmanuel
Franco in *La
cucina*, 2019

back over the time when Agler was at the helm, it is easy to imagine the
frustrations and tribulations that faced him year after year. It had been a time
of great change for Wexford Festival Opera, and also for the environment in
which the Festival was operating. Agler had steered the Festival through the
rough times following Jerome Hynes' death, had repositioned himself in the
company at that time to support the functions that needed to get done. He
delivered two Festivals when Wexford Festival Opera was without a permanent
home, giving the highest regard to maintaining standards at this transitional

Andrew Gavin and Sarah Shine at Barkers Pop-Up Event, 2020

time. He brought opera back to the bigger stage of the new Opera House, and he sought to ensure that the artistic funding was ringfenced so that he could deliver quality productions each year.

Agler was instrumental in finding a solution to the orchestra and chorus issues at Wexford. He realized early on that the national media, and indeed the Arts Council, were unforgiving of Wexford Festival Opera's use of international orchestras and chorus members. He set about developing a Wexford Festival Orchestra and subsequently a Wexford Festival Chorus, which both turned out to be very important decisions in driving Wexford's success.

Agler was a traditionalist – he didn't care for the Opera House being named the 'Wexford Opera House' and canvassed for the new building to retain the title of the 'Theatre Royal'. He invested a lot of time in building relationships with the press, in particular the international press, who valued his candid style and were impressed with what he had achieved for Wexford. As Andrew Clark of the *Financial Times* wrote to Agler:

> Thank you for taking the trouble to write to me and bring to the fore the still-warm experiences of Wexford that I will always cherish. In

recent times your personal welcome was an important aspect of that experience, as well as the shrewd and stylish way in which you wrestled with Wexford's peculiar challenges. Critics have a lot of comparisons to fall back on. You continue to make Wexford special.[15]

It was fitting that Agler was awarded an Honorary Fellowship of the Royal College of Surgeons Ireland (RCSI) for his outstanding contribution to the arts in Ireland. The Fellowship was conferred at a ceremony in Dublin just days before the 2019 Festival opened. Other notable recipients included Seamus Heaney and Sir Bob Geldof. The President of the RCSI, Kenneth Mealy, spoke at the event, stating that:

> At RCSI, we recognize the contribution the arts can play in improving physical health and wellbeing, providing ways to nurture creativity, tackle social and health conditions, and support long healthy lives. We greatly admire David for his work cultivating the Wexford Festival Opera – a truly international festival. With the unwavering support of the local community and the Arts Council of Ireland, the Festival has flourished. David has led an ambitious festival that has explored the neglected and often obscure opera repertoire and continued to surprise and intrigue audiences. We applaud him for those achievements and celebrate his vision, determination and success over his 15 years in Wexford …[16]

Agler loved Wexford, the town and its people and he understood the importance of engaging with them, and making time to listen to their comments, praise and criticisms. Agler described his time at Wexford as his 'happiest time'. During his tenure, he surrounded himself with kindred spirits – including Brian Dickie and Elaine Padmore – who also looked back on their time in Wexford as a very special and important time in their lives. He left Wexford in very much the same way that he had arrived, without any fuss or grandeur.

Cucchi entered the scene, full of enthusiasm for what lay ahead and keen to make an impression. The Festival Board met in February to discuss plans for the coming season and there was a real sense of optimism borne out of the fact that 2019 had turned out to be a successful year, following a bleak start. The full programme, developed around the theme of Shakespeare, was announced

– *Ein Wintermärchen* by Carl Goldmark, Ambroise Thomas' *Le songe d'une nuit d'été* and *Edmea* by Alfredo Catalani. Festival highlights would include a gala concert with full orchestra by the well-known Lisette Oropesa. Rossini's *Petite messe solennelle* was also listed as part of the programme and the ShortWorks would be renamed 'Pocket Operas' and would also follow a Shakespeare theme.

Cucchi was particularly interested in the development of an academy for young Irish artists and she had already enlisted the support of many eminent artists to act as mentors for these young singers. The Academy would be known as 'The Wexford Factory' and by early 2020 the auditions had already taken place for the coveted places on the programme.

2020, however, was quickly committed to the annals as being the bleakest year of all. No one could have predicted the profound impact that Covid-19 would have on the world, on the arts sector in general, and on Wexford Festival Opera in particular. Four weeks after the February Board meeting, where Cucchi had described her ambitions for the coming Festival, the government announced the immediate lockdown of all non-essential venues, shops, theatres, restaurants and cafés. The world watched in disbelief as every continent succumbed to the new virus that was spreading at a ferocious rate.

From the outset, all the thinking and contingency planning was short term. The lockdown was due to last for two weeks, after which time, life would return to normal. But this did not turn out to be the case. Although not impacted as badly in terms of illness as other countries, Ireland's social and business life came to a standstill and the impact was profound.

It became clear early on that the 2020 Festival was in danger. In its 69 years, there was only one year that the Festival had not taken place – the reason being to allow for renovations to the old Theatre Royal. The Finance Committee, a sub-committee of the Board under the chairmanship of Kevin Mitchell, worked diligently with Cucchi to explore many scenarios. The most immediate impact would be on the availability of priority booking and a decision needed to be taken as to when to make any announcements at all in such a fluid environment. Booking continued and patrons continued to show their support for the Festival, until it became clear that it would not be possible to run a Festival at all in the manner in which it had been imagined.

This was a very difficult decision, and a particularly disappointing one for Cucchi, in her first year in the role. The Board met regularly during these weeks, and Cucchi started to develop a contingency plan which imagined

Wexford Festival Opera going online for 2020, the theme being 'Waiting for Shakespeare'. Within weeks, the Board was left with no choice but to postpone the Festival planned for 2020 and seek to work with Cucchi on her new concept.

In a joint statement, Cucchi and McLoughlin addressed the Wexford Festival supporters:

> That spirit which enabled a small provincial town to create a world-renowned opera festival continues to this day, inspiring Wexford, with the support and guidance of its board of directors, to develop a crisis-inspired formula by presenting a reimagined, online Festival. We are determined to leave no stone unturned to ensure the Festival remains active, dynamic and fully prepared to welcome audiences back to Wexford to celebrate the Festival's 70th anniversary in 2021. The reimagined Festival aims to bring together audiences and the wider worldwide Wexford community through the power of music.[17]

The Wexford Factory academy went ahead in September of 2020 as planned, with some changes to the design of the programme. It was still not possible to bring many people together in the National Opera House, so the masterclasses were structured so that some of the mentors were streamed live into the Opera House, where the young singers were based for a number of weeks. The mentors included world-renowned tenor Juan Diego Flórez, Irish soprano Celine Byrne, renowned soprano Ermonela Jaho, as well as Ernesto Palacio of the Rossini Opera Festival and Dmitry Vdovin, head of the Bolshoi's Young Artist programme. Wexford Festival Opera director Roberto Recchia, classical music journalist Michael Dervan, movement specialist Sara Catellani and Rosetta Cucchi also provided instruction. Anthony and Myca Arnhold, avid supporters and long-time bursary sponsors of the Festival, provided sponsorship towards the programme.

It was a more solemn opening to the Festival than Wexford had ever before experienced – no fanfare or fireworks on the quay, no patrons in black tie attire arriving at the National Opera House, full of anticipation of the operatic treats that might lie ahead. On 11 October, the 2020 reimagined Festival opened with a performance of Rossini's *Petite messe solennelle*, a beautiful and melodic work, which was fitting as a dedication to the memory of the victims of the Covid-19 pandemic. Wexford Festival supporters tuned in to RTÉ's Lyric FM to hear the performance, hosted by Paul Herriott. Wexford Festival Opera's strengthening relationship with RTÉ proved crucial to enabling this online Festival to take place, and those that watched the live stream of the performance on RTÉ Culture or on RTÉ Player would note the sobering reminder of the virus that had changed everything – many of the performers on stage were wearing face masks to shield against the spread of infection. The performance was conducted by Kenneth Montgomery with Finghin Collins and Carmen Santoro playing piano and Andrew Synnott playing the harmonium. The soloists were Claudia Boyle, Tara Erraught, Pietro Adaíni and John Molloy and they were joined by the Wexford Factory singers.

Andrew Synnott, artist-in-residence, was invited by Cucchi to create a new opera for the 2020 season. *What Happened to Lucrece* was the result of an intensive period of writing for Synnott and was written with an online audience in mind. Based on the Shakespearean poem, *The Rape of Lucrece*, Synnott created three separate endings to his opera, performed on three separate days during the week-long Festival. The work was well received, and was performed by participants of the Wexford Factory, including Sara Richmond, Rory Musgrave, Sarah Shine and Kathleen Norchi, with pianist Giorgio d'Alonso.

Across the Festival week then, Giuseppe Verdi's *Falstaff* was performed, in fifteen-minute episodes across six days by the members of the Wexford Factory. It was fitting that the participants of the Wexford Factory played such a crucial role in ensuring that the 2020 Festival could proceed. Their presence in the National Opera House at the time when the Festival would have been going on was the only physical reminder that this was opera time, and the energy and excitement in the otherwise closed National Opera House was a welcome addition.

Two Dr Tom Walsh lectures took place virtually this year. Luigi Ferrari was invited back for the first lecture and the second was a conversation between Clara Hamer, granddaughter of Dr Tom Walsh, opera director Jack Furness and Feargal Hynes, son of the late Jerome Hynes, all of whom had close connections with Wexford Festival Opera.

In order to bring some of the Festival atmosphere to the town, albeit in a muted way, Cucchi organized a series of multi-disciplinary pop-up performances to take place at different locations in the town each day. Many of these took place behind closed doors and were streamed live to grateful audiences, and some took place outdoors on the streets. Although these events were curtailed somewhat in 2020 due to the various restrictions in place about social distancing and gatherings, the performances were very well received and it was clear that Cucchi had exciting plans for the future in this regard.

Irish soprano Celine Byrne was invited to give a dinner time recital on the second day of the Festival, again available live on Lyric FM or through live stream at RTÉ Culture. Byrne had also participated as a mentor in the Wexford Factory programme. A Gala Concert, entitled 'Remote Voices', was one of the highlights of the Festival this year. Taking place on the Friday night of Festival week, Cucchi managed to assemble an impressive cast of internationally renowned singers to participate remotely in the concert, as she and Marty Whelan, well-known broadcaster, now with RTÉ Lyric, commentated from the stage of the National Opera House. Interestingly, all the participants had performed in Wexford at some stage in their careers and had special regard for Wexford and its Opera Festival. It was a beautiful concert, but a poignant reminder of how things had changed in a short number of months, as those that tuned in looked out at the empty Opera House, one that should have been buzzing with anticipation and excitement at this time of year. Juan Diego

Stefania Panighini and Filippo Mancini with Factory singers doing Flashmob on the Quay, Wexford

Flórez, Joseph Calleja, Helena Dix and Ermonela Jaho were among the singers that took part.

The Festival closed on 18 October with a concert by Irish soprano Claudia Boyle and Sicilian tenor Pietro Adaíni, who were joined by the Wexford Festival Orchestra and conductor Francesco Cilluffo. Boyle and Adaíni replaced the American soprano Lisette Oropesa who was unable to travel given the travel restrictions into the country. Wexford Festival Opera was proud of what it had achieved, and Cucchi was praised for the enthusiasm and passion that she displayed, ensuring that the Festival went ahead in 2020. But the town and the local economy were reeling from the double blow of the impact of the Covid-19 pandemic, which affected their businesses since March, and now the absence of the Festival that they had come to rely upon for nearly seventy years. The comments of President Michael D. Higgins, patron of the Festival, reflected the power of this surreal Festival, and the importance of staging a Festival albeit under nearly impossible circumstances:

> The dedication of Rossini's solemn Mass to the victims of Covid-19 reminds us that one of the great qualities of the Wexford Opera Festival has always been its will to speak to all citizens, creating a cultural space that belongs to the people in all their diversity and in their different circumstances, rejecting, thus, any notion that such a space is the preserve of an elite.
>
> That principle of solidarity is so much at the heart of this year's Festival, despite the challenging circumstances under which it is taking place. As always, the power of music to connect and unite is the driving force of the Festival and its role as a major worldwide cultural event is equal to, but not greater than, its role as an accessible and inclusive community event.[18]

Higgins' words will resonate for some time to come, as the solidarity shown in delivering the 2020 *Festival in the Air* will be required again in 2021. The global pandemic has begun to show signs of abating, and there is hope and optimism coming, with the deployment of a vaccination programme for all citizens. For now, the 2021 Festival is being planned, with contingency planning again to the fore of the preparations. As Wexford Festival Opera navigates through yet another significant turning point in its history, it is as important as ever to realize that there is no room for complacency. As Walsh so accurately deduced:

> Opera is a business, but it is a business in its own right and must be run by people whose business is opera. When opera becomes an appendage, however important, to something else, be it a social occasion or a commercial promotion, then it is being deflected from its true artistic purpose. I am well aware that both commerce in one or other form and the social occasion are and always have been essential for the survival of opera, but one must guard that the tail is not allowed to wag the dog. To ensure that this does not happen, one must continually ask the question – what has been achieved? You see, it all boils down to a matter of results … In opera as in every other business there is either progress or regression. There can be no standing still.[19]

And the future? The Festival had survived what it believed to have been its most testing times, but it is more obvious than ever that there will always be challenges around the corner for Wexford Festival Opera. The Festival has become embedded in its community, to the point that this community cannot imagine an autumn in Wexford with no Festival. The loss of the physical Festival to the town in 2020 was palpable. At the same time, it will take a mammoth act of solidarity to ensure its viability into the future. In this struggle, Wexford is not alone. The presence of the current pandemic has taught us that we cannot take anything for granted, and in the world of culture and the arts, the vulnerability is especially stark. Wexford has always relied on certain ingredients to cement its success – its volunteers, its private donors, its sponsors, the strength of its artistic programme and its insistence on quality. Everything else will change – but these elements cannot.

The incredible spirit of resilience of this unique Festival has carried it through the last seventy years. Remembering the sentiments of Bernard Levin, the Festival was, and is, built to last. Throughout its history, Wexford Festival Opera has faced many challenging times. On each occasion, belief, courage, ingenuity, determination and the occasional minor miracle has seen it pull through the most testing of times. The current challenges will be no different, but fundamentally, we still believe in miracles at Wexford.

Emily Pulley and
Festival Chorus
in *Susannah*, 2005.
2006 Irish Times
Theatre Awards

EPILOGUE

President Michael D. Higgins

President of Ireland and Patron of Wexford Festival Opera

The Wexford Opera Festival is a hugely important event on Ireland's cultural calendar. Over the past decades, since its establishment in 1951, it has also become a major European cultural event – about forty per cent of attendees at the Festival come from overseas, travelling to Wexford to hear some of the great forgotten gems of the opera world, those long buried and almost forgotten masterpieces which are so beautifully revived by the many talented people behind this event, delighting new generations of devoted opera audiences.

The Wexford Festival Opera stands as a great tribute to the many people who have worked so hard over the past decades to create one of the most significant classical music events in Europe. It is amazing to consider that such an important cultural landmark began with an informal gathering of like-minded friends who simply came together to listen to some music on the gramophone. Out of that social occasion a music and arts festival was born which soon grew into the major musical occasion it is today. We owe an enormous debt to the festival's first director Dr Tom Walsh, the amateur musician and man of great imagination and foresight who steered this festival through its first decade-and-a-half, ensuring the mark it left on Ireland's cultural landscape would be deep and enduring.

All great works of art, be they in the fields of music, song, drama, literature or dance, have the power to stir us to great emotion; to cause us to reflect and to dig deeply into our feelings and sentiments as we experience the artist's own emotions being transmuted into unforgettable plays, songs, poetry, melodies, harmonies and stage performances. Opera, however, is a union of all of these art forms, a great coming together of the skills of the writer, the singer, the actor, the musician, the choreographer and the visual artist. It is, in many ways, the most complete work of art, a remarkable bringing together of each distinct form of creativity into one absolute and mesmerizing piece of work.

There can be no doubt that we are living through challenging times. Events like the Wexford Festival Opera are a crucial element in ensuring that we have the confidence and the foresight to retain a cultural space, a space that does not become marginal, tangential or even abandoned.

When I was inaugurated as President of Ireland I committed to championing creative communities. I believe that encouraging the development of creativity in our communities and ensuring opportunities for creative expression will lay the groundwork for sustainable employment in creative industries and enrich our social, cultural and economic development. The arts and culture is a unique sector, not just in its capacity to rouse our passions and imagination on a deep personal and communal level, but also in its employment-creation potential and its capacity for regional dispersal and the economically attested high multiplier it generates for local economies.

One of the great attributes of this festival is its ability to speak to all citizens and to create a cultural space that is accessible, that is not colonized or seen as the preserve of an elite. The Festival's role as a major cultural event sits comfortably alongside its role as an important community event and a part of a larger inclusive space.

I would like to commend all of those involved in the Wexford Festival Opera for their extraordinary hard work and commitment – an event of which I am delighted and very proud to be patron.

Go raibh míle maith agaibh go léir.

Sinéad Campbell, Paula Murrihy,
Noah Stewart, Glenn Alamilla,
Matthew Nelson, Peter Barrett,
David Crawford in *Transformations*, 2006.
2007 Irish Times Theatre Awards

'MY WEXFORD':

SOME PERSONAL REFLECTIONS

Geoffrey Wheatcroft (*journalist and writer*)

Fifty-one Wexfords

In October 1969, I took the Fishguard train from Paddington bound for the Rosslare ferry and four nights at White's which, for all that prices were somewhat lower then than now, was a fair part of my very modest salary as a twenty-three-year-old employee in a London publishing house. I've never felt my money better spent, otherwise I wouldn't have returned to the Wexford Festival every year since then, apart – of course and alas! – from last year. If I write about Wexford in personal terms, that's how I feel about it, as part of my life. It really is my favourite music festival, of very many. I love the Schubertiade at Schwarzenberg in the hills of western Austria, I've been solemnly impressed by Wagner at Bayreuth, but no one has ever called opera-going there fun, which Wexford pre-eminently is.

When I look back to my early Wexfords, I'm astonished by the roster of artists. Where are they now? Well, they're all over the place, men and women who were unknown then but are now world-famous. When Sir David Pountney was knighted not long ago, I said to him that he would be congratulated by many people, but not by many who'd been present at the first night of *Kát'a Kabanová* at Wexford in 1972, his first professional production, and when Jane Glover, that heroic pioneer for women conductors, became Dame Jane at the

New Year, I said likewise that not many writing to her would have been present at *Eritrea* in 1975, her first professional performance.

And then when I looked again at the programme for *L'infedeltà delusa* at my very first Wexford, who should have been playing harpsichord continuo in the pit but the twenty-two-year-old Mark Elder, now Sir Mark and Music Director of the Hallé Orchestra and sometime Music Director of English National Opera? When that lovely Martiniquan soprano Christiane Eda-Pierre died recently, I thought back straightaway to her enchanting performances at Wexford in *Lakmé* and *Les pêcheurs de perles* a lifetime ago. And who among those who were present at *Grisélidis* in 1982 will forget the western debut of the great Russian baritone Sergei Leiferkus?

Happy thoughts of Wexford are tinged with sorrow. Very long before the magnificent new theatre, now rightly the National Opera House, in rougher-and-readier shoestring days, Mozart's little bon-bon *Il re pastore* in 1971 was designed by the delightful Elisabeth Dalton. She enlisted my dear friend Rodney Milnes and myself to help finish painting the scenery in the storeroom at the Celtic Laundry. Liz died of cancer well before her time, followed by Rodney five years ago, after we had heard scores of operas together here, and the list of friends in Wexford who have left us is too long.

Over these years, no country I know anywhere has changed more, for worse and for better, than Ireland, and Wexford has been a microcosm of that change. One thing which hasn't changed is the ritual of 'Amhrán na bhFiann', and I would shyly point out, not for the first time, that Wexford is the only one out of the very many opera houses in Europe and America I know where the national anthem is played nightly. The Festival has also had its ups and downs, some glorious nights at the opera and some ghastly clunkers. Kindly oblivion can draw a veil over the worst, but to name one delightful recent memory it would be Ferdinand Hérold's *Le pré aux clercs* in 2015, a real case of an unjustly neglected work and also something you almost never hear in France today, a French opera sung by a French-speaking cast, one of the great achievements of David Agler's distinguished tenure.

Biology dictates that I shan't have another fifty-one Wexfords, but I'm game for a few more. And I shall count every one gratefully.

Larisa Kostyuk and Matjaz Robavs
in *Švanda dudák*, 2003.
2004 Irish Times Theatre Awards

The Ghosts of Versailles, 2009. 2010 Irish Times Theatre Awards

Virginia, 2010. 2011 Irish Times Theatre Awards

Terry Neill (*Chair of the National Development Council, Wexford Festival Opera*)

Beginnings

I was a professional musician long before Rosetta Cucchi – or even David Agler. Five shillings and sixpence a month, with a shilling each for weddings and funerals. The head choirboy of Bangor Abbey was doubly rich – the shillings and the wonderful music. My voice broke. I joined my father in the (amateur) ranks of the basses. Budget cut. On to Trinity Choral Society, first visits to Dublin Grand Opera Society, sharing Trinity rooms with an oboe player ... the blessings of being surrounded by music. Alfredo Campoli played the Bruch in the Exam Hall. Wondrous. I think I got to Wexford in 1967.

Solti's 50th

Trips to Wexford in the early 80s. We moved to Chicago. Lyric Opera regulars. By the 1990s, we were in London. Solti celebrated his 50th anniversary at the Royal Opera. *Otello* with Te Kanawa and Domingo. Afterwards, Solti got a cake, and a parade of many of the great names of the previous 50 years ... Schwarzkopf, Hotter, Bergonzi, Nilsson ... and many more. Magic. Wexford became a regular trip. In 2004, Barry Douglas asked me to chair Camerata Ireland. We had magical nights with the orchestra in Rome, Madrid, Paris, Barcelona, New York ... as well as the concerts and young musicians at the annual Clandeboye Festival.

Wexford every year

Since the mid-2000s, it's been Wexford every year, bar one dose of 'flu. (I missed *Silent Night*.) Every production is good, and sometimes it's magical ... hairs on the back of the neck stuff, maybe a tear in the eye. The good nights bring me back, the magical nights mean long term loyalty and commitment.

An Adès meeting of minds

I am not a fan of Thomas Adès' music. Marjorie and I sat through the premiere of *The Exterminating Angel* in Salzburg. The cast of stars included Thomas Allen, who was in Wexford the following year to deliver the Tom Walsh lecture. David Agler introduced us. I said to him 'We saw you in Salzburg in *The Exterminating Angel*'. I was trying to conjure a polite comment. Before I could find the words, Sir Thomas said 'My God, it was bloody awful – wasn't it?'

The 'magic of Wexford'

Why Wexford? We usually come with 20 or 30 friends. We love the music – all of it. We get all the religions (and none) to Ger Lawlor's sung Mass. We love the food, the town – the whole social experience. When I recruit, the response is often 'Wexford? Isn't that the place that does the weird opera? I say 'No. Just come and try it'. When I get them to Wexford, the vast majority want to come back every year. Along the way, David Agler and Rosetta Cucchi have become wonderful friends.

Grove got it right

I have an old *Grove Dictionary of Opera*. It says 'Wexford's tradition is to stage three seldom performed operas – one for the head, one for the heart … and one for fun'. Long may it continue. Rosetta's artistic imagination and leadership mean that the dates in late October will continue to be the first entries in any new diary.

Angela Meade (*soprano*)

My time in Wexford happened by accident or maybe it was destiny. I had been contracted elsewhere but when the opportunity to sing an obscure opera in the bel canto canon arose in the land of my ancestors, I jumped at the opportunity. I would never have imagined that I would meet my future husband in this quiet little Irish town, as it seemed such stories were only for fairy tales or opera plots. Maybe it was the Irish hospitality and the unencumbered way of life in Wexford that thrust us together or maybe it was spending time at Cappuccino's, the local coffee house, savouring not only every morsel of a traditional Irish scone and a pot of tea, but on each other's conversation as well. We spent days together as colleagues at the opera house in Mercadante's *Virginia* surrounded by the warm-hearted staff and the magnificent interior of the newly opened Opera House, with its honeyed wood and lavender seats inviting people in with a modern juxtaposition of the medieval town that lies just beyond its doors. Wexford Opera gave me not only the occasion to make my international debut but also my love and my life. Wexford is a magical place that had me spellbound from the moment I arrived and its magic continues its hold on me more than ten years later as I await the chance to return to its enchanted Irish shores.

John O'Donoghue (*former Minister for Arts, Sport and Tourism*)

I was appointed as Minister for Arts, Sport and Tourism in June of 2002 at a time when there was a serious deficit in our arts and cultural infrastructure. I introduced Access 1 which was followed by Access 2 and these programmes provided much-needed funds for capital projects across the country. By then, the campaign for the construction of a new Wexford Opera House had been under way for several years.

I first attended Wexford Opera Festival in the Autumn of 2002. I was warmly welcomed by the chairman, Paul Hennessy, and the chief executive, Jerome Hynes. I did not realize it at the time but it would not be the last time I met them! In fact, they were to become a part of my life for a couple of years! They turned up regularly to meet me (and sometimes in the most unlikely places) over the following couple of years to make the case for a new Wexford Opera House. It came to the stage that if somebody told me that they were with MI5 I would probably have believed it!

They made the case again and again that for over half a century Wexford Festival Opera had been recognized as the world leader in the production of rare opera and urgently needed a proper home. They pointed out that the Theatre Royal in Wexford was centuries old and no longer fit for purpose. They argued that the Festival bedrocked an important part of our cultural reputation as a major player on the global cultural scene, and consistently punched above its weight. They wanted to build a world-class venue on the footprint of the old Theatre Royal which would be Ireland's first purpose-built opera house.

I took Paul and Jerome's case to government and approved a grant of €26 million towards the estimated cost of €33 million for the new Wexford Opera House on the site of the old Theatre Royal in December of 2006. The balance of €7 million was to be provided by Wexford Festival Foundation led by Liam Healy and the building was to be completed within two years. It was erected on time and within budget.

Now known as the National Opera House, this magnificent building haunts the skyline of Wexford town and provides Wexford with – not alone a first-class, state-of-the-art opera house for the twenty-first century – but also a centre of cultural and arts activity for the people of Wexford, the south-east and Ireland as a whole. It is a world-class venue and a fitting legacy to the panache, entrepreneurial spirit and vision of the late Jerome Hynes who passed away at such a young age in 2005. It is a true codicil to his and Paul Hennessy's boundless energies.

I am proud and honoured to have had the opportunity to work with Paul, the late Jerome and so many others to enhance Ireland's and Wexford's cultural and artistic infrastructure in such a significant way. In this regard, it would be remiss of me if I did not acknowledge the efforts of Wexford's public representatives at that time and in particular my Oireachtas colleagues, Tony Dempsey, John Browne and Jim Walsh.

Wexford's National Opera House is surely a monument to the immortal words of Thomas Edison: 'Our greatest weakness lies in giving up. The most certain way to succeed is always to try just one more time.'

Chorus member in *Silent Night*, 2014. 2015 Irish Times Theatre Awards

Alessandro Luciano, Rubens Pelizzari,
Ekaterina Bakanova in *Il bravo*, 2018.
2019 Irish Times Theatre Awards

'THIS MUSIC CREPT BY ME UPON THE WATERS'

Colm Tóibín

Wexford has a strange beauty in the washed light of late October. The town still looks like a medieval port, with narrow streets leading from the quays to a single long main street, also narrow. Wexford got its name from the Vikings, but its tone was set by the Normans. Half the surnames of the people are Norman, and in the plainness of the architecture, and the lack of pretension in the citizens, there is a Norman austerity. The other elements include not only the Gaelic, but also the English and Huguenot.

The train journey along the river Slaney between Enniscorthy and Wexford passes through what is for me one of the most moving and resonant landscapes. In that silvery still afternoon light, for several miles you see no roads and hardly any buildings, just trees and the calm strong river. If you are travelling to Wexford in late October, with the promise of music, these ten or fifteen minutes offer a special happiness.

There is a line from Shakespeare's *The Tempest* that goes: 'This music crept by me upon the waters'. In Wexford, the autumn light over wide estuary water, by some miracle, has over seventy years been the light beneath which a great opera festival takes place.

I saw my first opera in Wexford precisely fifty years ago, in 1971 when I was sixteen. Those of us in school who wanted to go to the dress rehearsal of the opera had to assemble every afternoon before study to listen to a recording and have the story explained. I have a clear memory of the stereo record-player being rigged up and the light from the sea shining through the long windows in a seldom-used room of one of the front buildings in the old St Peter's College.

The opera was *The Pearl Fishers*. At home, we had a record of John McCormack singing the famous duet with a baritone. The soprano in Wexford that year was to be Christiane Eda-Pierre.

The yellowish lighting of the opening scene is vivid in my mind, and the extraordinary precision of the singing of the chorus and the heightened emotion. As I write this, the word *motif* comes back to me. In the talks about the opera each afternoon, we were told to watch for motifs, but that did not sink in. Now, as I sat in the old Theatre Royal in Wexford, I recognized the motif which came before the first duet and I was ready for those soaring moments when the two voices merge and move apart and compete and merge again.

What is extraordinary about the Wexford Festival Opera is how much has changed, but how much the sacred core has been preserved. The Festival is longer; the opera house is new. But there is something wonderful and special about walking those streets in your best clothes on those Festival nights, when you know that you are going to see an opera you will probably never see again, an opera that deserves to be better known, or has strange and interesting flaws or contains hidden, forgotten treasures.

It is important to remember that the celebration of beauty did not happen in Wexford by accident. It belongs to a spirit that has nourished this place for a long time. A spirit that lives, for example, in the work of the novelist John Banville and the playwright Billy Roche. A spirit that, in the 1790s, distributed pamphlets about liberty and studied the example of the French Revolution and the American Revolution. A spirit that enticed Pugin, the greatest church architect of the age, to Wexford to design the cathedral at Enniscorthy, the chapel of St Peter's College and other churches in the county.

A spirit that created a Festival which specializes in the creation of pure magic and giving this, as the years have gone on, greater scope, larger possibilities, sharper resonances.

NOTES

Chapter 1: The most ambitious venture in years, 1951

1   Quoted in Gus Smith, *Ring Up the Curtain* (Dublin, 1976), p. 29.
2   Joseph Groocock, *A General Survey of Music in the Republic of Ireland* (Dublin, 1961), p. 5.
3   Larchet, *A Plea for Music*, p. 508, in Harry White, *The Keeper's Recital* (Cork, 1961), p. 130. Larchet was Professor in UCD from 1921 to 1958.
4   Aural Interview with Nellie Walsh, John Bowman, RTÉ 1.
5   Aural Interview with Tom Walsh, John Bowman, RTÉ 1.
6   Smith, pp 41–2.
7   Compton Mackenzie, *My Life and Times* (London, 1970).
8   Letter Mackenzie to Walsh, 21 Oct. 1950; Walsh files.
9   Smith, p. 51. It is not known where this quotation is from or how accurate it is.
10   Walsh, 'How It All Began', Wexford Arts Centre newsletter (1977). Gus Smith had indicated in his book that two hundred guineas were sought and five hundred were received – but Walsh refuted this personally in 1977.
11   Walsh, 'How It All Began', Wexford Arts Centre newsletter (1977).
12   *The Bohemian Girl* was Balfe's most acclaimed work, but *The Rose of Castile* had achieved success at Drury Lane when it was first produced on 29 Oct. 1857, Smith, p. 35.
13   Walsh, 'How It All Began', Wexford Arts Centre newsletter (1977).
14   Smith, p. 57.
15   Report on Tom Walsh, RTÉ Archive.
16   Letter Walsh to Ó hAnnracháin, 23 Feb. 1951, RTÉ Archive.
17   Letter Walsh to Ó hAnnracháin, 23 Feb. 1951. RTÉ Archive.
18   Letter Ó hAnnracháin to Walsh, 3 Mar. 1951, RTÉ Archive.
19   Letter Walsh to Ó hAnnracháin, 28 Sept. 1951, RTÉ Archive.
20   Letter O'Dwyer to Ó hAnnracháin, 12 Sept. 1951, RTÉ Archive.
21   Letter Ó hAnnracháin to O'Dwyer, 14 Sept. 1951, Walsh files.
22   Letter Walsh to Ó hAnnracháin, 15 May 1951, RTÉ Archive.
23   Ibid., 3 July 1951, RTÉ Archive.
24   Letter Ó hAnnracháin to Walsh, 12 July 1951, RTÉ Archive.
25   Letter Walsh to Ó hAnnracháin, 13 July 1951, RTÉ Archive.
26   Ibid.
27   It was Walsh's singing teacher, Viani, who had founded the DOS.
28   Ibid., 13 July 1951 in *The Wexford Festival – An Historical Appraisal*, 21 May 1977, Speech to the Faculty of Anaesthetists, Royal College of Surgeons in Ireland.
29   *Free Press*, 20 Oct. 1951. Also in Smith, p. 35. Dickie and Springer became acquainted at Wexford and were subsequently married.
30   Copy of agreement re. Radio Éireann orchestra, 1–4 Nov. 1951, Walsh files.
31   Memo, Ó hAnnracháin, 24 Sept. 1951, Walsh files.
32   Letter Stephenson to O'Dwyer, 25 Sept. 1951, Walsh files.
33   Letter Ó hAnnracháin to O'Dwyer, 20 Sept. 1951, Walsh files.
34   Letter Dargavel Concerts Ltd to O'Dwyer. Letter re Programming notes, 9 Oct. 1951.
35   Letter C.E. Kelly to O'Dwyer, 23 Oct. 1951, RTÉ Archive.
36   Walsh, 'How It All Began', Wexford Arts Centre newsletter, 1977.
37   Moriarty founded the Cork Ballet Company.
38   Letter Moriarty to O'Dwyer, 29 Nov. 1951, Walsh files.
39   *Irish Independent*, 5 July 1963.
40   Letter Mackenzie to Walsh, 21 Nov. 1951, Walsh files.
41   Letter Mackenzie to Walsh, 11 Jan. 1952, Walsh files.
42   *Evening Herald*, 15 Oct. 1951. Also in 1952 Festival programme book.
43   *Irish Independent*, 10 Nov. 1951, in 1952 Festival programme book.
44   *Sunday Times*, 28 Oct. 1951, in 1952 Festival programme book.
45   *Boston Globe*, 13 Nov. 1951, in 1952 Festival programme book.
46   1951 Festival programme book.
47   Fanny Feehan, 'Tom Walsh: the Operatic Doctor', *Hibernia*, 20 Oct. 1972, Walsh files.
48   Report on Walsh, RTÉ Archive.

Chapter 2: An amateurish affair, 1952–5

1   1952 Festival programme book.
2   Nellie Walsh, *How Many Times Has the Festival Been in Danger?*, Photocopy, Nellie Walsh files.
3   Walsh aural interview, presented by John Bowman, RTÉ 1.
4   Smith, p. 44.
5   Elvina Ramella (soprano); Nicola Monti (tenor); Gino Vanelli (baritone); Cristiano Dallamangas (Greek bass) sang in Wexford's 1952 production of *L'elisir d'amore*, ibid.
6   *Echo*, 8 Nov. 1952.
7   Interview with Bryan Balkwill, Jan. 2000.
8   Letter Ó hAnnracháin to Walsh, 5 Feb. 1953, RTÉ Archive.

9　Letter Walsh to Ó hAnnracháin, 25 Mar. 1953, RTÉ Archive.

10　Letter Ó hAnnracháin to Walsh, 20 Apr. 1953, RTÉ Archive.

11　Letter Ó hAnnracháin to Walsh, 27 Apr. 1953, RTÉ Archive.

12　Letter Walsh to Ó hAnnracháin, 28 Apr. 1953, RTÉ Archive.

13　Letter Ó hAnnracháin to Walsh, 1 May 1953, RTÉ Archive.

14　Letter Walsh to Ó hAnnracháin, 28 Apr. 1953, Walsh files. The artists who had been engaged by the end of April were Nicola Monti as Ernesto; Elvina Ramella as Norina; and Cristiano Dallamangas as Don Pasquale.

15　Ibid., 4 May 1953, RTÉ Archive.

16　Ibid.

17　Letter Ó hAnnracháin to Walsh, 7 May 1953 and Walsh to Ó hAnnracháin, 22 May 1953, RTÉ Archive.

18　Ibid., 7 May 1953.

19　Ibid.

20　Ibid., 12 June 1953.

21　Letter Walsh to Ó hAnnracháin, 13 June 1953, RTÉ Archive.

22　Ibid., 22 June 1953, RTÉ Archive. Monti's fee was subject to Éire income tax and it was presumed that Radio Éireann would accept to pay for half of his return air fare to Ireland.

23　*Irish Independent*, 1953.

24　Ibid. Sir Compton was joined on the panel for the Forum by Lord Longford, Eoin O'Mahony and Dr J. Liddy.

25　Smith, p. 51.

26　1954 Festival programme book. Nicola Monti and Marilyn Cotlow were the soloists this year. Cotlow had previously sung in a Metropolitan production of *L'elisir d'amore*; Smith, p. 58.

27　*Creation* (Éire), 15 Oct. 1958, Walsh files.

28　Balance sheet for 1955 expenditure account, Walsh files.

29　Balance sheet for 1955 income account, Walsh files.

30　1955 Festival programme book.

31　Festival programme books.

32　*New York Times*, 14 Mar. 1993.

33　Ibid.

34　Kevin Collins, 'Festival is a Jewel, says Opera Expert', newspaper article (undated), Walsh files.

35　Charles Acton, 'Wexford Needs to Stress Irishness', newspaper article, 1 Nov. 1969, Walsh files.

36　This was due to the lack of a coherent archival system to record the history of the Festival in the early years.

37　Letter Moran Caplat to Fintan O'Connor, 3 Nov. 1955, Glyndebourne Archive.

38　Letter O'Connor to Caplat, 12 Oct. 1956, Glyndebourne Archive.

39　Ibid., 16 Jan. 1956, Glyndebourne Archive and 20 June 1956, Wexford Festival Archive.

40　Festival Council minutes, 22 Aug. 1956 and 10 Oct. 1956. Wexford Festival Archive.

41　Charles Acton, 'Wexford Needs to Stress Irishness', newspaper article, 1977, Walsh files.

42　John Mulcahy, newspaper article, 1977, Walsh files.

43　Wexford Festival minutes, 1956–68, Wexford Festival Archive.

44　*RTÉ Guide*, 21 Nov. 1969.

Chapter 3: The burden of carrying it on, 1956–9

1　1956 Festival programme book.

2　Letter Mackenzie to Walsh, 19 Apr. 1956, Walsh files.

3　Balance sheet, as at 7 Jan. 1957, Walsh files.

4　Letter Mackenzie to Walsh, 11 Feb. 1957, Walsh files.

5　Festival Council minutes, 20 June 1956, Wexford Festival Archive.

6　Ibid., 4 July 1956.

7　Ibid., 20 June 1956.

8　Ibid., 4 July 1956.

9　Ibid., 3 Oct. 1956.

10　Ibid., 21 Nov. 1956.

11　Ibid., 22 Aug. 1956.

12　Ibid., 19 Dec. 1956.

13　It is indicated in the minutes that this subsidy had been received prior to the 1956 Festival although evidence from further minutes shows the difficulty that the Festival Council encountered even into 1957 when trying to claim this subsidy for the 1956 season. By 21 November the Wexford Council had received a promise of £500 from the German Legation for the 1955 season but no mention was made of a subsidy for 1956. By 19 Dec. the Council realized that it was highly unlikely that they would receive money from the German contingent for their 1956 Festival.

14　Festival Council minutes, 3 Oct. 1956, Wexford Festival Archive.

15　Telephone interview with Terry Sheehy, Jan. 2000.

16　Moran Caplat, *From Dinghies To Divas* (London, 1985), p. 194. Significantly, the DGOS had never asked Walsh for operatic advice, although Walsh said he never expected them to.

17　*People*, 31 Oct. 1959, Walsh files.

18　Interview with Terry Sheehy, Jan. 2000.

19　1957 Festival programme book. Bryan Balkwill conducted, Peter Ebert produced and Joseph Carl was the designer for both operas in this year.

20　Letter O'Connor to Caplat, 12 Oct. 1956, Glyndebourne Archive.

21　Festival Council minutes, 20 Feb. 1957, Wexford Festival Archive.

22　Ibid., 28 Aug. 1957.

23　Ibid., 9 Sept. 1957.

24　Letter Mackenzie to Walsh, 11 Feb. 1959, Walsh files.

25　Festival Council minutes, 27 Nov. 1957, Wexford Festival Archive.

26 Smith, p. 77.
27 Ibid. Born in 1903 to an American mother, he was a Conservative who came into Parliament in 1931. Beit inherited most of his uncle's affairs in South Africa, including the trusteeship of the Beit Trust, a charity organization for medical and educational care in Central Africa.
28 Interview with Moran Caplat, Jan. 2000.
29 1958 Festival programme book. Due to the illness of Frans Boerlage, *I due Foscari* was produced by Peter Ebert.
30 Festival Council minutes, 19 Nov. 1958, Wexford Festival Archive.
31 *Evening Herald*, 2 July 1958.
32 1958 Festival programme book.
33 Ibid.
34 Festival Council minutes, 11 Dec. 1957, Wexford Festival Archive.
35 Ibid., 11 Dec. 1957. The Artistic section covered artists, publicity, scenery, structural alterations to theatre, printing of programme; Business – payment of artists, transport, advertising, insurance, accounts, income tax, accommodation, grants, ordering of goods, hiring of films and return thereof; Theatre and Box Office – brochure, preparation of tickets etc., bookings, card index system, stewarding, cleaning and decoration of theatre, seating; Finance – budget, control of finance, receiving of all cash, banking, keeping of a/c books; Illuminations – town lighting, fireworks, opening ceremony, decoration of town.
36 Ibid., 18 June 1958.
37 Ibid., 22 Oct. 1958.
38 Smith, p. 78. The Calouste Gulbenkian Foundation was operated from Lisbon but had a London office. Beit acted as Wexford's ambassador in the hope of gaining a grant from the foundation, as he had previously been acquainted with the Portuguese Ambassador in London.
39 Festival Council minutes, 18 June 1958, Wexford Festival Archive.
40 Ibid., 30 Apr. 1958.
41 Ibid., 12 Mar. 1958.
42 Ibid., 21 Jan. 1959.
43 This view was confirmed by another Council member, Dr Des Ffrench, who had had conversations with artists during the previous Festival to that effect.
44 Festival Council minutes, 21 Jan. 1959, Wexford Festival Archive.
45 Letter Walsh to Ninette Lawson, 5 Apr. 1959.
46 Letter Mackenzie to Walsh, 11 Feb. 1959, Walsh files.
47 Letter Walsh to Ninette Lawson, 5 Apr. 1959, Walsh files.
48 Festival Council minutes, 29 Jan. 1959, Wexford Festival Archive.
49 Ibid., 11 Feb. 1959.
50 Ibid., 2 Sept. 1959.
51 Ibid., 26 Nov. 1959.

52 Ibid., 29 Sept. 1959.
53 *People*, 31 Oct. 1959.
54 Ibid.
55 'The Wexford Festival, Something of which the Country is Proud', *People*, 31 Oct. 1959.
56 1959 Festival programme book.
57 *Irish Times*, 31 Oct. 1959.

Chapter 4: On the musical map of the world, 1960–3

1 *People*, 31 Oct. 1959.
2 Festival Council minutes, 11 Jan. 1960, Wexford Festival Archive.
3 Memo, 'The Wexford Festival and its Future', Alfred Beit to Walsh and Colonel Price, 6 Nov. 1959, Walsh files.
4 Ibid.
5 There is no evidence to suggest that Walsh replied to this memo but his actions thereafter suggest that he took Beit's suggestions very seriously, whether he agreed with them or not. After all, he was left with little choice.
6 Letter Raymond Corish to Walsh, 19 Dec. 1959, Walsh files.
7 Marese Murphy interview with Walsh, newspaper article (undated), Walsh files.
8 Festival Council minutes, 4 Dec. 1959, Wexford Festival archive.
9 Ibid., 11 Jan. 1960.
10 Interview with James O'Connor, Wexford, Mar. 2000.
11 Festival Council minutes, 1 Mar. 1961, Wexford Festival Archive.
12 1961 Festival programme book.
13 Festival Council minutes, 1 Mar. 1961, Wexford Festival Archive.
14 'The Wexford Festival', by Marese Murphy, Nov. 1961, Walsh files.
15 Festival Council minutes, 5 July 1961, Wexford Festival Archive.
16 Ibid., 1 Mar. 1961.
17 Ibid., 5 July 1961.
18 Letter Beit to Walsh, 23 Aug. 1961, Walsh files.
19 Ibid.
20 Festival Council minutes, 20 Dec. 1961, Wexford Festival Archive.
21 Ibid., 20 Dec. 1961.
22 Ibid. (undated, 1962).
23 Ibid., 3 Jan. 1962.
24 Ibid., 10 Jan. 1962. The Liverpool Philharmonic had been paid £2,500 in 1961.
25 Ibid., 10 Jan. 1962.
26 Ibid., 23 Aug. 1962.
27 Ibid., 10 Jan. 1962.
28 Ibid.
29 Ibid., 25 Jan. 1962.
30 Ibid., 14 Mar. 1962.
31 Ibid., 10 Apr. 1962.

32 Interview with Jim Golden (May 2000), voluntary backstage worker (Props) at Wexford Opera Festival. Later, he became chairman of the Festival Council.
33 Festival Council minutes, 10 Apr. 1962, Wexford Festival Archive.
34 Ibid., 29 May 1962.
35 Ibid., 2 Sept. 1962.
36 1962 Festival programme book. Bernadette Greevy and Veronica Dunne, both Irish artists, performed the Mascagni work.
37 Ibid.
38 Ibid.
39 Festival Council minutes, 5 Nov. 1962.
40 Ibid., 28 Nov. 1962.
41 Ibid.
42 Ibid., 14 Aug. 1962.
43 1963 Festival programme book.
44 Letter Walsh to Gerard Victory, 1 June 1963, Wexford Festival Archive.
45 Festival Council minutes, 13 Nov. 1963, Wexford Festival Archive.
46 *Irish Independent*, 5 July 1963.
47 Festival Council minutes, 13 Nov. 1963, Wexford Festival Archive.
48 Ibid., 2 Dec. 1963.
49 Ibid., 27 Dec. 1963.
50 Ibid., 5 Feb. 1964.

Chapter 5: Walsh and Wexford, Antony and Cleopatra, bacon and eggs, 1964–9

1 Tony Grey, '"Let's Make an Opera Festival" – said the five mad men of Wexford' (no date), Walsh files.
2 *Irish Independent,* 21 Feb. 1964.
3 *Irish Times*, 24 Feb. 1964.
4 Interview with Alan Wood, East Sussex, Jan. 2000. Wood was in charge of Guinness advertising.
5 Festival Council minutes, 3 Mar. 1964, Wexford Festival Archive.
6 1964 Festival programme book.
7 Ibid.
8 Festival Council minutes, 10 Mar. 1965, Wexford Festival Archive.
9 Festival Council minutes, 2 June 1965, Wexford Festival Archive.
10 Letter Walsh to Beit, June 1965, Walsh files.
11 Festival Council minutes, 9 Aug. 1965, Wexford Festival Archive.
12 1965 Festival programme book.
13 Confidential memo from Walsh to Jackson, 13 Dec. 1965, Walsh files.
14 Letter Beit to Walsh, 8 Jan. 1966, Walsh files.
15 Ibid. It is not clear what type of relationship Beit had with the Guinness group, although Alan Wood, in charge of Guinness advertising, said that Beit found the Guinness involvement hard to accept.
16 Ibid.
17 Letter Walsh to Beit, 10 Jan. 1966, Walsh files.

18 Ibid.
19 Festival Council minutes, 5 July 1966, Wexford Festival Archive.
20 Ibid., 25 Apr. 1966, Wexford Festival Archive.
21 Special meeting of the Wexford members of the Executive Council, 17 Aug. 1966, Wexford Festival Archive.
22 Festival Council minutes, 23 Sept. 1966, Wexford Festival Archive.
23 Ibid., 7 Nov. 1966, Wexford Festival Archive.
24 1966 Festival programme book.
25 Festival Council minutes, 5 July 1966, Wexford Festival Archive.
26 Letter Mackenzie to Walsh, 11 Feb. 1967, Walsh files.
27 Mackenzie to Walsh, 11 Feb. 1959, Walsh files. Mackenzie actually remained as President of the Festival until his death in 1972.
28 Interview with Jim Golden and interview with Nicky Cleary, voluntary workers with the Festival at the time. Also in Smith, p. 102.
29 Festival Council minutes, 7 Nov. 1966, Wexford Festival Archive.
30 *The Wexford Festival – An Historical Appraisal,* 21 May 1977, Speech to the Faculty of Anaesthetists, Royal College of Surgeons in Ireland. Walsh files.
31 *Sunday Times*, 29 Oct. 1967.
32 Brian Quinn, 'Wexford without Walsh' in *Hibernia*, Oct. 1967, Walsh files.
33 Fanny Feehan, 'Tom Walsh – An Operatic Doctor' in *Hibernia*, 20 Oct. 1972, Walsh files.
34 *Hibernia*, 20 Oct. 1972, Walsh files.
35 Ibid.
36 *Hibernia*, 20 Oct. 1972, Walsh files.
37 Letter Brian Dickie to Reverend B. Viney of Sussex, 13 Nov. 1968, Walsh files.
38 'The Dwarfs without Snow White', *Free Press*, 20 Sept. 1968, Walsh files.

Chapter 6: The professional amateurs, 1967–73

1 Festival Council minutes, 27 Jan. 1967, Wexford Festival Archive.
2 Ibid., 11 July 1967.
3 Ibid.
4 Ibid., 16 Aug. 1967.
5 *Sunday Independent*, 29 Oct. 1967.
6 Festival Council minutes, 3 Nov. 1967. James O'Connor had made a comment to the press regarding this. O'Connor defended his line by saying that he had stated that 'it *would* be considered', not that 'it *had* been considered'.
7 Ibid.
8 Ibid., 23 Jan. 1968.
9 Ibid., 27 Mar. 1968.
10 *Irish Times*, 10 June 1968.
11 *Evening Press*, 26 Oct. 1968.
12 Festival Council minutes, 3 Jan. 1969, Wexford Festival Archive.
13 Ibid.

14   Ibid., 14 May 1969.
15   Ibid., 26 June 1969.
16   Michael Yeats, 'Poor Standard at Wexford', *Evening Press*, 27 Oct. 1969, Wexford Festival Archive.
17   Festival Council minutes, 5 Nov. 1969, Wexford Festival Archive.
18   Letter Brian Dickie to Charles Acton, 1 Feb. 1972.
19   Festival Council minutes, 5 Nov. 1969, Wexford Festival Archive.
20   Ibid.
21   Ibid., 9 Sept. 1970.
22   *Enniscorthy Echo*, 10 Oct. 1970.
23   Festival Council minutes, 20 Jan. 1971, Wexford Festival Archive.
24   Robert Henderson, press cutting, Nov. 1971, Wexford Festival Archive.
25   *Country Life*, press cutting, 11 Nov. 1971.
26   *Hibernia*, 8 Nov. 1971.
27   *New York Times*, 14 Feb. 1971.
28   Festival Council minutes, 9 June 1971, Wexford Festival Archive.
29   Report on meeting of local Council members, 16 Nov. 1971, Wexford Festival Archive.
30   Festival Council minutes, 2 Dec. 1971. Wexford Festival Archive.
31   Ibid.
32   Ibid.
33   Festival Council minutes, 24 July 1972, Wexford Festival Archive.
34   Ibid., 26 Jan. 1972.
35   Ibid., 24 July 1972.
36   *Evening Herald*, 9 June 1972.
37   Letter Sean Scallan, Chairman, to Brian Dickie, 12 Feb. 1973.
38   Festival Executive Council minutes, 15 Dec. 1972, Wexford Festival Archive.
39   Letter Walsh to Mackenzie's wife, 10 Dec. 1972, Walsh files. Mackenzie had been married three times and was pre-deceased by his first two wives. His latter two wives were sisters.
40   Wexford Festival development Council minutes, 16 Dec. 1972. Wexford Festival Archive.
41   Festival Council minutes, 2 Feb. 1973, Wexford Festival Archive.
42   Ibid., 9 April 1973.
43   Ibid.
44   Ibid., 21 Feb. 1973.
45   Ibid., 21 Mar. 1973.
46   Publicity policy report to Wexford Festival Council, Apr. 1973, Wexford Festival Archive.
47   Festival Council minutes, 8 June 1973, Wexford Festival Archive.
48   Ibid., 28 Nov. 1973.
49   Ibid., 27 July 1973.
50   *Sunday Times*, 4 Nov. 1973.
51   'Irish Opera Company Needed', press cutting, 1973, Wexford Festival Archive.
52   *Glasgow Herald*, 3 Nov. 1973.
53   Wexford Festival Development Council report, Dec. 1973, Wexford Festival Archive.
54   Ibid.
55   1974 Festival programme book.

Chapter 7: Not so much a festival as a way of life, 1974–85

1   Festival Council minutes, 3 Jan. 1974, Wexford Festival Archive.
2   Report on Arts Council subvention in Festival Executive Council minutes, 4 June 1974, Wexford Festival Archive.
3   Festival Council minutes, 17 Sept. 1974, Wexford Festival Archive.
4   Tony O'Brien, 'Live Music is Dead in Wexford', *New Ross Standard*, 7 Sept. 1974, Wexford Festival Archive.
5   Festival Council minutes, 4 Feb. 1975, Wexford Festival Archive.
6   *Wexford People*, 24 Oct. 1975.
7   Nicholas Furlong, 'Wexford Festival no Anglo-Saxon Remnant', *Irish Post*, 13 Dec. 1975, Wexford Festival Archive.
8   Festival Council minutes, 30 Sept. 1976, Wexford Festival Archive.
9   Letter from Alfred Beit to Sean Scallan, 13 February 1975.
10   Festival Council minutes, 8 Dec. 1976, Wexford Festival Archive.
11   Rodney Milnes, 'Wexford Ho!', *Opera*, 1976, Wexford Festival Archive.
12   *Wexford People*, 5 Nov. 1976.
13   Festival Council minutes, 15 Feb. 1977, Wexford Festival Archive.
14   *Sunday Independent*, 28 Feb. 1977.
15   Letter F.X. Butler to Dick Jefferies, Chairman, 9 Feb. 1977.
16   1977 Wexford Festival programme book.
17   Festival Council minutes, 15 Aug. 1978, Wexford Festival Archive.
18   1978 Wexford Festival programme book.
19   Festival Council minutes, 15 Jan. 1979, Wexford Festival Archive.
20   Ibid., 16 Jan. 1979.
21   Ibid., 15 May 1979, Wexford Festival Archive.
22   Letter Dinah Molloy, Music Officer, Arts Council, to Richard Jefferies, Chairman, 7 Mar. 1979.
23   *Irish Times*, 6 Nov. 1979.
24   Festival Council minutes, 15 May 1979, Wexford Festival Archive.
25   1979 Wexford Festival programme book.
26   Festival Council minutes, 15 Jan. 1979, Wexford Festival Archive.
27   Ibid., 12 Feb. 1980.
28   Ibid., 11 Mar. 1980.
29   Ibid., 24 Sept. 1980.
30   Ibid., 9 Dec. 1980.

31 Brian Quinn, press cutting, 1980, Wexford Festival Archive.

32 Festival Council minutes, 23 June 1981, Wexford Festival Archive.

33 Kenneth Loveland, 'Another Triumph at Wexford', *South Wales Argus*, 30 Oct. 1981, Wexford Festival Archive.

34 Festival Council minutes, 8 Dec. 1981. Wexford Festival Archive.

35 Ibid.

36 Ibid., 4 Feb. 1982.

37 Letter Adrian Slack to Jim Golden, 9 May 1981.

38 Festival Council minutes, 4 Feb. 1982. Wexford Festival Archive.

39 Ibid., 13 July 1982.

40 Ibid., 12. Oct. 1982.

41 Repertory committee report, 4 Jan. 1983, Wexford Festival Archive.

42 Letter to Ian Fox, 7 Feb. 1983, Wexford Festival Archive.

43 *Enniscorthy Echo*, 14 Jan. 1983.

44 Festival Council minutes, 16 Feb. 1984, Wexford Festival Archive.

45 Letter Jim Golden to Elaine Padmore, 20 Jan. 1984

46 Letter Elaine Padmore to Chairman and Council members, 17 Mar. 1984.

47 Letter George Waters, Director General of RTÉ to Ted Nealon, TD, Minister of State at the Dept. of the Taoiseach, 5 Mar. 1984.

48 Festival Council minutes, 20 Nov. 1984, Wexford Festival Archive.

49 *Irish Times*, 2 Nov. 1984.

50 Festival Council minutes, 15 Jan. 1985, Wexford Festival Archive.

Chapter 8: Walsh's final farewell, 1986–8

1 Festival Council minutes, 12 Dec. 1985, Wexford Festival Archive.

2 Letter from Jim Golden to Sean Scallan, 5 Dec. 1985.

3 Festival Council minutes, 17 Feb. 1986, Wexford Festival Archive.

4 Ibid., Finance Officer's Report.

5 Notes from Wexford Festival meeting, 17 Feb. 1986, Wexford Festival Archive. It is unclear by whom this was written but it is obvious nevertheless that tensions were extremely high at this point.

6 Statement from Wexford Opera Festival Council, 20 February 1986.

7 'A Plan to Save the Wexford Festival Opera', February 1986.

8 Festival Council minutes, 3 Mar. 1986, Wexford Festival Archive.

9 Letter from the Manager of the Bank of Ireland to John O'Connor, Wexford Festival Council, 18 March 1986.

10 Festival Council minutes, 20 May 1986, Wexford Festival Archive.

11 Letter Barbara Wallace to Máirtín McCullough, 14 Apr. 1986.

12 Chairman's Address at Guinness reception, 23 June 1986.

13 Festival Council minutes, 27 Aug. 1986, Wexford Festival Archive.

14 Chairman's Address at Guinness reception, 23 June 1986.

15 'Festival Fanfare', *People*, 24 Oct. 1986.

16 Festival Council minutes, 1 Dec. 1987, Wexford Festival Archive.

17 Festival Council minutes, 8 Dec. 1987, Wexford Festival Archive.

18 Letter Barbara Wallace to Beit, 21 Dec. 1987, Wexford Festival Archive.

19 Festival Council minutes, 20 May 1986, Wexford Festival Archive.

20 Bernard Levin, 'Doctor Tom's Final Curtain', *The Times*, 14 Nov. 1988. Reprinted in Ian Fox (ed.), *100 Nights at the Opera* (Dublin, 1991), pp 135–7.

21 'Dr Tom Walsh – Founder of the Wexford Festival', *Guardian*, 1988, Wexford Festival Archive.

22 Festival Council minutes, 10 Dec. 1989, Wexford Festival Archive.

Chapter 9: We still believe in miracles at Wexford, 1989–2003

1 Festival Council minutes, 18 Sept. 1989, Wexford Festival Archive.

2 Letter Barbara Wallace to Sean Scallan, 31 Mar. 1989.

3 Letter Sean Scallan to Wallace, 2 Mar. 1989, Wexford Festival Archive.

4 Memo from Barbara Wallace, 31 Mar. 1989, Wexford Festival Archive.

5 'Some Reasons for Examining the Existing Structure of Wexford Festival Opera', by Barbara Wallace, 1990, Wexford Festival Archive.

6 Meeting of Wexford Festival Council, 4 Sept. 1990.

7 Wexford Festival Council meeting, 11 Oct. 1990.

8 Letter Elaine Padmore to Patricia Quinn, 9 Nov. 1990.

9 Festival Council minutes, 3 Dec. 1991, Wexford Festival Archive.

10 Meeting of Wexford Festival Council, 23 Apr., 1991.

11 Briefing document from Jerome Hynes to Dr A.J.F. (Tony) O'Reilly, Nov. 1992.

12 Wexford Festival Council minutes, 11 June 1991, Wexford Festival Archive.

13 Paul Hennessy, Wexford Festival Opera – Corporate affairs and statutory compliance report, Aug. 1992.

14 1992 Wexford Festival programme book.

15 Elaine Padmore to Jerome Hynes, 21 Jan. 1992.

16 'Air on a Shoe-String: There was Only One Economic Miracle in 1992: the Wexford Festival Opera', *Arts Review*, Dec. 1992.

17 Letter Elaine Padmore to John O'Connor, 31 Aug. 1992.

18 Wexford Festival Council meeting, 6 Oct. 1992.

19   1994 Wexford Festival programme book.

20   1995 Wexford Festival programme book.

21   2000 Wexford Festival programme book.

22   Festival Council minutes, 28 Mar. 1994, Wexford
      Festival Archive.

23   Memo from Jerome Hynes to the Board of
      Directors, 6 Sept. 1994.

24   Festival Council minutes, 30 Oct. 1995, Wexford
      Festival Archive.

25   1996 Wexford Festival Trust, the Chairman's
      statement, Wexford Festival Archive.

26   Letter Jerome Hynes to Tony O'Reilly, 15 Jan. 1996.

27   Minutes of Board of Directors meeting, 6 Mar.
      1996.

28   *Wexford People*, 30 Oct. 1996.

29   *Wexford People*, 29 May 1996.

30   Minutes of meeting of Board of Directors of
      Wexford Festival Opera, 25 Mar. 1997.

31   Minutes of meeting of Wexford Council, 27 Oct.
      1997.

32   Letter Jerome Hynes to Thomson Smillie, 1997.

33   Letter Kevin Myers, journalist, to Jerome Hynes, 6
      Oct. 1997.

34   Festival Council minutes, 23 Mar. 1999, Wexford
      Festival Archive.

35   Minutes of meeting of Board of Directors, 7 Sept.
      1999.

36   Message from President Mary McAleese, 2001
      Festival programme book.

37   Message from the Taoiseach, Bertie Ahern, 2001
      Festival programme book.

38   Interview with Luigi Ferrari, Feb. 2004.

39   *The Guardian*, 25 Oct. 2002.

40   *Wexford People*, 13 Mar. 2002.

41   *Classical Music*, 25 Oct. 2003.

42   Weber had begun composing the music for *Die drei
      Pintos*, a comic opera. It was completed 65 years
      later by Mahler.

43   *Irish Times*, 14 Oct. 2003.

44   *Irish Times*, 29 May 2004.

45   Interview with Luigi Ferrari, Feb. 2004.

**Chapter 10: The best of times, the worst of times,
2004–5**

1   *The Echo*, 20 Oct. 2004.

2   'Wexford Opera', Editorial comment, *Irish Times*, 9
      Aug. 2004.

3   In the end, there were 780 seats in the main
      Auditorium, and 175 in the Jerome Hynes Theatre.

4   'High Tide and Strong Wind Devastate Town', *Irish
      Times*, 29 Oct. 2004.

5   'The Wexford Singers Who Fell on Their Arias',
      Myles McWeeney, *Irish Independent*, 16 Oct. 2004.

6   Roderic Dunnett, 'Land of the little opera', 20 Oct.
      2004.

7   'No Irish Need Apply?', Michael Dervan, *Irish
      Times*, 28 Oct. 2004.

8   Incidentally, Vladimir Jurowski became Music

      Director at Glyndebourne Festival Opera in 2001.

9   'The Heir Apparent', Tom Mooney, *The Echo*, Oct.
      2004.

10   'The Man to Give Wexford a New Angle', Michael
      Dervan, *Irish Times*, 2 June 2005.

11   Letter David Agler to Paul Hennessy, Chairman, 16
      Feb. 2005.

12   'Orchestral Services for Wexford Festival Opera',
      Memo from David Agler to Paul Hennessy and
      Jerome Hynes, 12 Jan. 2005.

13   'Inside Wexford Festival Opera', Pat O'Connell, *The
      Echo*, 26 Oct. 2005.

14   Letter David Agler to Paul Hennessy, Chairman, 16
      Feb. 2005.

15   Board members had all played their part in
      imagining a concept for the new building, and
      many of them had visited other opera houses in
      Europe, to bring back any ideas that might be of
      benefit in the concept and construction of Wexford's
      own Opera House.

16   Interview with Paul Hennessy, July 2020.

17   'Festival Opera Names Jerome's Successor', Patrick
      O'Connell, *Independent*, 21 June 2006.

18   Floyd had travelled to Wexford with his sister in
      1980 for a performance of *Of Mice and Men*.

19   David Tucker, *Irish Independent*, 21 Oct. 2005.

20   Interview with Paul Hennessy, July 2020.

Chapter 11: One hell of a ride, 2006–8

1   Email Hennessy to Agler, 8 Dec. 2005.

2   'Theatre of Dreams', Jo Kerrigan, *Irish Examiner*, 14
      Dec. 2005.

3   Email Hennessy to Agler, 27 Jan. 2006.

4   Email Hennessy to Agler 30 Jan. 2006.

5   'Cleary & Doyle Get Contract', *Wexford Echo*, 14
      June 2006.

6   'Opera 2006 Announced', *New Ross Echo*, 24 May
      2006.

7   'Where Opera is Concerned, it's a Case of All or
      Nothing', Bruce Arnold, *Irish Independent*, 21 Nov.
      2006.

8   Email Vaněk to Agler, 14 Nov. 2006.

9   'La Behemoth', Ferghal Blaney, *Irish Mail on
      Sunday*, 6 May 2007.

10   Email Vaněk to Agler, 25 Apr. 2007.

11   Email Agler to Vaněk, 8 May 2007.

12   Email Hennessy to Agler, 3 Aug. 2007.

13   Michael Parsons, *Irish Times*, 1 June 2007.

14   News Items, 'Wexford Festival Foundation: Update',
      Press Pack, Wexford Festival Opera, Johnstown
      Castle, 31 May–17 June 2007.

15   'Wexford Festival Shifts Location – and Season',
      Michael Dervan, *Irish Times*, 28 Feb. 2007.

16   'The Gospel of Excellence', Tom Mooney, 2019
      Festival programme book.

17   'Opera Rocks', Sophie Gorman, *Irish Independent*,
      26 May 2007.

18   Ibid.

19 Chairman's Message, Paul Hennessy, 2007 Festival programme book.
20 'Wexford Opera Chief Granted Injunction to Stop Dismissal', *Irish Times*, 23 June 2007.
21 'Dispute between Opera Festival and Executive Settled', Mary Carolan, *Irish Times*, 3 July 2007.
22 'Another Fine Mess in Wexford', Deirdre Falvey; *Irish Times*, 7 July 2007.
23 'Opera House to Sustain Artistic Growth', Paul Hennessy, *Wexford Echo*, 15 Oct. 2008.
24 'New Theatre Heralds a New Gilded Age', *Wexford Echo*, 27 Aug. 2008.
25 Memo from Paul Hennessy to the Board, 19 July and 17 Sept. 2008.
26 'Festival Foundation Still Needs €2.5m to Pay for Opera House', *Wexford People*, 8 Oct. 2008.
27 Matt O'Connor to Agler, 27 Feb. 2017.
28 Agler to Sue Graham-Dixon, 3 Sept. 2008.
29 'Why Wexford Should Open its Doors to the Nation', Fintan O'Toole, *Irish Times*, 25 Oct. 2008.

Chapter 12: Just one of those crazy things, 2009–12

1   'Just One of those Crazy Things', Michael Dervan, *Irish Times*, 16 Oct. 2008.
2   Andrew Clark, *Financial Times*, 22 Oct. 2008.
3   Dick O'Riordan, *Sunday Business Post*, 26 Oct. 2008.
4   Michael White, *Catholic Herald*, Oct. 2008.
5   Foreword from outgoing Chairman, Paul Hennessy, 2009 Festival programme book.
6   Email from David Agler to Hennessy and Thomas de Mallet Burgess, 7 July 2009.
7   Memo from Agler to the Board of Wexford Festival Opera, 7 Feb. 2009.
8   Unfinished report in response to the Arts Council's Opera Provision proposals, 14 Aug. 2009.
9   Memo from David Agler to the Board of Wexford Festival Opera, 7 Feb. 2009.
10 Ibid.
11 'Cullen's Final Operatic Act', Dick O'Riordan, *Sunday Business Post*, 28 Mar. 2010.
12 Memo from David Agler to the Board of Wexford Festival Opera, 7 Feb. 2009.
13 'Hanafin Signals More Cuts on Way for the Arts', Conor Kane, *Irish Independent*, 29 Apr. 2010.
14 Chairman's Message, 2010 Festival programme book.
15 'Opera House again Strikes Right Note with Architects', Olivia Kelly, *Irish Times*, 25 May 2010.
16 'Town Mourns Loss of Former Opera Festival Chairman John O'Connor', 13 May 2010.
17 Dr Tom Walsh had chosen Donizetti's *Don Pasquale* in 1953, and it was produced again in 1963.
18 Brian Dickie to David Agler, 26 Oct. 2010.
19 The name of the Department changed from 'Arts, Sport and Tourism' to 'Tourism, Culture and Sport' in May 2010.

20 'No One Ever Asked Us to go Home', Colm Tóibín, *Irish Times*, 9 Aug. 2011.
21 'It's Curtains for National Opera Plans', Stephen O'Brien, *Sunday Times*, 29 May 2011.
22 'Opera Ireland's Tragic Final Act', Dick Riordan, *Sunday Business Post*, 12 June 2011.
23 Ibid.
24 'It's Curtains for National Opera Plans', Stephen O'Brien, *Sunday Times*, 29 May 2011.
25 '€1.7m for Opera Festival', *Wexford People*, 16 Mar. 2011
26 Ibid.
27 'New Festival Chorus Replaces the Prague Chamber Choir', David Looby, *Wexford Echo*, 27 Sept. 2011.
28 'Zurich Sponsors Opening Production at 60th Wexford Festival Opera', *Irish Broker*, 14 Sept. 2011.
29 'A Voluntary Night at the Opera', Voluntary Arts Ireland website, *The Thought Collective*, Kevin Murphy, 4 Nov. 2011.
30 Ger Lawlor, 2011 Festival programme book.
31 Translation from the German article *Die Zeit*, 17 Sept. 2012.
32 'Reduced Festival Blow to Wexford', *Wexford Echo*, 15 Nov. 2011.
33 2014 Festival programme book.
34 'Launch of the American Friends of Wexford Opera', 2012 Festival programme book.
35 'Report on the 2011 Festival', Memo from David Agler to the Board, 10 Jan. 2012.
36 Memo by Brian Byrne re the use of a marquee V use of Jerome Hynes Theatre, 22 Feb. 2012.
37 'Rare Opera Too Rare – Even for Wexford!', *Wexford People*, 8 Feb. 2012.
38 'Teenage Stars of the Opera', *Wexford People*, 25 Sept. 2012.
39 'Irish Eyes are Smiling at a Russian Star', David Mellor, *Mail on Sunday*, 4 Nov. 2012.
40 'Is Wexford Opera Back in Full Voice?', Michael Dervan, *Irish Times*, 31 Oct. 2012.
41 Letter from David McLoughlin to John O'Kane, the Arts Council, 20 Nov. 2012.

Chapter 13: The purpose of opera is to change the world, 2013–16

1   Artistic Director's message, 2013 Festival programme book.
2   Colm Tóibín speech, Opera Europa Conference, Wexford, 2013.
3   Brian Dickie to Agler for the 2013 Festival programme book – email 3 Sept. 2020.
4   Padmore to Agler, 12 Nov. 2004.
5   Loretta Brennan Glucksman was the American Friends of Wexford Opera Honorary Patron at the time.
6   Errol Girdlestone was one of the founding members of the Hilliard Ensemble, a British male vocal quartet originally devoted to the performance of early music.

7   Artistic Director's Message, 2013 Festival programme book.
8   Email DMCL to the Board, 13 Dec. 2013.
9   'The Greatest Job', Wexford's David Agler talks to John Allison, *Opera*, Oct. 2013.
10 'Stirring Rendition of Enescu's Octet Closes Festival', Michael Dervan, *Irish Times*, 10 July 2013.
11 'The Greatest Job', Wexford's David Agler talks to John Allison, *Opera*, Oct. 2013.
12 Ibid.
13 2014 Festival programme book.
14 Agler to Brian Dickie, 11 Nov. 2014.
15 'The Gospel of Excellence', Tom Mooney, 2019 Festival programme book.
16 Joe Csibi to Agler, 18 Oct. 2014.
17 Change of Department name from 'Tourism, Culture and Sport' to 'Arts, Heritage and the Gaeltacht' in June 2011.
18 Lawlor to the Board, 19 Oct. 2014.
19 *Spectator*, 2015.
20 'Liam Healy, An Appreciation', Paul Hennessy for the 2016 Festival programme book.
21 Hennessy to David McLoughlin, 1 Nov. 2016.
22 *Opera News*, Brian Kellow, Feb. 2017.
23 'My Opera City – Wexford', Brian Kellow, *Opera* magazine, Nov. 2016.

Chapter 14: A place like no other, 2017–20

1   Agler to Joe Csibi, 25 July 2016.
2   Proposal submitted to the Arts Council re Bid for Main-Scale Opera Provision 2018–20, 2 Apr. 2017.
3   Agler to Brian Dickie, 18 Oct. 2017; Agler to Elaine Padmore, 23 Oct. 2017.
4   'Does Medea Belong in a Gym or a Palace?', Emer O'Kelly, *Irish Independent*, 8 Jan. 2018.
5   'Barbara Wallace-McConnell, Memorial tribute by Ian Fox, 2017 Festival programme book.
6   Agler to Hennessy, 28 June 2018.
7   Pre-release update by McLoughlin to WFT and NOH Board, 18 Oct. 2018.
8   Paul Hennessy had taken on the role of chairman of the Wexford Opera House in January 2017.
9   Gail Henry, Producer, RTÉ Lyric FM to Agler, 28 Oct. 2018.
10 Wednesday 5 Dec. 2018, McLoughlin to members of the Executive and members of the Board.
11 Agler to Padmore, 8 Feb. 2019.
12 Letter from David Agler to Mary Kelly, Chairwoman of Wexford Festival Opera, 20 Jan. 2019.
13 McLoughlin to Board, 21 Mar. 2019.
14 Dr Tom Walsh served as artistic director from 1951 to 1966, although there was no Festival in 1960.
15 Andrew Clark to Agler following Clark's retirement from the *Financial Times*, 14 Sept. 2014.
16 News Updates, RCSI website, 11 Oct. 2019.
17 'Blow to Town as Wexford Festival Opera is Postponed Until Next Year', Maria Pepper, *Wexford People*, 16 June 2020.
18 President Michael D. Higgins, Online opening address for the 2020 Wexford Festival.
19 Transcript of speech by Walsh, *c*.1970, Walsh files.

LIST OF ILLUSTRATIONS

Photographic credits

Front cover and vi–vii, viii, 202, 213, 217, 218, 223, 229, 232, 236, 241, 242, 245, 246, 250–1, 253, 256, 257, 267, 270–1, 273, 276, 279, 280, 281, 287, 288, 290, 293, 294, 297, 306, 309, 314, 319, 320 Clive Barda photography, ArenaPAL; 196 Joanne Grant photography; 298, 303 Pádraig Grant photography; 140, 149, 155 John Ironside photography; back cover, 195, 203, 204, 210, 225, 226, 310 Ger Lawlor photography; 69, 79 Ger Leahy, Wexford Festival Archive; 41, 42, 53, 65, 66, 72, 89, 90, 106, 110, 115, 125, 128, 133, 134, 137, 161 Denis O'Connor estate, c/o Denise O'Connor-Murphy; 63 Denis O'Connor estate, c/o Lucy Small; 192 Mike Savage, 21Stops.com; ii, 162, 163, 164, 167, 168, 169, 170, 173, 176, 180, 183, 186–7, 191, 198–99, 201, 313 Derek Speirs photography; xii, 23, 24, 27, 31, 32–3, 35, 36, 37, 40, 48, 49, 50, 54, 56, 85, 86, 93, 94, 99, 105 TJW estate, c/o Victoria Walsh-Hamer; 2, 5, 6, 9, 10, 13, 14, 17, 28, 44, 47, 60, 70, 75, 76, 118, 138, 152, 158, 214 Wexford Festival Archive.

INDEX

by Eileen O'Neill. Page references in **_bold italic_** refer to images. Years in () refer to the year that the work was performed at the Festival. For a full list of past productions please go to https://www.wexfordopera.com/about-us/past-productions/